# ENDORSEMENTS

**Pierre Dillenbourg:** Academic Director of the EPFL Center for Digital Education and head of the CHILI Lab: "Computer-Human Interaction for Learning and Instruction," Lausanne, Switzerland

The EDC adventure started many years before tablets and tabletops were known in the public. The urban planning application was the first example I encountered that illustrated how this technology may actually re-shape social interactions. In this case, it also created new forms of participation in societal decisions. The story and results reported in this book will inspire developers who aim to have an impact.

**Morten Fjeld, Ph.D.:** Professor, Director of the t2i Lab, Chalmers University of Technology, Sweden

This is a timely and interesting book and one that is rewarding to read. Offering a substantial contribution to Human-Centered Informatics, this book is well suited for computer science graduate students with an interest Human-Computer Interaction, Interaction Design, and CSCW. Students of urban planning and digital architecture are also likely to benefit. The book is well written and well illustrated and is a treasure for anyone wishing to better understand how emerging interactive technologies will affect the practice of collaborative planning. Drawing on the Envisionment and Discovery Collaboratory (EDC) project, the book presents more than 20 years of pioneering research into collaboration technology. This research has brought about revolutionizing tech innovations such as touch-based user interfaces, interactive tabletops, and large visualization walls. Such products and prototypes have later instigated radical shifts in certain professions, such as energy management, urban planning, and crisis management.

**Gerry Stahl:** Editor-in-Chief, *International Journal of Computer-Supported Collaborative Learning* and Professor Emeritus, College of Computing and Informatics, Drexel University, Philadelphia, PA, U.S.

The powerful idea driving this book is that judiciously integrated systems of software components for design and communication can be developed to facilitate challenging problem solving by communities of stakeholders. This pushes the use of technology far beyond the automation of well-understood tasks or the augmentation of individuals' skills. These new environments must effectively support the tight collaboration of group reflection, design, and construction, as well as provide timely and informative feedback and visualizations. The EDC featured here, and the DODEs preceding it, pioneered this approach. The book reflects on the considerable theoretical, technical, and experimental effort that was required to move from vision to functional success. It reveals the details in which the devil of software design for collaboration hides. Leading-edge efforts today at building environments that integrate construction of visual, table-top, virtual-reality, or tangible artifacts with group discourse and system feedback must build on the heritage meticulously documented in this volume to make further progress.

**Emily Talen, Ph.D.:** Professor, School of Geographical Sciences and Urban Planning at the Arizona State University, Fellow of the American Institute of Certified Planners, and Co-editor of the *Journal of Urbanism*

There is a lot of talk today about "bottom-up" planning, but without the right tools for effective exchange, local knowledge is hard to tap into. Excellent communication, in other words, is the key to successful planning. This book on EDC technology shows how this communication relies on good visual tools—that we need more than verbal transaction to keep the lines of communication flowing and productive. It shows that professionals need the input of clients just as much as clients need the input of professionals. However, more importantly, it provides practical understanding of how to successfully engage, with insight about the methods for mutual learning and active consensus-building—not passive "stakeholder" meetings. This is crucial for tapping local knowledge and, ultimately, making better cities.

**Richard Byyny:** Former Chancellor, University of Colorado, Boulder, U.S.

As a lifelong learner, educator, practitioner, problem solver, and leader I found this book compelling on account of the authors' new ideas, revelations, and advanced methodologies to support creativity, learning, and design. The authors describe interdisciplinary team-based problem solving combined with table-top computing environments to support participation in the action design and planning. They successfully integrate technical systems with computational simulation and social systems for more effective individual and collaborative design and decision making by helping people work together in creativity and problem solving. Their methodologies also greatly enhance experiential learning. This is an important read for those in many fields working on creativity, design, problem solving, and learning.

**Paul Tabolt:** Former Vice Chancellor for Administration, University of Colorado, Boulder, U.S.

I didn't know what to expect when I was initially exposed to concepts espoused in the Envisionment and Discovery Collaboratory more than 15 years ago. I was accustomed to observing the tension and conflict often found in practical urban planning conversations. During years' worth of experiences with the Collaboratory platform I observed exciting breakthroughs as technology coupled with social engagement enabled a refinement of problem analysis and understanding at multiple levels in a community. I had the unique opportunity to participate and observe dramatic shifts in the tone of normally hard-lined conversations as urban planning and technologically driven simulation models and table-top exercises encouraged, fostered, and stimulated dialog. The application and lessons learned from research and tools outlined in this book can lead to more productive, informed, and enlightened conversation as well as better decision making in many different fields and endeavors.

# The Envisionment and Discovery Collaboratory (EDC)

*Explorations in Human–Centered Informatics with Tabletop Computing Environments*

# Synthesis Lectures on Human-Centered Informatics

Editor

**John M. Carroll**, *Penn State University*

Human-Centered Informatics (HCI) is the intersection of the cultural, the social, the cognitive, and the aesthetic with computing and information technology. It encompasses a huge range of issues, theories, technologies, designs, tools, environments, and human experiences in knowledge work, recreation and leisure activity, teaching and learning, and the potpourri of everyday life. The series publishes state-of-the-art syntheses, case studies, and tutorials in key areas. It shares the focus of leading international conferences in HCI.

The Envisionment and Discovery Collaboratory (EDC): Explorations in Human-Centered Informatics with Tabletop Computing Environments
Ernesto G. Arias, Hal Eden, and Gerhard Fischer
www.morganclaypool.com

ISBN: 9781627055703 print
ISBN: 9781627055710 ebook

DOI 10.2200/S00670ED1V01Y201509HCI032

A Publication in the Morgan & Claypool Publishers series
*SYNTHESIS LECTURES ON HUMAN-CENTERED INFORMATICS #32*
Series Editor: John M. Carroll, Penn State University

Series ISSN 1946-7680 Print 1946-7699 Electronic

# The Envisionment and Discovery Collaboratory (EDC)

*Explorations in Human–Centered Informatics with Tabletop Computing Environments*


**Ernesto G. Arias**
University of Colorado, Boulder and Universidad de Costa Rica
**Hal Eden**
University of Colorado, Boulder
**Gerhard Fischer**
University of Colorado, Boulder


*SYNTHESIS LECTURES ON HUMAN-CENTERED INFORMATICS #32*

## ABSTRACT

The *Envisionment and Discovery Collaboratory (EDC)* is a long-term research platform exploring immersive socio-technical environments in which stakeholders can collaboratively frame and solve problems and discuss and make decisions in a variety of application domains and different disciplines.

The knowledge to understand, frame, and solve these problems does not already exist, but is constructed and evolves in ongoing interactions and collaborations among stakeholders coming from different disciplines providing a unique and challenging environment to study, foster, and support *human-centered informatics*, *design*, *creativity*, and *learning*.

At the *social level*, the EDC is focused on the collaborative construction of artifacts rather than the sharing of individually constructed items. It brings individuals together in face-to-face meetings, encouraging and supporting them to engage, individually and collectively, in action and reflection. At the *technological level*, the EDC integrates tabletop computing environments, tangible objects, sketching support, geographic information systems, visualization software, and an envisioned virtual implementation.

This book is based on 20 years of research and development activities that brought together interdisciplinary teams of researchers, educators, designers, and practitioners from different backgrounds. The EDC originated with the merging of two research paradigms from disparate disciplines to build on the strengths, approaches, and perspectives of each. This book describes the artifacts and scenarios that were developed, with the goal of providing *inspiration* for human-centered informatics not focused on technologies in search of a purpose but on the development of systems supporting stakeholders to explore personally meaningful problems.

These developments have inspired numerous research and teaching activities. The challenges, prototypical systems, and lessons learned represent important milestones in the development and evolution of the EDC that are relevant for future research activities and practices in human-centered informatics.

## KEYWORDS

human-centered informatics, tabletop computing environments, design, creativity, learning, collaboration, participatory design, design environments, urban planning, ill-defined problems, problem solving, decision-making, emergency management, energy sustainability, physical games and simulations, inspirational prototypes

# Contents

# Foreword

It's rare for a research team to stay together, productively, for over 20 years. The unifying bond in the joint work of Ernesto Arias, Hal Eden, and Gerhard Fischer is their common desire to move "away from the computer as the focal point toward an understanding of the human, social, and cultural system that creates the context for use."

They are not the first to go beyond the computer or its user interface to the user experience and its cultural context. This shift reframes research to deal with the distinctly human experiences of learning, creativity, collaboration, and community. The authors dig deeply into these contemporary concerns providing numerous stories from diverse projects that contribute to conveying how technology-mediated human experiences work in realistic situations. Of course, breakdowns in the human experiences of learning, creativity, collaboration, and community are also part of their study, and often key to understanding what leads to success and failure.

The book's core consists of the rich insights from the authors' 20+ years of collaboration at the leading edge of human, social, and cultural system innovation. They build on the grand dreams of the socio-technical systems thinkers of the 1960s, carrying those themes to realizations by way of advanced tabletop technologies, yet persistently focused on the human, social, and cultural systems that surround them and their users.

Arias, Eden, and Fischer give us a language for talking about technology-mediated human experiences. Their language grows out of the pioneering work of influential thinkers such as Herb Simon, Donald Schön, Horst Rittel, and Christopher Alexander, who provide terminology for many key concepts such as satisficing, reflection-in-action, wicked problems, and cultures of design, respectively. The authors also enthusiastically draw from other research leaders to describe concepts such as participatory design, tacit knowledge, and boundary objects.

In addition, the authors build on these concepts by identifying new ones such as meta-design, Renaissance communities, and the Seeding, Evolutionary Growth, and Reseeding (SER) Model. As in any boisterous new language community, there are many colorful phrases, overlapping concepts, and variant uses. All of this swirl of new ideas can be thrilling for readers whose minds are tickled by these gusty and gutsy concepts.

The authors' capacity to see what others have missed, and interpret it for us, is what makes this book so valuable. They do more than understand and teach us about what they have seen; at their best they elevate what they have learned into actionable guidance for future researchers, system designers, organizational change agents, and visionary thinkers.

There are many themes, but I encourage readers to pay special attention to the following.

- **Motivation:** Arias, Eden, and Fischer tell their readers that "it is one of the most important forces determining human behavior." This is the big message for the next 100 years. Never before have technologies provided such immensely powerful and exquisitely focused tools for raising human motivation (or squelching it) to improve health behaviors (diet, exercise, smoking cessation, etc.), conflict resolution, financial decisions, or learning opportunities. Triggering a cascade of motivational energy could change civilization even more vigorously than a nuclear chain reaction.

- **Participation:** Getting individuals, families, teams, organizations, communities, and cultures to become more engaged so as to give generously to others, engage in civic systems, contribute to community safety, etc., is now more possible than ever. Yet, our theories of participation and how to catalyze it are weak, incomplete, and sometimes misguided. This book moves our thinking forward in how to redesign systems to dramatically increase participation.

- **Reflection:** Arias, Eden, and Fischer are men of action, but they are also profoundly men of reflection. I think they would like to be remembered for promoting deep reflection by more people, more of the time. I think the kinds of reflection they seek are far deeper than casual reconsideration of past actions, but more in the spirit of how can my past experiences change our communal future? Reflection can have its quiet meditative moments, but I think the authors are after the adrenalin-induced intensity that leads to innovation and new possibilities.

- **Responsibility:** I was pleased to see how well the writing recognizes the importance of individuals stepping forward to take more responsibility for their own performance and for the success of their teams. I think design to clarify, encourage, and reward responsibility for success (and accountability for failures) will become a major theme for the coming decades.

Finally, even though the authors never use these terms, every page seems to be about trust and empathy. These vital human features are what make human, social, and cultural systems succeed. In recent decades, cybersecurity and privacy advocates have discussed design to improve trust in systems by users, but empathy has as much power to shape learning, creativity, collaboration, and community. Design discussions about raising trust and empathy seem to be just becoming possible now.

The additional happy news about this book is that it is infused with human values and ethical considerations. Reading the stories of diverse projects conveys a great deal about the human values that they seek to foster and the ethical practices that are part of their research as well as their offerings to readers. The collection of stories offers powerful lessons for many researchers.

Ben Shneiderman, University of Maryland
August 2015
ben@cs.umd.edu,

# Preface

The *Envisionment and Discovery Collaboratory (EDC)* is a socio-technical environment serving as a long-term research platform to explore *conceptual frameworks* for *design*, *creativity*, and *learning*.

Over the last two decades, we have published numerous articles documenting specific aspects of the EDC—but no coherent document exists to describe the numerous different facets of our research effort. Even without such a document, the EDC has generated over time interest in different communities. Other researchers have emphasized the importance of the EDC, for example Dillenbourg and Evans (2011) remarked the following about the EDC in a special issue of the CSCL journal *Tabletop Interfaces for CSCL* by stating: "A primary contribution of this work <the EDC> was to lay a foundation for much work cited in this article and continuing to this day."

## AUDIENCES FOR THE BOOK

The frameworks and developments described in the book are relevant for several different disciplines (and specific results have been reported in the journals and conferences of these research communities)—the major ones being as follows.

- *Human-Computer Interaction (HCI)* with a publication (Arias et al., 2001) demonstrating that the EDC shifts developments away from the computer as the focal point toward an understanding of the social and cultural systems creating the context in which the system is embedded. This shift facilitates to explore key conceptual principles such as establishing shared understanding among various stakeholders, contextualizing information to the task at hand, and creating objects-to-think-with in collaborative design activities.

- *Computer-Supported Collaborative Learning (CSCL)* with a publication (Fischer and Sugimoto, 2006) arguing (1) for the importance of self-directed learning taking place among heterogeneous groups of people and (2) the need supporting communities, mindsets, and cultures that embrace lifelong learning.

- *Design of Interactive Systems (DIS)* with a publication describing our efforts to develop integrated design environments linking physical and computational dimensions to attain the complementary synergies that these two worlds offer.

- *Creativity and Cognition (C&C)* with a publication (Fischer et al., 2005) illustrating how individual and social creativity can be integrated, how the creation of shareable externalizations and boundary objects can be enhanced, and how new design competencies are emerging.

- *Participatory Design (PD)* with a publication (Fischer et al., 2002) discussing the Seeding, Evolutionary Growth, and Reseeding (SER) model that broadens the historical focus of participatory design beyond the initial design of a system.

- *End-User Development (EUD)* with a publication (Fischer and Giaccardi, 2006) arguing that the challenge of design is not a matter of getting rid of the emergent, but rather of including it and making it an opportunity for more creative and more adequate solutions to problems and introducing meta-design as a conceptual framework aimed at defining and creating social and technical infrastructures in which new forms of collaborative design can take place.

- *Computer-Supported Cooperative Work (CSCW)* with a publication (Fischer and Ostwald, 2005) differentiating communities of practice and communities of interest by analyzing the challenges of collaborative design that involve stakeholders from different practices and backgrounds requiring constructive interactions among multiple knowledge systems.

- *Conflict Resolution, Informed Participation, and Decision Analysis (CR&IP)* with publications (Arias, 1996; and Arias et al., 2001) introducing the use of decision-support games and simulations to enhance informed participation in community planning, urban planning and design.

For researchers and practitioners in different application domains, the book describes in urban planning (Chapter 2), campus planning (Section 5.1), emergency management (Section 5.2), energy sustainability (Section 5.3), student projects in different domains (Sections 7.1.2 and 7.1.3), and EDC inspired projects by two of our scientific collaborators (Sections 7.2.1 and 7.2.2).

While some themes pursued in the context of the EDC are more connected to one of the specific research and practice activities mentioned, the most important contribution of the EDC is that it has facilitated an interdisciplinary dialogue between these different disciplines.

# Acknowledgments

The three authors formed the core design and development team for the EDC. But the research activities described in this book would not have been possible without the extensive involvement of numerous other participants contributing their expertise and generously giving their time over the last two decades. We are especially grateful to the support and contributions of:

- *Ph.D. students* (specifically Eric Scharff and Jonathan Ostwald);

- *Undergraduate Research Apprentices* (specifically Kyle Bygott, Jack Elston, and Anuradha Kumar);

- *Students* in our courses in the Computer Science department and the Research Methods courses in the College of Architecture and Planning;

- *Research Scientists* working in $L^3D$ (specifically: Alexander Repenning, Elisa Giaccardi, and Andrew Gorman);

- *Visiting Scientists* (specifically: Masanori Sugimoto, Eva Hornecker, Shin'ichi Konomi, and Andy Warr);

- Collaborators and supporters representing the content areas of our case studies:

  - from CU Boulder: Richard Byyny (as Chancellor at the time); Paul Tabolt (as Vice-Chancellor for Administration at the time); Bruce Ekstrand (Vice-Chancellor for Research) whose support was critical to the founding of the Center for LifeLong Learning & Design ($L^3D$); and Risa Palm (Vice Chancellor for Research) providing the start-up funding for the Urban Simulations Laboratory (SimLab);

  - the Regents of the University of Colorado and the Members of the Boulder City Council (as pictured in Figure 5.2 during a joint planning session);

  - representatives from the transportation and the emergency department of the City of Boulder; and

  - Robert Harriss from the National Center for Atmospheric Research (NCAR), Boulder.

Finally, we owe a big "thank you" to different directorates and program directors at the National Science Foundation (NSF) that have generously supported our research over many years, specifically through the programs in *Human-Centered Computing*, *Science of Design*, and *Creativity and IT*.

The third author was supported during the writing of the book by a fellowship from the Hanse-Wissenschaftskolleg Institute for Advanced Study at Delmenhorst, Germany (HWK; http://www.h-w-k.de/en/hwk-overview.html).

The first author's participation in writing this book was supported by the Offices of the Rector and the Vice Rector of Research of the Universidad de Costa Rica.

# CHAPTER 1

# Introduction

## 1.1 THE EDC IN A NUTSHELL

The *Envisionment and Discovery Collaboratory (EDC)* is a socio-technical environment (Fischer and Herrmann, 2011; Mumford, 1987; Trist, 1981) serving as a long-term research platform in exploring *conceptual frameworks* for *design*, *creativity*, and *learning* in the context of specific case studies and contributing to an improved quality of life for all citizens. Its development is grounded by the research methodology of the Center for Lifelong Learning and Design ($L^3D$) pursuing "basic research on real problems." The conceptual frameworks and the EDC are related to each other in a *mutually beneficial relationship*: the design of the EDC was grounded in the conceptual frameworks and in return, the research and developments with the EDC allowed us to evolve and enrich the conceptual frameworks.

While the EDC framework can be applied to many application domains, its test bed domains have been focused on urban planning and decision making, emergency management, and energy sustainability (requiring primarily *locational decisions*). The knowledge to understand, frame, and solve these problems or resolve these conflicts does not already exist, but is constructed and evolves in ongoing interactions and collaborations—an ideal environment to study design, creativity, and learning.

At the *social* level, the EDC supports more democratic planning, decision making, and design processes and it addresses the following challenge from the President's Council on Sustainable Development (PCSD, 1996):

> "How can more than 261 million individual Americans define and reconcile their needs and aspirations with community values and the needs of the future? Our most important finding is the potential power of and growing desire for decision processes that promote direct and meaningful interaction involving people in decisions that affect them. Americans want to take control of their lives."

To empower all stakeholders involved in problem solving and decision making processes (bringing together neighborhood communities, local governments, states, and other organizations), the EDC supports participatory design processes to be examined systematically, controversial issues to be explored, and decisions be reached that reflect a democratic process based on a robust assessment of alternatives. It represents a fundamentally different approach compared to other settings and alternative uses of technology dominated by planners and technocrats who provide answers that are to be taken at face value and used as an objective basis for decisions with little or no interest and concern for public participation in decisions.

At the *technical* level, the EDC (1) supports face-to-face problem-framing and problem-solving activities (by bringing together individuals who share a common problem), (2) pioneers the use of tabletop computing environments and innovative interaction techniques including tangible objects, sketching, visualization, and simulation support, and (3) integrates external tools (such as geographic information system (GIS), Google Earth, the COMET program, and others).

## 1.2    ORGANIZATION AND READING GUIDE

The book contains ten chapters, organized around topics with important relationships between them (as illustrated by Figure 1.1). The importance of individual chapters is based on the readers' disciplinary backgrounds and interests.

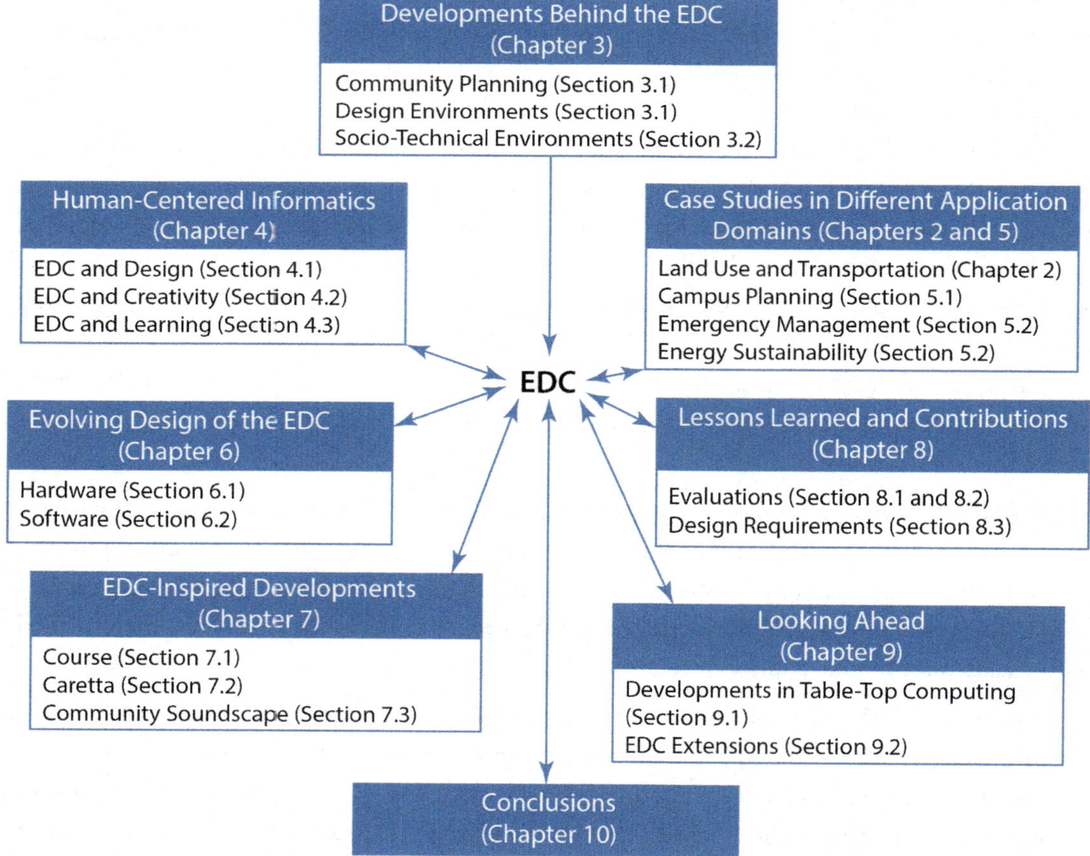


Figure 1.1: Overview of the organization of the book: topics and chapters.

Chapter 2 "A Scenario Illustrating the EDC in Use" provides an overview of the various functionalities of the EDC (including the integration of action and reflection spaces) of the EDC needed to support a community of stakeholders in transportation planning by exploring land use, the design of a bus route, and the location of bus stops through the neighborhood. The aim of this scenario is to contextualize the reading of the subsequent chapters by providing the basis for a critical understanding of their content and their intended relationships.

Chapter 3 "Research Activities and Developments Behind the EDC" provides a historical context to understand the background and evolution of the EDC from its inception to its present form by describing the integration of two paradigms: (1) the *community based tools paradigm (Co-Plan)* from urban planning and design and (2) the *domain-oriented design environment paradigm (DODEs)* from computer science.

CoPlan is based on our research activities using physical media in the form of tabletop games and simulations to support more effectively decision-making in planning, and to address design problems and conflict resolution arising from the "what," "how much," and "where" behind the location of urban activities, as demonstrated by the joint project with a neighborhood community in the City of Denver (Arias, 1996). The *physical* tabletop games and simulations incorporated a language of objects in order for the users to make explicit their tacit understandings to frame and resolve design problems through collaborative descriptions, evaluations, and prescriptions of situational contexts (Arias et al., 1995).

DODEs (Fischer, 1994a) represent research activities not only to make computers more powerful but to support people to be more productive. These systems are an attempt to empower people working in different application domains to interact with computational artifacts by not only facilitating human computer interaction but by building layered architectures in support of *human problem-domain interaction* (Fischer and Lemke, 1988).

The integration of these two paradigms provided the foundation for the design and development of the *INTERactive SIMulation* Station (Intersim), a horizontal computational surface serving as an initial prototype of what later became known as *tabletop technologies*. The Intersim along with physical-digital objects (created to interact with the tabletop games and simulations) supported *tangible interfaces* (Hornecker, 2011) to facilitate the interaction between participants and the tabletop environment. These developments are explored in more detail in Chapter 6.

The chapter also provides an introduction of the $L^3D$ research agenda and its synergistic relationship with the EDC, i.e., how the EDC's development *influenced* and *was influenced* by such an agenda. The developments from physical to digital media attained through the integration of these paradigms, along with the advancements to our research agenda, demonstrate the value of interdisciplinary collaborations in the creation of innovative systems to support and advance developments and knowledge in the area of human-centered informatics.

Chapter 4 "Contributions of the EDC to Human-Centered Informatics" presents a theoretical framework from which the other chapters of the book can be understood individually and in terms of the relationships with each other. *Human-Centered Informatics* in the context of this book represents the "intersection of the cultural, the social, the cognitive, and the aesthetic with computing and information technology" instantiating the overall objective of the Synthesis Lectures of Morgan & Claypool (http://www.morganclaypool.com/toc/hci/1/1) in a particular context.

The first section introduces *design* and its relationships to the EDC in terms of four central aspects: (1) design methodologies; (2) design communities; (3) boundary objects; and (4) the seeding, evolutionary growth, reseeding (SER) model. The second section analyzes the mutual relationship between the EDC and *creativity* by exploring (1) the concepts of individual and social creativity; (2) the impact of distances and diversity in creativity; and (3) a description of the unique features of the EDC in supporting creativity. The third section introduces *learning* (1) by describing its multi-dimensional aspects and (2) by illustrating how various conceptions of learning can be explored and supported by the EDC.

Chapter 5 "Case Studies in Different Application Domains" presents three selected real-world case studies in which our research team has collaborated with stakeholders from different application domains: (1) *campus planning* in collaboration with CU Boulder and the City of Boulder; (2) *emergency management* with a focus on creating training and operational environments to cope with wildfires; and (3) *energy sustainability* to create environments supporting smart grids and smart meters to motivate and support citizen to engage in environmentally responsible behaviors.

Chapter 6 "The Evolving Design of the EDC" describes the evolution over time of EDC's architecture. Our incremental trial-and-error approach for hardware innovations moved the EDC's hardware development from the original design of the (1) Intersim to (2) Smart Boards (integrating touch and projection) to (3) the PitA-Board (allowing users to interact in parallel and new tangible interfaces with smart objects). On the software side, AgentSheets provided an important foundation for moving the physical media design games into a horizontal game-board format and the corresponding initial language of objects to attain interaction with the tabletop game board. As the evolution continued, the EDC's software went from those early efforts to the Squeak-based version and subsequently to the current EDC system architecture.

Chapter 7 "EDC-Inspired Developments" describes a selected set of examples that the EDC inspired in our own work as well as that of others. The first section discusses our teaching, learning and research experiences with the EDC and describes two experiences in detail: (1) Mr. Roger's Sustainable Neighborhood and (2) an urban dynamics application to study its impact on climate change. The second section presents two examples of applications inspired by the EDC developed by other researchers (Masanori Sugimoto and Elisa Giaccardi): (1) the linking of shared and individual spaces supporting interactive learning by Japanese children with the *Caretta* environment;

and (2) the *Community Soundscapes (CoS)* system exploring the integration of sound as a means of supporting new notions of understanding landscapes as cognitive soundscapes.

Chapter 8 "Lessons Learned and Contributions" represents an attempt to distill the experiences that we have learnt in our work with the EDC into a set of design requirements that are simultaneously theoretically grounded (in the frameworks described in Chapter 4) and empirically derived from the specific developments conducted in the case studies. A major finding resulting from a synthesis of individual design requirements is that future evaluation developments must find a path that proceeds from artificial experiments to authentic design contexts. This will require the creation of models of increasing sophistication including the transition from single studies to multi-sessions and longitudinal studies.

Chapter 9 "Looking Ahead" describes future developments that we consider important based on the research undertaken with the EDC so far. Tabletop computing environments (hardware and basic software substrates) are still limited in their commercial availability and in their potential features spaces that are needed for stakeholders using them to pursue their objectives. Based on identifying limitations in our research project, we outline the rationale for three extensions: (1) capturing more of the interactions and communications between the participants gathered aorund the table; (2) additional support for meta-design and cultures of participation; and (3) to create a virtual extension of the EDC that would complement the face-to-face interactions by supporting collaborations among participants that are not co-located.

Chapter 10 "Conclusions" briefly revisits the contributions of the EDC and articulates our hopes that the developments and contributions described in this book are steps forward towards the long-term objective of human-centered informatics.

CHAPTER 2

# A Scenario Illustrating the EDC in Use

This chapter introduces a scenario to provide an illustration of the capabilities of the EDC supporting *collaborative decision-making processes* in the participatory planning of a bus route. It presents a specific version of the EDC as it was used in numerous sessions as a socio-technical environment that supports informed participation in domains. The scenario will provide "anchoring episodes" for human-computer interaction in design, creativity, and learning, as well as specific technological configurations that will be described and discussed later in the book.

## The Conceptual Architecture of the EDC

Figure 2.1 depicts the EDC in use by a group of stakeholders (including city planners, transportation specialists, and neighborhood representatives engaged in a planning and decision making session) to improve public transportation by establishing a new bus route through a neighborhood. The conceptual architecture of the EDC instantiates Schön's conceptualization (Schön, 1983) of "reflection-in-action" and "reflection-on-action" as a supporting framework for decision making and conflict resolution.

The horizontal *tabletop environment* in the foreground is an interactive surface coupled with a projected display of a computational information environment using graphical information systems (GIS) and other contextual information. Tangible interaction with the environment takes place by the stakeholders moving the computationally enhanced language of physical objects that are sensed by the interactive table. The horizontal tabletop represents the "action space," supporting participants to make decisions and effect design actions in a collaborative space. The face-to-face configuration allows all participants in creating externalizations of their ideas and objectives, using the pieces to emphasize their convictions behind the associated actions. Thus, the tacit knowledge of each individual is externalized and made explicit allowing for the development of informed compromises that form the basis of the shared understanding necessary for the resolution of conflict in the solution of design problems (Arias et al., 2001).

Figure 2.1: The EDC: action and reflection spaces.

In the background of Figure 2.1 are two vertical interactive whiteboards that provide extended information related to the activity happening in the action space, including: argumentation contextualized by the actions, visualizations of planning and design information (e.g., provided by Google Earth perspectives), for the players and the audience beyond the table (if there is one).

## The Problem: Revising an Existing Bus Route

The company operating public transportation noticed that the ridership in a bus route through one outlying area of town is much lower than expected. Transportation planners have decided to try to change the existing route and its bus stops to better serve the needs of the neighborhood and encourage the residents to use the bus more often. The objectives of the redesign are to maintain a commercially viable and lively downtown area, decrease the use of the private car transportation, improve the connection to a Park & Ride station connecting the region through regional bus lines, thus addressing also environmental and energy concerns of the region.

Rather than focusing solely on the technical planning aspects of the problem and developing a top-down design, the planning team wants to understand what behavioral and social issues underlie choices the residents make regarding their transportation needs and hope to cultivate greater participation from the residents in the planning of public transportation at the urban and regional levels.

To address the objectives above, the transportation planning team develops a set of scenarios to support a series of meeting with residents to explore possible alternatives, understand the interests and motivations of different stakeholders, and analyze the impacts and benefits of different transportation choices.

Changes to the bus route (such as changing the path it takes and either relocating or adding stops) can add to the time it takes to complete a "cycle" of the route. If these changes are too great, it can require significant additional expense to accommodate them. The planners have determined that there is time in the schedule for changes of 5–10 min and have identified which streets are wide enough for the buses to drive on. This information gives the participating residents an idea about how much they can change the route without requiring extra buses or significant additional funding for infrastructure changes. The bus route may be expanded or changed, provided it meets the constraints described. Neighbors are encouraged via public announcements and neighborhood fliers to participate in the route design activities and make recommendations to the planners on path of the route and the location of bus stops.

## Creating an Agenda for the Transportation Session

The activities for the sessions were designed by city planners and EDC developers and are divided into several phases that there can be different foci at different phases of the session. This agenda and descriptions of the respective phases and their foci are documented in the reflection space, as shown in Figure 2.2.

The Envisionment and Discovery Collaboratory

EDC Home | Project Home |
[View]    [Edit]  [Print]  [Lock]  [References]  [Attachments]  [History]  [Home]  [Changes]  [Search]  [Help]

**Route 205**

Welcome to the EDC Transportation Forum!

The Boulder 205 bus route is underutilized, particularly by the outlying Gunbarrel neighborhood. Transportation planners have decided to try to change the existing route to better serve the needs of the neighborhood to encourage the residents to use the bus more often. The bus route may be expanded, re-routed, or have bus stops relocated. The planners have already determined that approximately five additional minutes could be added to the portion of the trip encompassing the neighborhood and identified the streets that are wide enough for the buses to drive on.

This meeting of interested enighbors, one of a series being convened, will consider what changes might be appropriate and make recommendations to the transportation planners. The transportation planners will consider the input from the meetings in the final realignment of this route.

The meeting will consist of several phases:

- Pre-Session Information
- Brief Overview of the technology being used
- Discussion of land use in the neighborhood and the current route alignment
- Information survey and introductions
- Walking distance discussion
- Redesigning the route
- Wrap-up discussion

Figure 2.2: An overview of the transportation session agenda.

## Phase I: Familiarizing Participants with the Technology

To make the participants more comfortable in the interaction with the new technology, Phase I familiarizes the participants with the operation of the tabletop environment. The technology supports participants in exploring how to use the language of physical pieces on the tabletop system (Figure 2.3 showing the action space and the gray command borders at opposite sides), how to pan and zoom in and out to show broader or narrower views of areas in the neighborhood or the streets, and how to access the various information and data resources that are available in the Reflection Space. The granularity of the interaction is fairly coarse (the underlying sensors were co-opted from an electronic chessboard technology as explained in Chapter 6 and the pieces need to be placed in the center of the (chessboard) grid squares where grey outlines are overlaid to guide the placement of pieces. Also, there are some "dead" spaces between the sensor grids where the pieces are not sensed at all. A special "administration piece" (admin piece) is used to control various parts of the interaction (such as the different zooming categories and selecting the phase or specialized map layers) by placing it on grey command squares located along opposite edges of the table.

Figure 2.3: Familiarizing participants with the tabletop environment.

To support *tangible interactions* (Hornecker, 2011), we developed physical pieces (Table 2.1) with embedded sensors that facilitated that all participants could express their ideas and objectives by focusing on their tasks rather than the computational mechanisms.

Table 2.1: Summary of some of the pieces used in the scenario

| Phase II: Land Use | | Phase III and IV: Introductions and Walking Distances | | Phase V: Redesigning Bus Routes | |
|---|---|---|---|---|---|
| | Light Industrial | | Query Tool | | Draw Bus Route |
| | Open Space, Parks | | Player 1 | | Bus Stop |
| | Commercial | | Player 2 | | |
| | Single-Family Residential | | Player 3 | | Bus |
| | Multi-Family Residential | | Player 4 | | |
| | Agricultural | | Player 5 | | |
| | Store | | Player 6 | | |
| | School | | Player 7 | | |

## Phase II: Exploring Land Use and Zoning

To better understand the design context for a bus route, the next phase engages the stakeholders in an exploration of the existing neighborhood environment. In addition of current bus routes, this includes how land is used within the neighborhood (Figure 2.4). Extensive data (data describing the current bus routes, the different types of land uses and the zoning categories in each use, and other simulation components to analyze bus movement) are available from various sources, including GIS sources maintained by local government and transportation agencies and are Internet accessible.

Even though land-use data are available for the neighborhood—providing the *official views* of land use distributions which represent the *potential* planned environment (Gans, 1991)—the EDC supports the notion that other valuable perspectives describing such aspects are brought to the table. In order to draw out these sources of information and to surface disparate views and conflicts, the rest of Phase II asks the participants to describe and discuss how they understand and perceive land use within their neighborhood, describing the *effective use* (Gans, 1991) of their environment by placing pieces representing land-use types on areas of the neighborhood that they are familiar with (Figure 2.4 indicates the different categories).

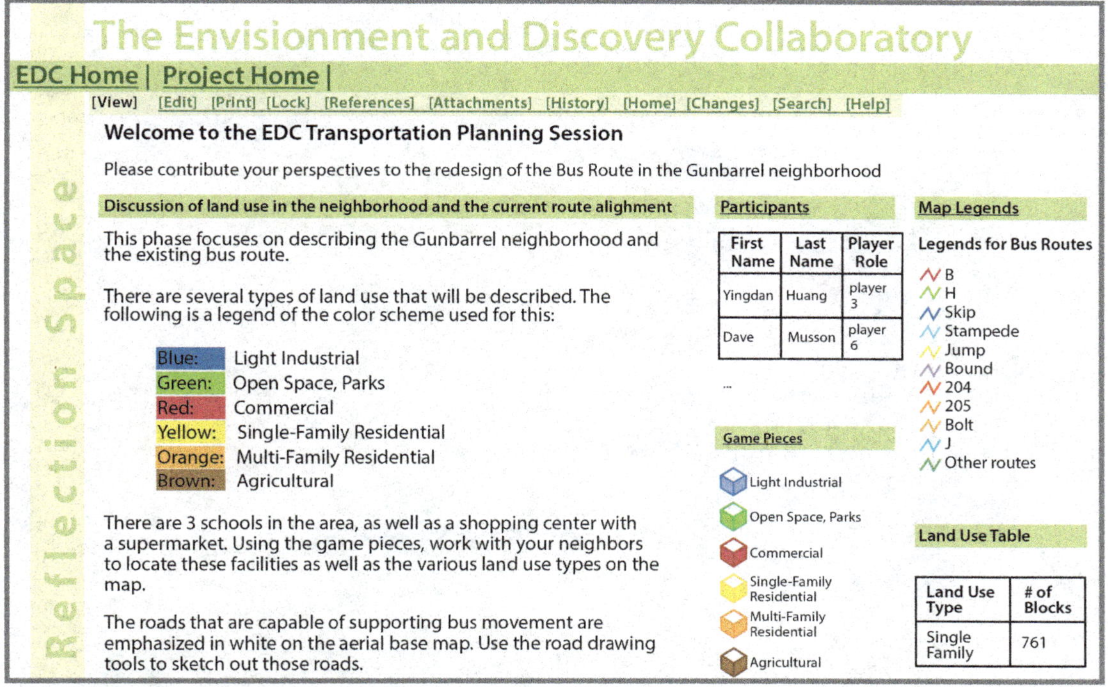



Figure 2.4: Reflection space information on land use types and existing bus routes.

As they proceed, various understandings are expressed and there may be general agreement on many of the associations made, or there may be areas where one person's different description that surfaces generates reactions, often tacit, from other participants perspectives—for example: some residents perceive the golf course as open space, but when they express this view, others point out that since fees are charged to use the course, this is more of a commercial venture.

The information provided by the participants is shown on the board with the associated colors in a geographic view (Figure 2.5) and is also shown in the reflection space in an analytic view, both tabular and graphical (Figure 2.6), summarizing how many of each land-use type has been labeled by participants. This data is updated dynamically as users make changes to the land-use description in the action space after discussions and represents a shared understanding of land uses arrived from individuals' informed compromises (Arias and Fischer, 2000). In addition, the distribution of land-use across the categories could be compared with distribution ratios of the official planning and zoning ordinances to critique the state of the neighborhood.

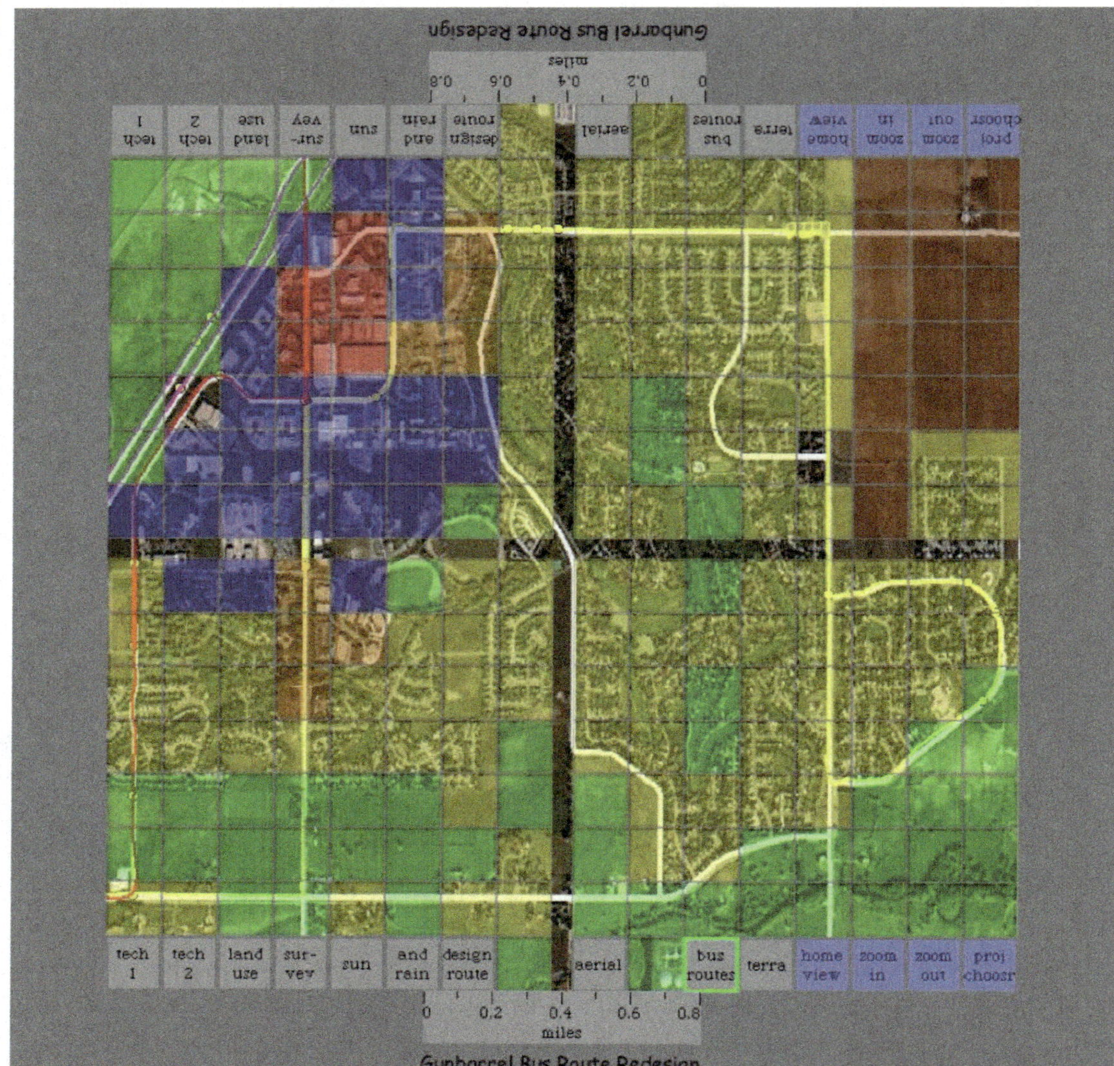


Figure 2.5: A land-use scenario in the action space as constructed interactively by neighbors.

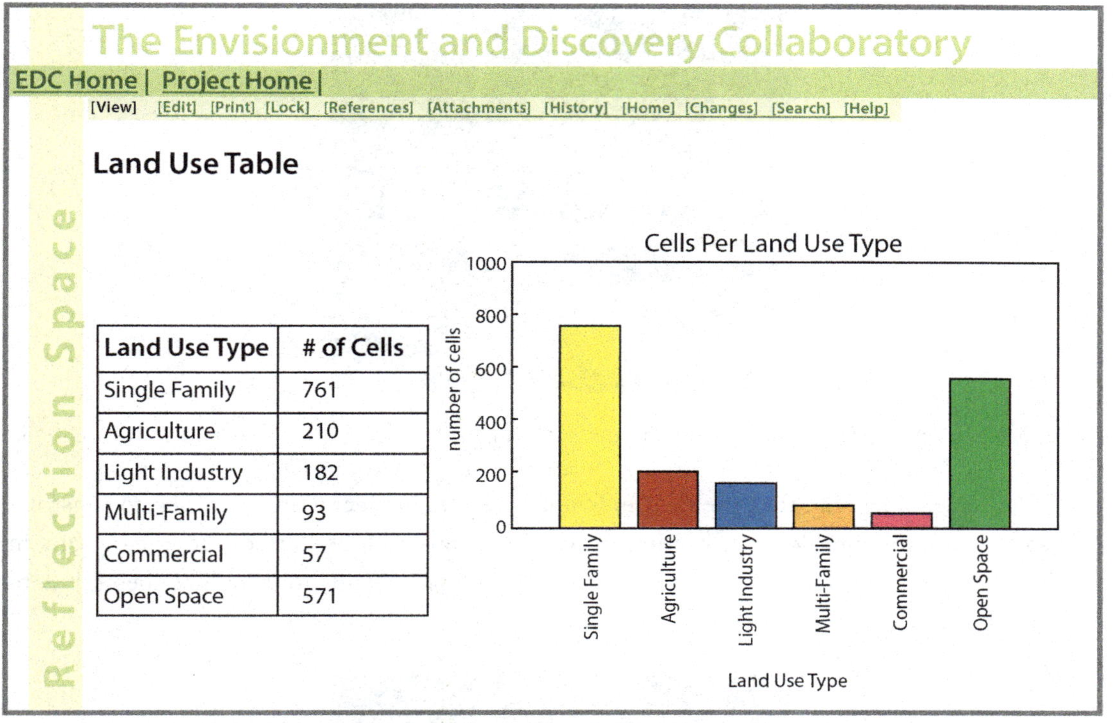


| Land Use Type | # of Cells |
|---|---|
| Single Family | 761 |
| Agriculture | 210 |
| Light Industry | 182 |
| Multi-Family | 93 |
| Commercial | 57 |
| Open Space | 571 |

Figure 2.6: Dynamically generated analytic view of land use in the reflection space.

## Phase III: Expressing Preferences/Introducing Each Other

For the discussions surrounding the redesign of the bus route, the background of the participants is crucial. In Phase III participants introduce themselves and the concerns and issues they bring to the meeting by interacting with various "kiosks" placed around the edge of the map on the action space. Participants utilize tangible people-shaped pieces of the language (representing themselves) to indicate where they live on the map, resulting in a house icon appearing at that spot (Figure 2.7).

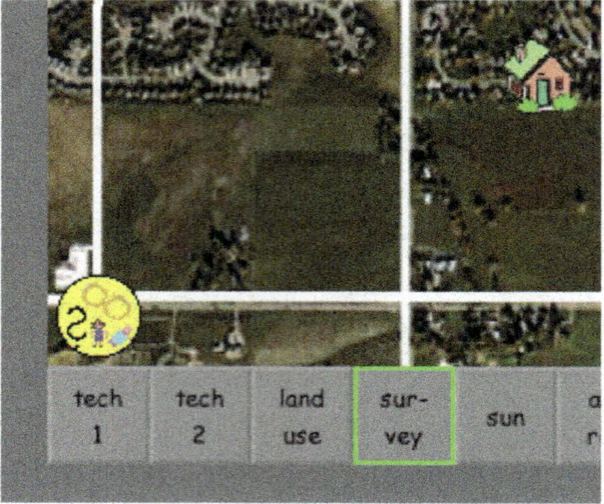

Figure 2.7: Showing "My House Placement" and a nearby kiosk.

The stakeholders can then use their individual piece to interact with the kiosks, to construct their socio-economic profile by answering various questions such as age, sex, how many cars in the household, etc. (Figure 2.8). This allows a way for all participants to introduce themselves to the others.

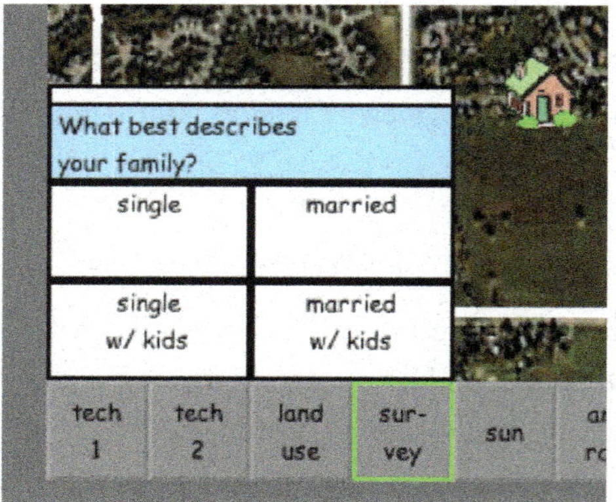


Figure 2.8: Allowing participants to describe their family status.

As discussed in Chapter 6, the most recent technology used in the EDC allows stakeholders to interact in parallel (Figure 2.3) working on their own tasks and no one paid attention to what others were doing. To address this shortcoming, a query-tool piece was developed that, when placed on the user's house icon, would present a bubble showing the neighbor's socio-economic profile (Figure 2.9).

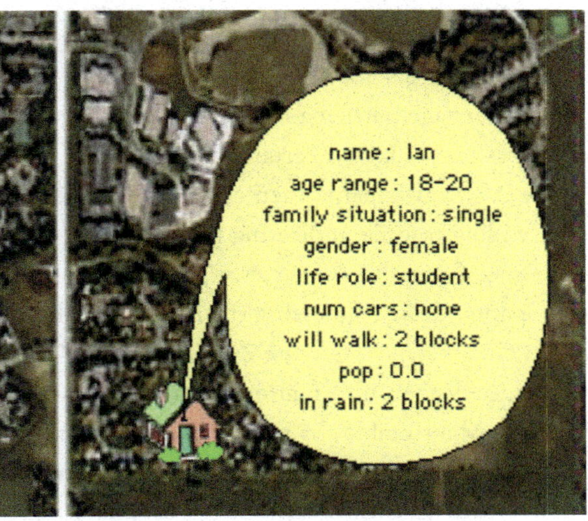



Figure 2.9: Query tool bubble.

This information is also displayed in the reflection space (Figure 2.10), allowing each stakeholder an opportunity to review and comment on the profile of other participants. This piece acts as a "talking stick"—a physical object in the language that can be passed around, allowing each participant a turn at speaking by virtue of possession of the object.

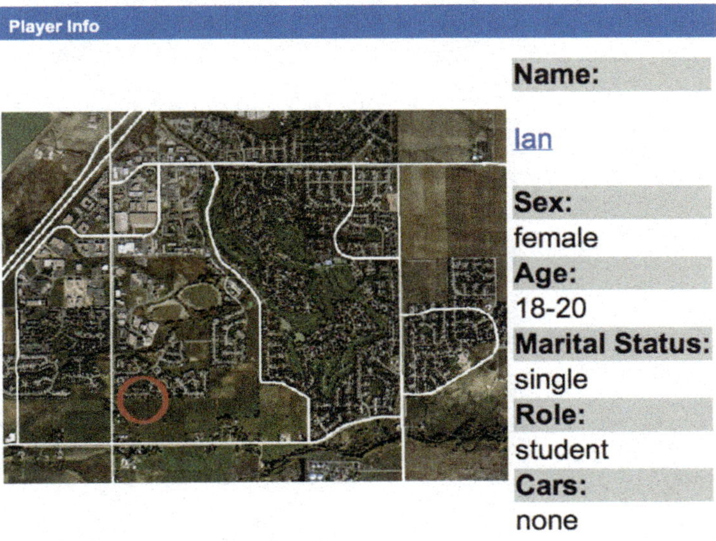



Figure 2.10: Displaying the user's socio-economic profile in the reflection space.

## Phase IV: Emerging Insight: Illustrating Multiple Walking Distances

This next phase focuses on a walking-distance activity to discuss the bus route's path and the location of bus stops. It is used to engage participants in understanding the interaction among their preferences and their willingness for walking a certain distance to the catch the bus. Having indicated where they live (Figure 2.7), participants then can use other kiosk items to articulate their choice as to how far they are willing to walk, indicating their different distances for "good weather" and for "bad weather." After specifying this information, colored circle appears around the house icons of the individual participants, clearly indicating the radius that they might be willing to walk to catch a bus under different circumstances (Figure 2.11).

As the participants all specify their information, the visualization shows emerging, overlapping patterns of areas that might be suitable for bus routes and locations of bus stops, providing information and perspectives that no individual had in their head prior to the exercise (as emergence is an essential aspect of creativity, this example serves as one of the "anchoring examples" for the Section 4.2). The process of the individual articulation of stakeholders how far they are willing to walk and to visualize the integrated result of individual actions can continue across multiple sessions. The outcomes of the sessions incrementally gather more data from additional neighbors and creates an more accurate understanding of the efficiency of a bus route and the convenience of bus-stop locations.

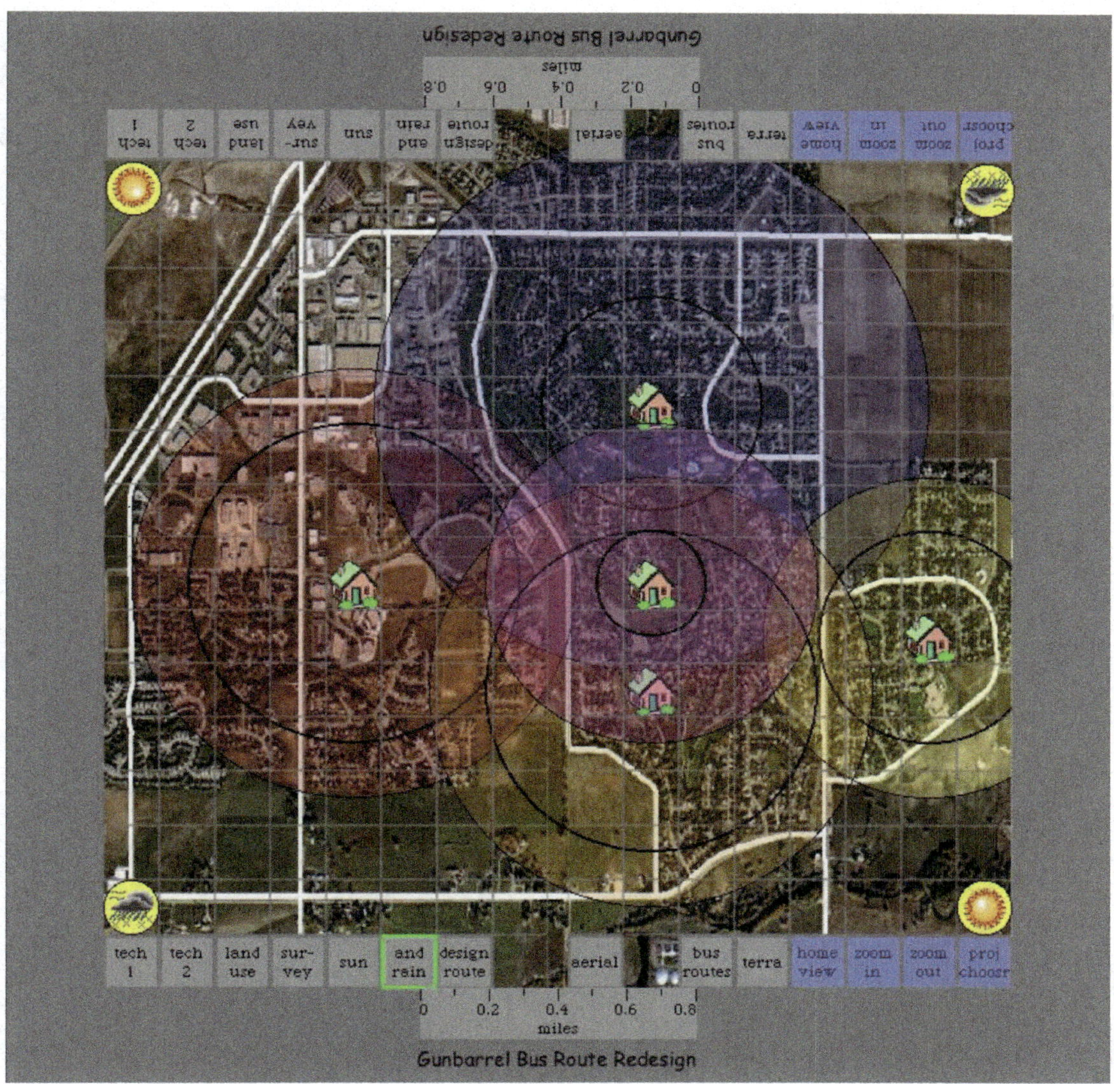



Figure 2.11: Walking-distance phase.

## Phase V: Sketching Alternate Routes

Based on their discussion and their stated preference so far, participants in this phase turn their focus on how the alignment of the bus route and the number and placement of bus stops could best meet their needs given their collective socio-economic characteristics behind their walking prefer-ences. Taking advantage of the sketching facilities provided by the EDC (that allowed the creation of multiple sketch layers, provided for ways to set aside a sketch, create new sketches, overlay existing sketches, and finally import desired sketches into the simulation), the participants could select a preferred option that optimizes the satisfaction of the neighborhood's collective needs, import it into the simulation to better evaluate the costs and benefits of the proposed vs. the existing route and stops location. This also allows the capability to associate it with a bus route object type, allowing it to be used as other bus-route objects.

Figure 2.12: Sketching a new bus route.

Once the participants have agreed on a bus route (either an existing one from GIS or a new one identified from their sketching), tangible bus-stop pieces can be used to place bus stops on the bus routes and relocate them as needed. The simulation component of the EDC will show the bus stopping at those new stops along with their service radius coverage. Additional design assumptions encoded in the simulation based on transportation prescriptive specifications about the placement of the bus stops provides feedback to participants on issues related to their design. Shown in the form of visual critics, these design constraints indicate whether stops are too close or too far apart (Figure 2.13). This allows for a visualization of any possible discrepancy that may exist between, for example, a specific case of an elderly couple or other special populations who may need to adjust the stop closer to their home to address their walking distance limitations.

Figure 2.13: Computational critics enriching the design process.

The activities of the session allow the engagement of the community in the design process, thus allowing the elucidation of various insights and perspectives that can support engineers and planners to develop more detailed designs, and bring those back to the community in subsequent sessions for an evaluation. On-line forums can allow discussion on specific issues to continue, as well.

In this manner, through interactive informed participation, the EDC has been able to support the neighbors in collaborative learning about the public transportation domain, and empower them through social creativity in the design of their bus route. The following chapters of the book will expand on the EDC's functionality, its contextual background and conceptual basis, its evolution and applications in real life domains, and an overarching assessment along with its future implications to human-centered-informatics.

## CONCLUSIONS

Various conclusions can be drawn from this brief introduction of the EDC and how it works in the scenario presented, such as the following.

- *Supporting Problem and Conflict Resolution.* First, the decisions behind establishing a bus route alignment and the location of its bus stops, while on the surface may appear to be trivial in nature, they, on the contrary, represent a complexity inherent in all locational decision-making of domains such as planning or design. The reason being that such decisions to frame and resolve this type of problems are inevitably in contexts where the many stakeholders involved either effect the outcomes or are affected by the outcomes, and therefore are found in a context which is usually associated with conflict. This is the challenge of technological environments face in supporting participation and collaborative design activities.

- *Functionality for Interactivity.* Second, interactivity support through the linkage of the reflection and action spaces and a tangible interphase in the EDC facilitate the interactions not only those between stakeholders and the technology, but also between the stakeholders themselves. This interactivity makes the tacit knowledge explicit and serves as a basis for stakeholders to resolve conflicts and to construct informed compromises.

- *Technology-domain Relationship.* Third, a "fit" between the EDC's functionality and the application to the transportation planning domain is an important design requirement in human-centered informatics. Domain knowledge, both theoretical and practical, is a fundamental building block for the design and development of socio-technical environments such as the EDC. The following two chapters expand on this conclusion.

CHAPTER 3

# Research Activities and Developments Behind the EDC

Chapter 2 introduced the EDC and its support functionality in a scenario addressing the collaborative and participatory design of a bus route. This chapter describes the development and research activities that eventually lead to the development of the EDC. The first two sections expand on the merging and integration of two research paradigms (Figure 3.1).

- *The Community PLANning (CoPlan)* paradigm about tabletop decision-games and simulations to support urban design and planning activities (conducted at the Urban Simulations Laboratory (SimLab) of the College of Architecture and Planning).

- *The Domain-Oriented Design Environments (DODEs)* paradigm focused on supporting domain workers in creating computational artifacts (conducted at the Center for LifeLong Learning and Design ($L^3D$) in Department of Computer Science at the College of Engineering).

The research and development activities explored with CoPlan and DODEs provide testimony that EDC did not spring forth from a vacuum. As illustrated by Figure 3.1, the merger of community-based urban design and planning tools in CoPlan and the computational support mechanisms explored with DODEs resulted in the initial version of the EDC.

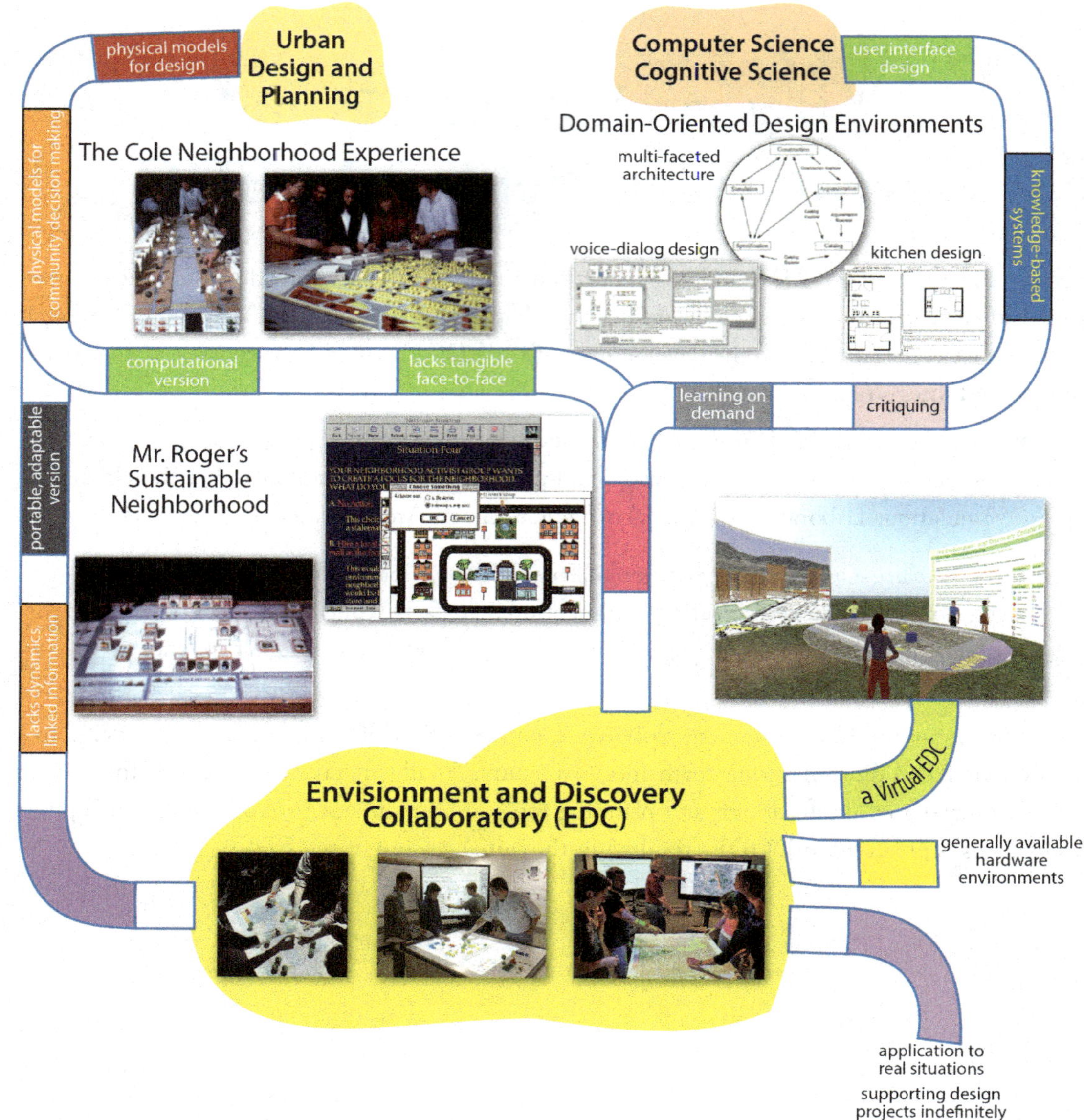


Figure 3.1: Integrating two research development paradigms: CoPlan and DODEs.

The first two sections of this chapter describe CoPlan and DODEs in some detail. The third section analyzes the mutually beneficial and reciprocally reinforcing research relationships between the EDC and the Center for LifeLong Learning and Design's (L$^3$D). The chapter concludes with the fourth section conceptualizing the EDC as a *socio-technical environment*.

# 3.1    COPLAN: COMMUNITY-BASED PLANNING TOOLS AND THE COLE NEIGHBORHOOD

## 3.1.1    TABLETOP GAMES AND SIMULATIONS SUPPORTED BY PHYSICAL MEDIA TOOLS

The central purpose of the tabletop games and simulations based on physical, non-computational media is to function as interactive tools and assist participants who "cannot plan or design" by helping them to frame planning problems, make decisions, identify compromises, resolve conflict, and learn from others gathered around the tabletop by transforming tacit knowledge into distributed understanding (Arias, 1995a; Polanyi, 1966). Given their applications on real problems, it is important that decision outcomes through the use of these tools are reliable and valid, and that all stakeholders understand and agree on the intended meaning provided by the interaction of the common language of the tools with their respective tabletop. The SIMlLab experience included the development of many of these tools for various contexts not only as decision support tools for resolving problems, but also for teaching and research applications in planning, design, and learning (Section 7.1 for specific examples) (Arias, 1995b).

Figure 3.2: Tabletop games and simulations at the SimLab: (a) left pane: *learning to design* urban movement systems and (b) right pane: *designing to learn* about urban land-use and zoning regulations.

These early experiences lead the initial ideas of integrating on-the-side technological functionality to the design games and simulations as was the case of the Cole Neighborhood tools presented in this chapter, and subsequently to the development of the interactive simulation gameboard, or Intersim (explained later in Chapter 6).

## The Development of the Physical Media Tools

From their inception, the initial efforts in the development of interactive decision-tools for collaborative planning and design were motivated by various real-world and academic experiences such as:

- the nature of planning and design and their importance on implementation and their direct influence on city center revitalization and growth management in various central cities in the U.S. (Wallace et al., 1979a, 1979b);

- an interest in participation and its value in housing and community planning, e.g., resident participation and residential quality in public housing or participation in squatter settlement improvements (Arias, 1988);

- the limitations of formal approaches such as (1) modeling of choice behavior using more well-defined approaches such as expressed preference methodology (Saaty, 1977), (2) multi-criteria and analytic hierarchy frameworks for locational analysis (Anselin and Arias, 1983), or (3) closed micro-analytic simulation approaches (e.g., SimCity; www.simcity.com/) in addressing the open-ended nature of wicked and ill-structured planning and design problems (Rittel and Webber, 1984);

- the notion of "behavior setting" in framing the relationship of the participants and the tabletop games (Barker, 1968);

- a perceived value in the integration of the physical and the digital (Arias et al., 1997a); and

- the pursuit of better approaches to teaching planning and design research methods utilizing the SimLab tools and applications (as discussed in Section 7.1) (Arias, 1995b).

The motivations above lead us to the initial developments of tabletop games and simulations as interactive decision-support tools for other contexts in addition to planning, such as learning activities. In addition, they provided central contributions to the functional capabilities of the tools as well as their subsequent extensions into digital media, for example:

- supporting *decision-making* as a basis of problem solving and conflict resolution (Mandelbaum, 1984);

- supporting *participation* as a means of empowerment, and ownership behind implementation (Arias, 1988; Arias et al., 1999);

- constructing *critical coalitions* of relevant stakeholders in collaborative planning to support identification of (i) problems and objectives in planning and urban design, and (ii) a political basis for the implementation of policies and plans (Arias, 2005; Grigsby et al., 1977);

- supporting *creativity* as a central human attribute of an individual or a group for innovation in the outcomes of architectural and urban design activities (Lang, 1987; Sternberg, 1999);

- evolving *simulations and game boards* from physical to computational (Arias et al., 1997a); and

- evolving (i) the "languages of 3D objects" into *tangible interfaces* (Hornecker, 2011), (ii) the role of the 'hand-object' relationship as a central to the notion behind the language of objects in interactive interfaces of the tools (Wilson, 1998), and (iii) the use of "by-the-side computers" into a *reflection space* (Arias, 1996).

As described above, while there is collaboration in design, planning processes on the other hand are fundamentally based on decision-making in a context of conflict (Mandelbaum, 1984). The reason being that the resolution of planning problems imply making decisions which bring together many stakeholders, and these decisions affect or are effected by them. Since these stakeholders represent different interests, the decisions are of a multiple-criteria and multiple-objective nature and consequently lead to their inherent conflict, i.e., *my problem is more important than yours*, or *that solution does not work for me* (Anselin and Arias, 1983). The information and knowledge associated with the decision making in these processes is both tacit and distributed among the different stakeholders in the *problem or conflict space*. These basic concerns led to the initial development of the tabletop simulations and games to support decision-making in planning and design (Arias et al., 1997a).

### Language-Based Simulations and Games: Supporting Planning and Design Decision-Making

For the *decision games and simulations* developed in the context of the CoPlan paradigm the concept of "winning or loosing" found in competition games does not exist. Rather, our concerns were to make players aware of the *benefits and costs behind different decision outcomes* and with the stakeholder's interpretation of what rank order and intensity between ranks of design actions are worthwhile pursuing in the application domain. We make a distinction between a simulation and a decision game.

- In a *simulation* the description of the physical systems, and all other relevant non-physical socio-economic systems of the setting being analyzed, are simulated with the descriptive language of objects over the board before any of the evaluative and prescriptive activities take place. In addition, no specific pre-conceived set of rules and protocols are defined, other than to understand the language of pieces, the functionality of a simulation board, and the relationships between the pieces and the board.

- In a *decision game*, a fundamental difference is that as opposed to simulations, the setting and its characteristics are pre-described so that players engage in a "what if" gamming approach focusing on either evaluative and prescriptive activities. In this manner games support players to identify the existence of problems, their intensity and their social or spatial distributions, along with the discussion and definition of possible solutions. They utilize the notion of chance or probabilities for events or actions to take place on the board. The game situations, pieces selections, and placements, along with supporting visualization information are activated through pre-established rules and protocols, e.g., each player or group of players rolls the dice, pieces are moved on the board provoking discussion, and decisions are made and the outcomes from physical or socio-economic relationships are visualized.

Wittgenstein introduced the concept of a *language game* and the view that the world is no longer a totality of logically connected "state of affairs," but rather a variety of related expressions in a language (Wittgenstein, 1953). Language in this sense covers what we do and what we say, and the connection of words and objects is just preliminary to the use of language. Taking this notion of *language*, as Habraken did with design (Habraken et al., 1987), we applied it to decision-making and constructed our tabletop prototypes, as *language games and simulations* (Arias, 1988). In developing games and simulations as physical media, we focused on locational decisions of urban activities over space and viewed urban planning or management of natural resources and hazards as "problem re-solution processes" (Anselin and Arias, 1983). The goal of these processes is to arrive at interventions (actions, plans, or policies) whose aims are simply the reallocation of resources and the change of behavior in either human or natural systems in the settings of concern. Change may be viewed as either the reinforcement or redirection of behavior, depending on the situation been perceived as "going well" or as "being bad," respectively. These experiences with CoPlan provided important foundations later for the seeding of the EDC's functionality for application experiences, as described in Chapter 5. The capability to support simulations and games was difficult to attain with our physical media games and simulation efforts whereas the EDC gives the interesting possibility to integrate both to enhance decision-making support (Arias et al., 1997a).

## Components and Affordances of Physical Media Tools

In the context of CoPlan, tools were developed to help users frame or address domain-specific problems and their associated interventions (for example, a simulation to analyze zoning decisions or a game to understand policies affecting neighborhood change) (Arias, 1995b). These tools included the following components:

- a language comprising three vocabularies of 3D physical objects. The vocabularies provide the tools with their descriptive, evaluative and prescriptive capabilities through their interactions with the game board (Figure 3.3 below), this language evolved later as the EDC's tangible interface described in Chapter 6;

- a simulation-game board representing the horizontal surface upon which simulations are constructed and/or games are played. By placing and moving the language of objects stakeholders can simulate or play to frame and resolve planning problems in a participatory manner (Figure 3.3). This component later becomes the digital tabletop of the EDC, as mentioned in Chapter 6;

- a set of rules and protocols developed for each game or simulation application to guide the interactions between players, and between the language and the game board. These protocols were developed to guide the player-player and player-tool interactions for the different application domains; and

- later inclusion of early use of *computers by-the-side* in the SimLab became a fourth element of the physical media, e.g., a driver linking SPSS and AutoCad for an early version of planning information systems or the integration of the early computer-based simulation for urban zoning) (Arias, 1994).

### A Physical Language of Objects to Support Collaborative Participation

The development of a common language of objects is considered central to the construction of "meaning" through the interactivity with the tabletop games and simulations in the physical media tools. The three-dimensional languages of the physical media are composed of three vocabularies of objects or 'languages of pieces' as users refer to them, with meanings associated to these pieces, for example, descriptions of land use in the neighborhood such as yellow or red blocks representing buildings of residential or commercial uses. To facilitate players' ease of understanding as well as valid and reliable associations, the physical elements in the language are developed across a spectrum of abstractness—from *high abstraction* to *high authenticity*—by using the three physical dimensions of shape, size, and color of the physical objects which in turn are associated to meanings through agreements by the players (Arias, 1995b).

The physical language is also designed to overcome the psychological anxieties of any interface that some stakeholders may initially experience in addressing problems through a participatory approach (Arias and Eden, 2002). Therefore, the language must appear simple enough so that all stakeholders feel sufficiently confident to understand what the different objects mean. To this end, the vocabularies of the language as tangible interfaces meet several requirements that themselves form the basis for evaluation of the physical media as follows.

- *Relevancy.* The language should emphasize relevant aspects of the situation and omit irrelevant ones. For example, the building materials used in a house do not figure in a zoning problem. Thus, the material should not be represented in the pieces in a zoning exercise.

- *Flexibility.* Degrees of freedom in decision-making must be reflected by the possible ranges of selection and arrangement of pieces. Location, orientation, and combination of pieces should correspond to aspects of the physical system that can be determined by the decisions to be made.

- *Verisimilitude.* The level of abstraction of game board and pieces must conform to the abstraction ability of the stakeholders. Along these lines, tools may also contribute to cognitive development by increasing the abstraction capabilities of players.

- *Transparency.* Mappings between aspects of the real situation and characteristics of the pieces should be as intuitive as possible. For example, the size of a house can better be visualized by the size of a piece than by its color.

- *Evolutionary adaptability.* The meaning of the language (game board and pieces) while developed specifically for each domain application, should allow for evolution through modifications by the players during use.

- *Simplicity.* Finally, the language (game board and pieces) should be as simple as possible, within the limits defined by the above requirements.

The physical media was applied in various contexts from academic research and teaching to actual planning situations. For example, the notion of tabletop games and simulations were found to be very useful in teaching and learning how to collaboratively explore problems to undergraduates at $L^3D$ and the SimLab under the NSF Undergraduate Research Opportunities Program and the Graduate/Undergraduate Education Enrichment Program at the University of Colorado (for further articulation of learning developments see Chapters 4 and 7).

In addition, these experiences provided valuable contributions to the initial and continuing development of the EDC's functionality to support design, creativity, and learning as elaborated in Chapter 4. Their use facilitated to contextualize the notion of research in the classroom and as such they became useful teaching vehicles as mentioned in Chapter 7. Beyond the academic and research applications they were utilized in real-world situations, as in the following case study about the redevelopment of the inner city neighborhoods of the Cole neighborhood in Denver, Colorado.

### Supporting Descriptive, Evaluative, and Prescriptive Thinking

Through the associations of physical attributes with meaning, and through the interactions between the language objects and the game board, the tabletop tool gains representational capabilities that facilitate the expression of the *descriptive, evaluative*, and *prescriptive thinking* of the stakeholders. These three phases are fundamental to the players' critical thinking and their capacity of creative problem and conflict resolution in a participatory manner (Arias, 1995a). Three types of objects are developed within the space of alternatives created by the three dimensions above (Figure 3.3).

1. *Descriptive thinking* is supported by objects of the vocabulary that represent the empirical aspects of the decision problem. It corresponds to the cognitive dimensions of perception and observation and addresses the question: *How are things (reality)?* It has as its outcomes the production of *images, representations*, and *models* of the world. It not only serves as a model of reality (and consequently it supports *predictive capacity*), but also allows for others to have access to reality without necessarily having had a direct contact with its objects and processes. Thus, the substantive and procedural descriptions of the existing setting or concern are developed through combinations of pieces and their placements on the board.

2. *Evaluative thinking* is supported by objects of the vocabulary that can express the evaluative aspects of both empirical and policy-making aspects of the problem. It corresponds to the cognitive dimensions of analysis and assessment and addresses the questions: *What is the state of things? Should I manipulate things (reality) given their state?* Its outcome is the *utilization of existing criteria and the attitudes and values behind them* that govern what should and should not be done. Thus, utilizing evaluative pieces over descriptive ones (in combination with simulations or visualization of impact analysis models by-the-side), the stakeholders can explicate their perceptions of watershed problems, their causes, effects, and intensity and their evaluations of the social and spatial distributions of the problems. In addition the notions of concurrence and non-concurrence are made explicit by the placement of each player's evaluative pieces;

3. *Prescriptive thinking* is supported by those objects that represent policies, plans, and decisions. It corresponds to the cognitive dimensions of *analysis and intervention* and addresses the question: *What do I want to do, and how can I manipulate things (reality) to accomplish it?* Its outcome is the supporting development of strategies to attain *objectives* (satisfy needs and wants) and *priorities* between them and it results in the modification of existing criteria or the creation of new ones to guide future behavior. Utilizing prescriptive pieces from the language (in combination with simulations or visualization of impact analysis models by-the-side), development and testing of pro-

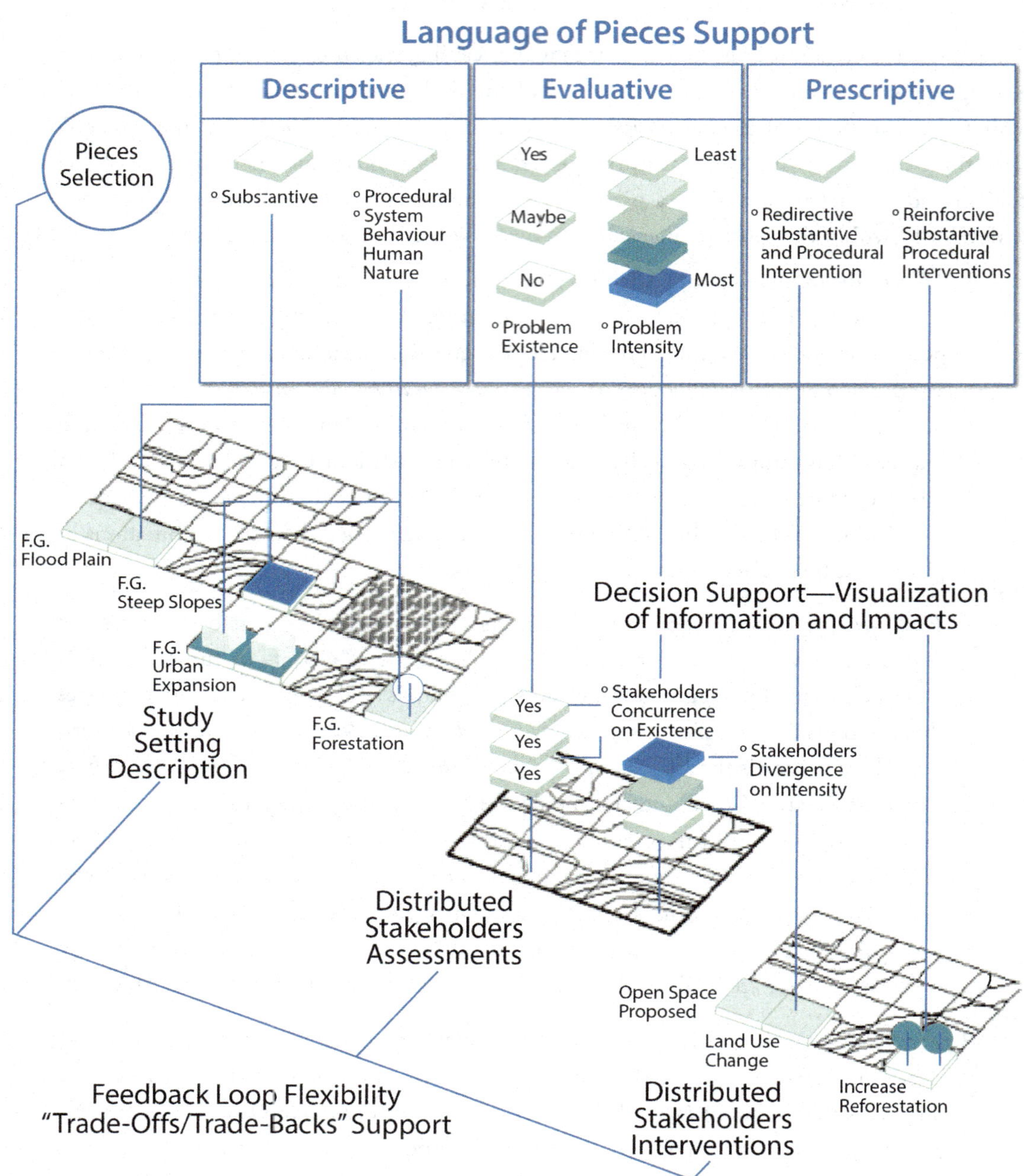


Figure 3.3: The *descriptive, evaluative* and *prescriptive language of objects*: through their placement over the gameboard players are able to describe the study setting, then make explicit their assessments of the perceived problems and their proposed interventions to address these problems.

posed reinforced or redirected actions are designed by the stakeholders, resulting in the reallocation of resources and the necessary changes in behavior.

Figure 3.4: Physical media tools: (a) sustainability indicators developed to research through the notions of gaming; and (b) urban zoning simulation to learn about its regulation impacts on the form of cities.

Many of the ground rules as to how a description is allowed to be developed are predetermined in the descriptive phase, for example, the laws governing vehicular movement can be defined by colors where red is stop or no movement, yellow is slow or caution, and green is free flowing movement; also different shades of green may mean different rates of speed. Much of the definition and use of the evaluative and prescriptive elements is left up to the participants to come-up with through a shared understanding or agreements. Thus, whereas the descriptive pieces more or less set the physical and legislative boundary conditions for problem solving, the meaning and uses of the evaluative and prescriptive pieces are often developed in each game or simulation through a complex process of social interaction between players. In fact, even new pieces are added to these vocabularies during the course of using the tool. Later on, computational functionality gave these objects of the language a tremendous flexibility to change, adopt, and adapt meanings in the tactile interphase of the EDC as explained in bus scenario of the previous chapter and in the different case studies and applications in Chapters 5 and 7.

The physical media was applied in various contexts from academic research and teaching to actual planning situations. For example, the notion of tabletop games and simulations were found to be very useful in teaching and learning how to collaboratively explore problems to undergraduates at $L^3D$ and the SimLab (for further articulation of learning developments see Chapter 7).

In addition, these experiences provided valuable contributions to the initial and continuing development of the EDC's functionality to support design, creativity, and learning as elaborated in the following chapter. Their use facilitated to contextualize the notion of research in the classroom and as such they became useful teaching vehicles, as mentioned in Chapter 7. Beyond the academic and research applications they were utilized in real world situations, as in the following case study where they were applied in the redevelopment of inner city neighborhoods like the Cole neighborhood in Denver, Colorado.

### 3.1.2   THE COLE NEIGHBORHOOD EXPERIENCE: A PHYSICAL MEDIA APPLICATION

#### Cole: A Case of Inner City Deterioration

Located to the northeast of the Denver central business district, the Cole neighborhood comprises a 4 square-mile area of 88 city blocks. According to the 1990 census, the neighborhood included about 5,000 people, inhabiting about 1,200 residential units and a mix of industrial and commercial activities. Hard hit during the 1980s by an ailing economy, rapidly increasing crime due to drugs and gangs, loss of some of its stable families that left for safer areas, housing vacancy rates close to 20%, deterioration and abandonment of over one-third of its housing stock, and the lack of institutional concern and support, by the 1990's Cole was considered one of the worst neighborhoods in Denver. The unemployment level was estimated at over 15%, which was more than double the citywide average of 6% at the time. Despite the neighborhood's proximity to downtown Denver, the conditions mentioned above reinforced high apathy and low pride of its residents. The neighborhood became a representative example of the deterioration and ailments facing America's inner-city neighborhoods (Arias, 1996).

#### The Need for Planning Assistance

Out of this dim picture in the late 1980s emerged an alliance of stakeholders including: a core group of residents, one bank, the school district, churches, the police department, and others—all of whom were devoted to changing trends in the social, economic, physical, and educational condition of the neighborhood. In response to this group of motivated stakeholders, the newly formed Neighborhood Planning Division of the mayor's office and the Denver Planning Department, selected Cole as one of three target neighborhoods for revitalization, instead of gentrification, and issued a $7.5M commitment to this effort. While not nearly enough to resolve all problems, the intent was to turn the downward trends around.

Cole became the initial test case for the city's planning initiative where the mayor intended the neighborhood revitalization to be a grass-roots effort that would permit the neighbors to decide how the money would be spent. To accomplish this goal, the Cole Neighborhood Coalition was formed, together with a Coordinating Task Force and a City Technical Team that provided support to the academic group of the SimLab. The neighbors were expected to participate through the coalition at all levels of issue identification, program development, and implementation.

During the initial meetings, the City Technical Team noted that the Cole residents were poor, with an average educational level not higher than elementary school, with very limited verbal and graphic communication skills, and a limited conception and understanding of "their" neighborhood (Foy, 1991). In addition, there was a lack of neighborhood information such as social, economic, and physical inventories (housing, crime, infrastructure, social services) which made "informed participation" (Arias et al., 1999; Brown et al., 1994) extremely difficult to attain. In addition, like in many preceding community planning efforts, conflicts started to arise among stakeholders when deciding how the money would be spent over the 3-year disbursement period. The *conflicts* arising out of the initial unstructured participation were of the type that frequently occur in framing a wicked problem-for example, "my street or block is in worse condition than yours" or "redevelopment of commercial areas is more important than parks and residential streets" or "why redevelopment funds for the street and not my house?" These conflicts threatened the process of objectively identifying priorities in the allocation of the redevelopment funds. Such observations raised concerns over the competence of the stakeholders, who were are asked to make valid and reliable revitalization decisions for the neighborhood as a whole.

Given such concerns, the Denver Planning Department asked the SimLab group in the College of Architecture and Planning to become involved in the intended "grass roots" revitalization by developing tools for the stakeholder group to participate in an informed manner in accomplishing their tasks to revitalize the Cole Neighborhood (Arias, 1996). The SimLab was asked to develop three major tools for the Cole neighbors to resolve conflicts during the planning of the revitalization of public areas, blocks, and streets, and as well as for private property improvement through a low-interest loan program. The neighbors named the tools "the neighborhood model" tool, "the street model" tool, and "the information system" tool. Development of the models represented a joint effort between the neighbors in the coalition, the Denver Planning and Community Development Department and more than a dozen planning and architecture students at the SimLab providing evidence. As mentioned later in this chapter and the next, our Cole experience represents an argument that our design methodology behind the EDC-CoPlan development was driven by real problems with real solutions, as illustrated by Figure 3.4.

## The Neighborhood Simulation Tool

This tool was developed to help the neighbors strengthen their perception of issues and opportunities distributed over the entire neighborhood. While interacting with a digital map of their community, the participants began collaborating by developing a common vocabulary. By identifying the physical elements on the board as "pieces", the participants started to move the pieces around the board to describe and evaluate the conditions of Cole. Together, they started to form a common language about their community, and thus were able to communicate about topics such as zoning and land use, concentrations of crime, vacancies and abandonment or specific condition of housing units, neighborhood blocks, and streets (Figure 3.5(a) and (b)) (Arias, 1995a).

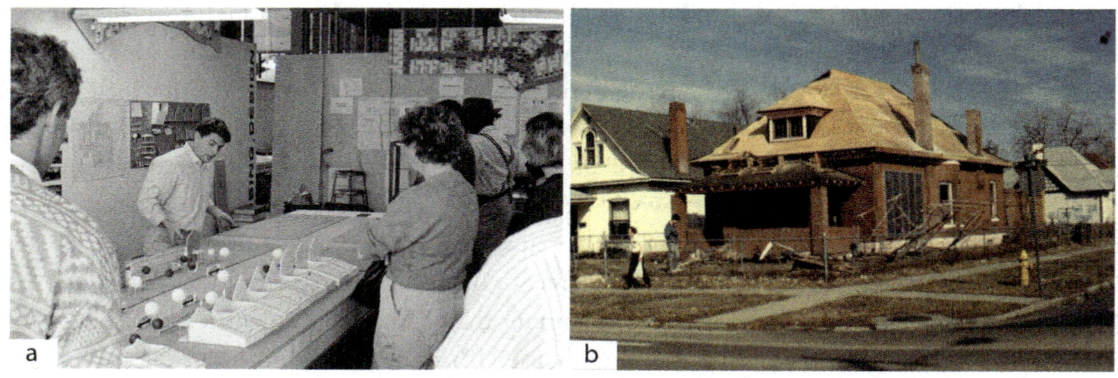


Figure 3.5: The Street Tool, supporting neighbors to attain housing improvements: (a) neighbor assessors learning to identify properties for the bank's low interest loans program for (b) real private property improvements in the neighborhood.

During extended design sessions, property-by-property descriptions of the Cole Neighborhood were created. These descriptions represented the neighbors' distributed understanding of the housing and other land uses in the neighborhood. Using the yellow pieces as a descriptive vocabulary they were able to represent the various types of housing from single-family detached to multi-family attached and their locations throughout the neighborhood. In a similar manner the representations of the other land-use types as described in the bus scenario of the previous chapter, e.g., commercial, industrial, recreational, etc., were achieved with the objects of the respective vocabularies (Figure 3.5.a). The shared evaluator vocabulary enabled the participants to evaluate the neighborhood in terms of various concerns such as crime, housing condition, and abandonment, or land-use incompatibility, among others (Figure 3.5.b). Discussions in the evaluative session were carried out on the outcomes of the descriptive session. These discussions were complemented and supported by other media in the information system such as videos, or slides of neighborhood streets, houses, buildings, and other data provided by the planning department. Once compromises were reached, neighbors placed evaluative pieces over the descriptive ones. For example, they placed a "black roof" piece over the yellow housing piece to indicate that the property was in "poor condition" or "abandoned" (Figure 3.5.b).

The distributed descriptive and evaluative understanding made it easier for neighbors to visualize the extent and spatial distribution of the physical and social problems in "conflict zones," as the neighbors called them. The conflict zones were described as abandoned structures affording high incidence of crimes. These zones enabled participants to further identify specific issues that could be addressed during revitalization, such as housing deterioration, street and alley improvements, commercial-zone revitalization, and improvements to neighborhood facilities. In doing so, neighbors were able to reach an informed compromise about priorities for intervention and funding allocation. The Neighborhood Tool also provided the participants with the capability of monitoring neighborhood change on an ongoing basis.

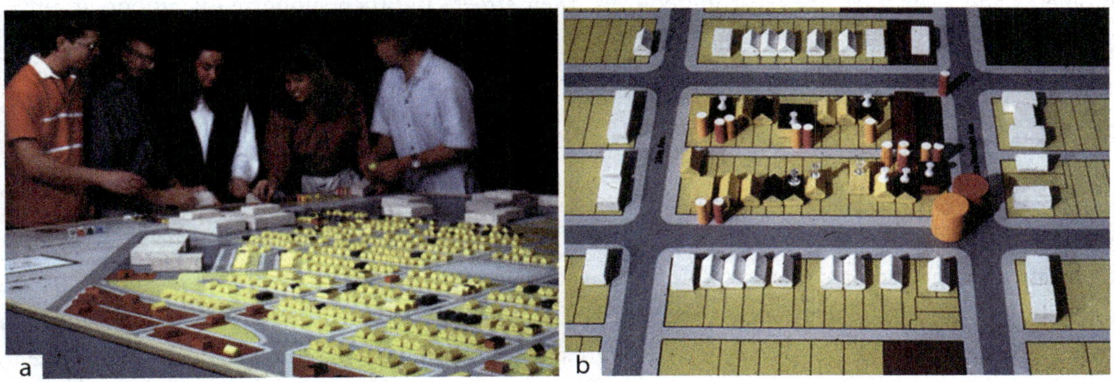

Figure 3.6: The Cole Neighborhood Simulation Tool: visualizing spatial distributions and intensity of neighborhood condition and problems using the descriptive and evaluative languages: (a) the neighborhood's existing characteristics (descriptive language) and (b) he perceived problems affecting condition of a neighborhood block (evaluative language).

Perhaps the tool's most important revitalization application was that it allowed neighbors to interact with each other and work together to visualize the distributed nature of the physical problems and their concentrations in certain areas of their neighborhood—for example, deterioration or abandonment along a street corridor or in certain blocks and not in others—or social problems across the neighborhood in terms of socio-economic characteristics of the population—for example, distributions and concentrations of crime or household unemployment. The interaction and visualization were important in forming informed compromises that lead to a shared understanding by neighbors that formed the basis for establishing intervention priorities for redevelopment. This common understanding continues to be a core objective of our research activities in design and learning with the EDC, as presented in Chapter 4 on the contributions to human-centered- informatics.

## The Street Simulation Tool

This tool allowed the neighbors to zoom in on priority areas for intervention that were identified using the Neighborhood Stimulation Tool (Figure 3.6). In a second stage of community planning, the Street Simulation Tool enabled participants to define a set of descriptive, evaluative, and prescriptive vocabularies about public right-of-ways for street improvements, and also for private-property improvements (Figure 3.5). It allowed neighbors living in the identified blocks of intervention priority areas to describe in more detail existing conditions along the streets and houses, as they knew them. The evaluative elements assisted them in identifying the existence of problems and their intensities distributed over "their street" and then supported neighbors in prescribing possible interventions.

The objects of the language in this tool were elements of high verisimilitude to reality, e.g., a tree was represented by a ball with a stick (Arias, 1995a). The descriptive set of existing street elements were all painted white. The evaluative pieces were pins with flags of different colors and a set of flags of a color were given to each so that he/she could place them to identify his/her perception where a problem existed along the street player. The prescriptive elements where the same as the descriptive but had color, so for example, trees were painted in green (Figure 3.6b). The prescriptive interventions were then attributed a second layer of vocabulary, which included the dimension of costs—for example, the costs of trees, streetlights, or traffic lights. This dimension then supported trade-offs (trading an item for another) and trade-backs (taking something back) after neighbors designed their "ideal street" improvements in a cost unconstrained manner.

Figure 3.7: The Street Simulation Tool: (a) Facilitators teaching neighbors how to use the street tool through manipulation of the language of objects to describe and evaluate their street; and (b) designing a safe intersection in their street through the placement of different street elements of the prescriptive language.

To support the discussion about the dimension of cost, the Street Stimulation Tool was programmed with the implementation costs for all prescriptive elements. When some of the neighbors physically placed elements to address a problem or change them, another neighbor used the computer on-the-side to keep track of costs associated with each prescriptive element (for example: street lights if security problems were perceived as security with dark areas of the street, or pedestrian lights if the problem was one of safety crossing a street). After all the participating neighbors completed their respective "ideal street," the neighbor in charge of tallying costs would let the participants know whether their prescribed solution(s) to a problem was within the agreed budget for that street or problem type. If it was not, then a phase of trade-offs and trade-back and compromises followed until an acceptable solution met the budget.

While we used a computer-by-the-side in CoPlan to complement these physical tools, the two environments were not integrated. This shortcoming emerged as an important design requirement for integrating the physical and the computational media as explained in more detail in the evolving architecture of the EDC in Chapter 6 (Arias et al., 1997a).

## The Neighborhood Information System

This computer information system was developed in a integrated fashion through computers-by-the-side with the neighborhood and street simulation tools above. Its purpose was to provide the neighbors with the necessary data and information about their neighborhood to make informed decisions using the simulation tools and to help them to manage the information generated from the different session using the simulation tools. In this manner, the neighbors could use the system over time to build the information base for making and tracking decisions.

A base map was digitized on a property-by-property basis with the legal property as its unit of analysis, thereby developing the capability to construct city blocks and larger areas of the neighborhood through aggregations of these units of information in the database (Figure 3.7). In this manner, the system was also correlated to the neighborhood and the street simulation boards, which were also developed on a property-by-property basis. The units, as semantic objects in the graphic maps, were given meaning by using the data associated with each property in the statistical database—value, land use, proximity to facilities, number of residents, or values of housing condition—as well as in the graphical database—for example, other information complementing numeric data such as photographs of buildings to visualize their physical condition, written text documents, or videos of drive-by trips along street corridors. This information was useful in helping neighbors use the tools to describe setting, evaluate situations, and prescribe redevelopment interventions to resolve problems. In this manner, the information system may be thought as the initial notion of what later became the EDC's reflection space (Arias, 1994).

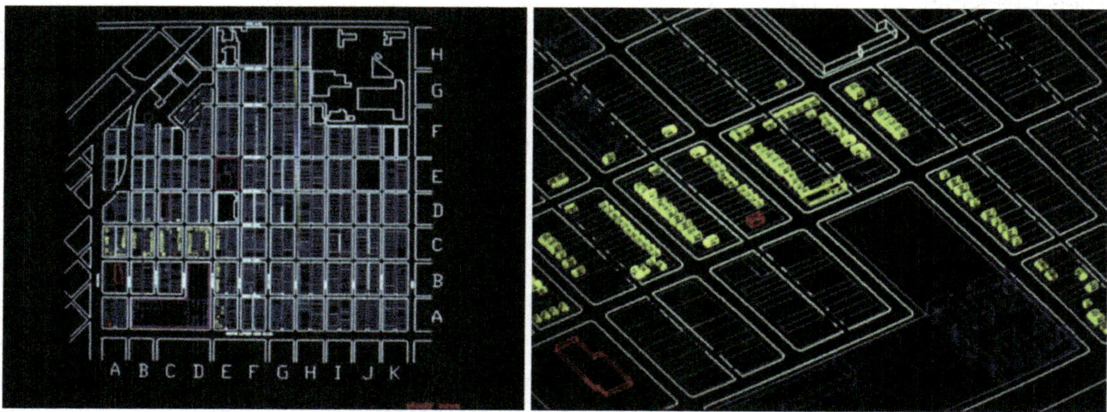

Figure 3.8: The Information Tool: predecessor of the EDC's reflection space: (a) the digital base map of COLE on a property-by-property basis with (b) the 3D visualization capabilities of different types of information to indicate a priority area for intervention.

Neighbors could deposit information generated from the other tools on a unit-by-unit basis. They also could retrieve information by searching for all objects with one or more attributes—"show me all houses that are abandoned or valued over $10,000"—or by displaying all attributes of one object—"show me the condition of this property." In this manner, support information in the system's database could be recalled to inform decisions in the physical simulation tools. It helped give meaning to pieces in the vocabulary, such as housing condition (good and poor) by recalling stored photographs to see examples of different building conditions, thus enabling neighbors to reach informed compromises and give a "shared meaning" when selecting a piece from the language (Arias, 1996).

## 3.1.3    LESSONS LEARNED FROM COPLAN

Some of the practical results included the identification of neighborhood high-priority areas that would receive funding over the period of the grant. Neighbors were able to make these decisions by using the neighborhood model (Figure 3.6). Likewise, they used the street model to propose street redevelopment efforts along the public rights-of-way (Figure 3.7), for example, sidewalks, landscaping, street crossings, lighting, tot-lots, and block gardens; and identified candidate private properties for low-interest restoration loans along streets in an intervention area of priority stored in the information system tool (Figure 3.8). Also, the neighborhood database in the information system was built in a comprehensive manner as a result of the information generated from the sessions using the tools over time. The ability to store information by this system in the computers by-the-side was a major limitation of the physical tools which also led us initially to think about moving from the physical boards computational table tops.

Reflecting on the Cole experience, and experiences with over 60 similar physical planning simulation and design games made us aware of some of their benefits and limitations compared to more traditional mathematical planning algorithms (Anselin and Arias, 1983) or close computer base simulations at the time, such as the initial versions of SimCity.

The *benefits* and *limitations* derived from the CoPlan paradigm have created an important foundation for the integration of computational functionality with physical tools that resulted in the EDC (Figure 1.1). The following features are some of the "added values" brought about by the real-time social interaction among neighbors, and made possible by the use of three-dimensional game boards and game pieces.

- *Continuity of argument.* Unlike computer-based simulations, the endowment of game pieces with meaning and the definition and redefinition of rules can take place without the cognitive interruption of a computer and its user interface. For example, as players move and place a piece representing a street light in a particular location, they argue the point that higher levels of illumination at night would make them feel safer as they walk from the bus stop to home. Their oral argument, including subjective factors such as intensity of conviction (emotion) or description of functionality (level of illumination), are complemented by the artifact (the three-dimensional language element) representing the objective factors of the argument (specific location or even higher levels of illumination). This continuity is especially important given recent findings that, even for friendly computer-user interfaces, the added value of real-time modeling and plan evaluation can be lost almost entirely in the cognitive burden of having to "work" the computer (Landauer, 1995).

- *Comprehension and retention.* For various reasons, the experiential characteristics of selection, placement, and replacement of the physical elements facilitate comprehension and retention more than in the case of computational simulation on a screen. For example, in the case of augmenting comprehension, capability to elicit the tacit knowledge of other points of view associated with a problem is greater and occurs more rapidly through face-to-face interaction among neighbors. The language supports the ability to describe, evaluate and prescribe (critical thinking) flexibility and interactively among a neighbor, the tool and other neighbors (Arias, 1995a). In the Cole experience, after the baseline survey of 115 neighbors, a greater understanding of the boundaries of the neighborhood was evident in the cognitive maps of "my neighborhood" by neighbors who had used the tools than by the ones who had not used them. The discrepancies between the cognitive and the political definitions of a neighborhood are relevant in that their existence represents limits to neighborhood participation in policy-making processes (Foy, 1991). For example, these limits can be apparent when addressing neighborhood revitalization needs through processes such as the capital improvement program. In such a process, it is fair to assume that neighbors are less motivated to participate in planning a capital improvement project that is beyond "their cognitive neighborhood" than a project that is within "their cognitive neighborhood."

- *Intuitive understanding.* If properly designed, the meanings associated with the physical three-dimensional attributes of the gaming simulation are intuitive. For example, using the colors green, yellow, and red for the evaluative vocabulary allows for an intuitive selection of an evaluative element by a player to express agreement, indecision, or disagreement within a simulation.

- *Ease of use.* Endowing the three-dimensional physical tools with meaning is something that neighbors can do easily through social interaction with each other. Thus, neighbors can develop a common language of gaming elements that can be easily used to make the selection, placement, and relocation of pieces on the game board closely follow the arguments and reasoning applied in their negotiations. This attribution is extremely difficult to support with our current set of logic formalisms used for computer representations (Winograd and Flores, 1986)

- *Conflict resolution, distributed understanding, and problem/solution ownership.* Taken collectively, the various benefits just described give the tools some advantages over their computational counterpart—e.g., SimCity—in the ability to resolve conflict by facilitating discussions and making tacit knowledge of problems from the different stakeholders explicit from which informed compromises can be reached. In addition, the face-to-face participation capability offered by these tools better affords shared ownership by the players of the solution to the problem and leads to the formation of critical coalitions that support implementation (Arias, 2005).

## Identification of Shortcomings of CoPlan

The development and application of the three-dimensional, simulation-games approach identified great potential in supporting critical thinking and distributed understanding via face-to-face interaction—both necessary in the resolution of ill-structured problems within contexts of conflict. However, the following shortcomings are associated with the physical nature of the board games and thus limit their applicability to various aspects and forms of policy-making. Concurrently they represented opportunities for our thinking in the development and integration of the physical media with the new digital media.

- *Process vs. state information.* The dynamic aspects of planning problems—for example, changes in rates and frequency of behavior in systems such as speed of vehicular flow in streets—are difficult if not impossible to represent with static three-dimensional game pieces and the tabletop simulation games. Appropriately to incorporate processes and the dynamic behavior of many urban systems into the tools of the CoPlan paradigm, the games and simulations must be endowed with computational functionality such as those presented in the bus scenario of Chapter 2.

- *Point vs. non-point phenomena.* While game pieces can easily represent the location of point phenomena such as a source of light or noise through location over the board, they are not well suited to represent non-point phenomena, intensity, and volume. Yet, especially in problems such as safety and noise in neighborhood streets, such phenomena as volume of traffic or noise generated by it are important aspects of the quality of a neighborhood and hence must somehow be incorporated into the functionality of a gaming-simulation tool. An example of this capability of the EDC was used in the community soundscapes prototype developments inspired mentioned in Chapter 7.

- *Aggregation/disaggregation.* The physical tools do not allow flexible aggregation and disaggregation of phenomena and processes. For instance, two separate tools had to be developed to address neighborhood-wide concerns, as in the neighborhood model, and the more specific issues at the block or street level, as the street model. Yet, computational functionality such as that found in geographical information systems (GIS) does allow efficient zooming in and out of particular areas, thereby permitting policy-making problems for various levels of spatial aggregation to be addressed. The support capabilities for such concerns are illustrated in both, the application domain cases of Chapter 5 and in the EDC's innovations in teaching and learning of Chapter 7.

### Outcomes of CoPlan: The Development of a Computational Gameboard

Based on the CoPlan experience and the displayed strengths of the three-dimensional approach and the need to ameliorate its inherent limitations found in the Cole experience, the development of a computationally INTERactive Simulation-gameboard (InterSim) was initiated (Figure 6.2) The InterSim project as a predecessor of the EDC had at its core the creation of a prototype to integrate systems that support new paradigms of interaction with simulations—with an emphasis on support for shared interaction to mediate social aspects of learning, design, and planning (Arias, 1996). To this end, it integrated the use of the physical objects-to support and encourage face-to-face interaction among the participants with virtual objects to provide computational support for the model underlying the simulation (Arias, 2000). The architecture of the InterSim development is presented later as part of the evolving architecture of the EDC in Chapter 6. The InterSim computational functionality enhanced the contributions of the physical simulation-games approach while retaining the participatory, experiential, and interactive characteristics and ameliorating most of their observed limitations of CoPlan (Arias et al., 1997a).

In conclusion, the three central outcomes of relevance from the CoPlan paradigm are:

1. the design idea to create a horizontal surface with computational capabilities upon which planning games and simulations could be carried out interactively utilizing the physical language of objects for tangible interactions;

2. based on the observed value in supporting participatory planning and design, CoPlan is responsible for the idea to continue utilizing these physical tools as an integrative part of design processes for idea generation of the computational functionality associated with the evolution of the EDC (Chapter 6); and

3. the impetus for merging the CoPlan and the DODEs paradigms (described next) in order to advance the development of the INTERSIM into its evolution as Smart Board and PiTA Board versions of the EDC (as discussed further in Chapter 6).

## 3.2    DOMAIN-ORIENTED DESIGN ENVIRONMENTS (DODEs)

The CoPlan paradigm supported collaborative planning and decision making with physical media. The DODE paradigm (Fischer, 1994a) explored a variety of different mechanisms that digital media could provide in supporting design. This section discusses the differences between physical and computational media and some unique characteristics of computational media; the interweaving of problem framing and problem solving; the development from domain-oriented construction kits to DODES; and illustrates these developments with an application of a DODE in the domain of architectural design.

### Differences between CoPlan and DODEs

While passive materials and artifacts cannot speak for themselves, computational materials can (Schön, 1983). This fundamental difference between computation and other design materials provides great leverage in improving the way designers work and learn. Printed media do not have interpretive power—they can convey information for designers, but they cannot analyze the work products created by them. Computational media can make information relevant to the task at hand thereby (1) reducing the information overload problem and (2) the need for decontextualized learning. They provide the foundation for all "on demand" notions (such as learning on demand, using information on demand, detail on demand).

### Intertwining Problem Framing and Problem Solving

DODEs are significant not only as technical achievements in computer science, but also as examples of principled analyses of helping humans to cope with complex design problems. Design is not merely a search through a well-defined space to find a best solution but it involves cognitive, social, organizational, and cultural issues. Computational support for design is not merely a function of computational power; it must itself be designed with an understanding of the fundamental challenges that design problems present.

One specific challenge is the need to intertwine problem framing and problem solving (Rittel, 1984), because the characteristics of a problem are not known precisely before attempts at a solution are made. Only through attempting to solve a problem do the characteristics come into focus and requirements can be articulated. A partially framed problem affects the process of creating a solution, and at the same time, this partially constructed solution affects the process of reframing the problem. The limitations and failures of design approaches that rely on directionality, causality, and a strict separation between analysis and synthesis have been recognized in architecture for a long time. A careful analysis of these failures could have saved software engineering the effort expended in finding out that waterfall-type models can at best be an impoverished and oversimplified model of real design activities.

### Domain-Oriented Construction Kits

The Pinball Construction Kit (Budge, 1983), an early example of a domain-oriented construction kit, is illustrated in Figure 3.9. It supports users to design a pinball game by arranging components (such as flippers and bumpers) and allows them to try out intermediate designs through simulation by playing a pinball game with the artifact they have created. This simulation capability allows users to evaluate their design by experiencing it. In this sense, designs created within the Pinball Construction Kit "talk-back" to the designer in a manner that is not possible with passive media, such as pencil and paper. If designers find out that the current design does not perform as expected, it can be easily modified and tested again thereby supporting an iterative design methodology within the limits of the kit of objects provided.

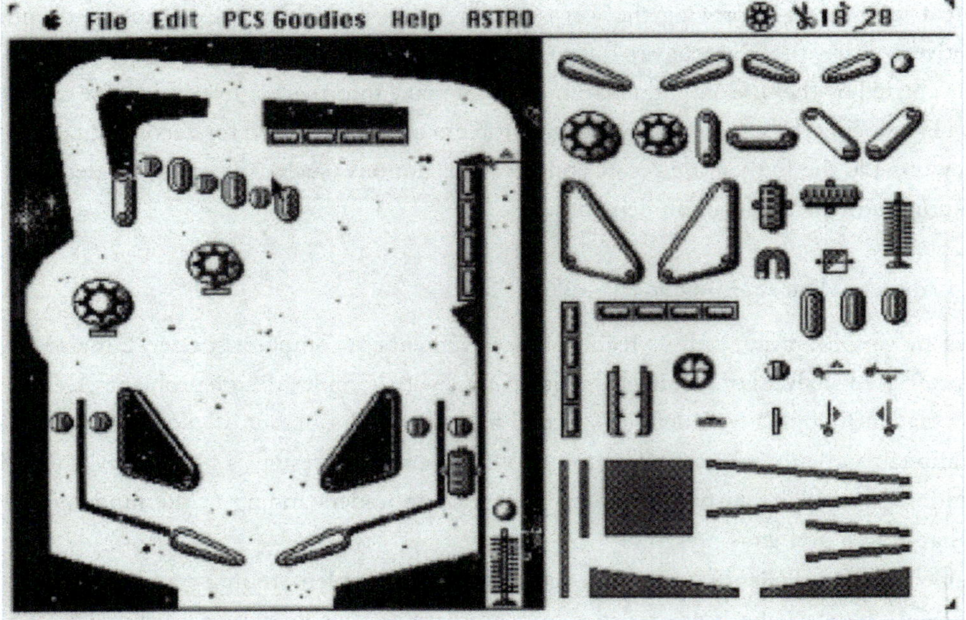


Figure 3.9: The Pinball Construction Kit: on the right side of the screen is a palette of pinball objects. On the left is a work area where the objects are arranged to design a pinball artifact. The work area supports simulations allowing pinball games to be played at any point in the design.

## From Construction Kits to DODEs

By implementing, using, and assessing domain-oriented construction kits, our research provided evidence that construction kits help designers to quickly and easily configure a design, but they provide little support in creating a good design. Although these systems provide domain abstractions to users, they had no knowledge about the quality of the design. Even with construction kits that support simulation, design errors that might have been avoided are not discovered until a great deal of work has been done, if at all. And when the designer has created a design that seems to work satisfactorily, there is no feedback from the system about how to improve the design. *Computational critics* (Fischer et al., 1998) supporting design perform a task that paper-based design materials cannot—they interpret the evolving design situation created by the designer, and actively signal when potential problems are detected.

## Illustrating DODEs: Janus: A DODE for Kitchen Design

Janus (Fischer, 1994a) supports kitchen designers in the development of floor plans. Janus-Construction (Figure 3.10) is the construction kit for the system. The palette of the construction kit contains domain-oriented building blocks such as sinks, stoves, and refrigerators. Designers construct kitchens by selecting design units from the palette and placing them into the work area. In addition to design by *composition* (using the palette for constructing an artifact from scratch), Janus-Construction also supports design by *modification* (by choosing existing designs from the catalog and modifying them in the work area).

The critics in Janus-Construction identify potential problems in the artifact being designed. Their knowledge about kitchen design includes design principles based on building codes, safety standards, and functional preferences. Figure 3.10 illustrates that the critics fired two critiquing messages, one of which stating "the length of the work triangle is greater than 23 feet." Designers who are not familiar with the concept of the work triangle, or who are not sure of the implications of violating this rule, can access relevant argumentation by clicking on the critiquing message. Clicking on the critiquing message invokes Janus-Argumentation and enters the argumentation at the location where the work triangle is discussed. The information about the work triangle rule includes a definition (the work triangle is the combined distances between sink, refrigerator, and stove), a graphical illustration, and arguments for and against following the rule.

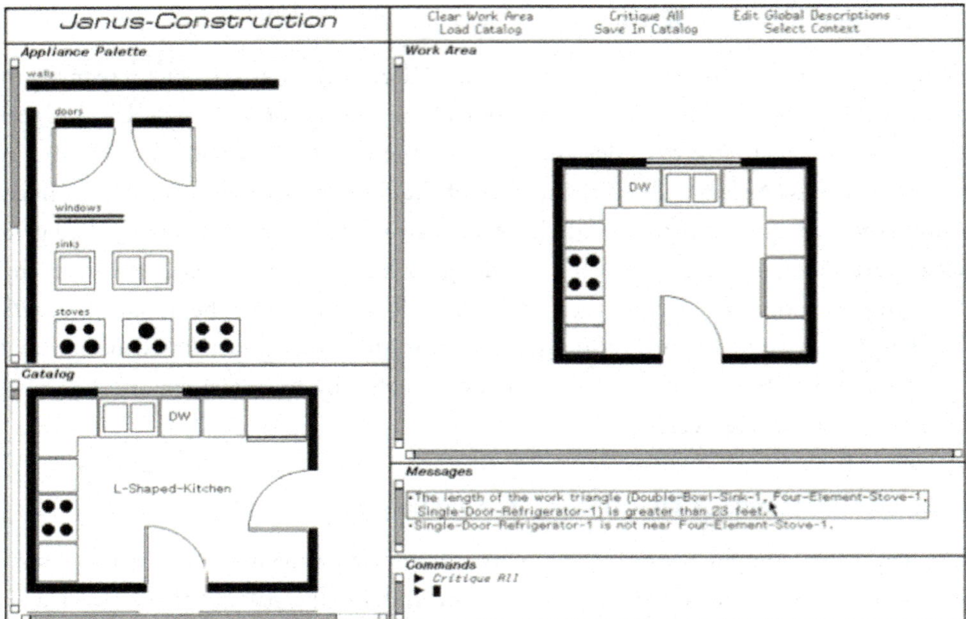


Figure 3.10: Janus-Construction: the work triangle critic. The construction component of Janus has an appliance palette of kitchen design objects and work area for constructing kitchen flow plans. Critic messages are displayed in the Messages window. Selecting on critic message takes the designer to the argumentation component.

Designers needing additional help to understand the argumentation about the work triangle can retrieve examples from the catalog (the top-right window in Figure 3.11) that obey the rule (or, alternatively, they can retrieve counter examples that do not obey the rule). The Argumentation-Illustrator applies the current critic (in this case, the work triangle critic) to the items in the catalog, retrieving items that satisfy the rule as examples, that or do not satisfy the rule, as counterexamples. Examples of other designs that either obey or do not obey a critiquing rule are helpful for designers to understand the rule, whether they should obey it or not, and how to do so.

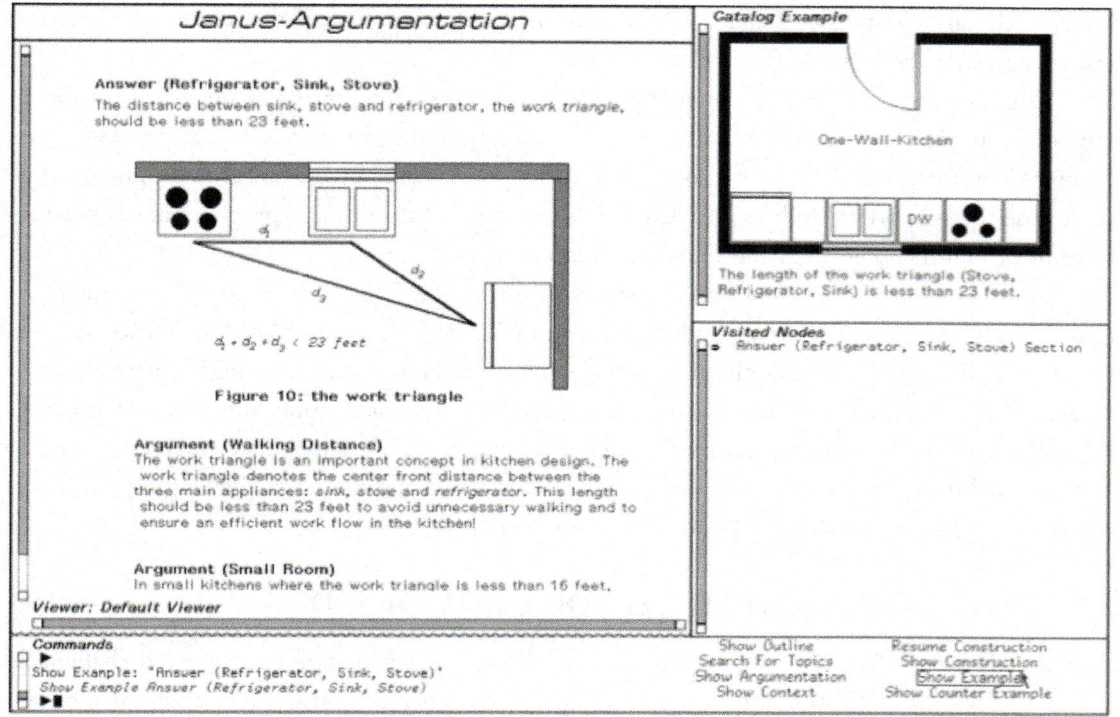


Figure 3.11: Janus-Argumentation: rationale for the work triangle rule. The main window of Janus-Argumentation presents issue-based information about a critiquing rule, in this case the "work triangle rule." Graphical representations help to contextualize and clarify the textual answers and arguments. Further clarification is presented in the Catalog Example window (top right), which displays a catalog entry.

## Insights Gained from DODEs for the EDC

DODEs support design as a "reflective conversation" (Fischer and Nakakoji, 1992): (1) beyond the possibilities of physical media as employed by CoPlan and (2) beyond the facilities provided by construction kits. DODEs provide the initial computational mechanisms supporting designers to incrementally create and modify both problem requirements and solutions.

Our research with DODEs inspired many capabilities and developments in the EDC including: (1) the linking between *action* and *reflection* spaces (Fischer et al., 1996); (2) allowing participants to interact at the level of the *problem domain* (Fischer and Lemke, 1988); (3) mechanisms to support *end-user modifiability* (Fischer and Girgensohn, 1990),; (4) *critiquing* to create awareness of questionable design decisions (Fischer et al., 1998); (5) interaction capabilities to *specify unique aspects* of design decisions (Nakakoji, 1993); and (6) the development of the *seeding, evolutionary growth, reseeding (SER) model* (Fischer et al., 2001).

The *fundamental new objective* of the EDC was not only empowering individual designers with a laptop as technology, but to support the collaboration of communities of designers with tabletop computing environments. An additional challenge addressed by the EDC developments was to increase the support capabilities of DODES as the complexity of design problems are increasing in terms of multiple objectives and multiple criteria.

Another extension of the DODE approach from single to multi-user approaches was pursued by Stahl (who contributed as a Ph.D. student to the development of DODEs) who directed a long-term design-based research effort investigating virtual math teams using a software environment that combined chat-based argumentation with a multi-user application for constructing dynamic geometry figures. He analyzed the *group cognition* (Stahl, 2006) that emerged from interaction within this design environment, as teams of students responded to challenging geometry problems and to the feedback of the dynamic geometry software.

## 3.3   THE RESEARCH METHODOLOGY OF L³D

Over the 20 years of its existence, the research in $L^3D$ has explored some fundamental challenges facing our society in the 21st century including lifelong learning and design in a variety of application domains including urban planning, energy sustainability, and cognitive disabilities. Within the University of Colorado, $L^3D$ built collaborative, interdisciplinary relationships with faculty in the:

- College of Engineering and Applied Science (http://www.colorado.edu/engineering/);

- Department of Computer Science (http://www.colorado.edu/cs/);

- Institute of Cognitive Science (http://www.colorado.edu/ics/);

- Alliance for Technology, Arts and Society (ATLAS) (http://atlas.colorado.edu);

- College of Architecture and Planning (http://www.colorado.edu/catalog/2012-13/architecture);

- School of Education (http://www.colorado.edu/education/);

- Coleman Initiative for Cognitive Disabilities (http://www.colemaninstitute.org); and

- Renewable and Sustainable Energy Institute (RASEI) (http://rasei.colorado.edu).

The EDC represents one of the major research projects of $L^3D$ and it has created a synergistic and beneficial relationship with the center in the following way: the EDC was conceptualized and designed taking advantage of existing frameworks of $L^3D$ and simultaneously transcended and enriched them by exploring new problems in collaborative design and decision making and taking advantage of new media and technologies (such as tabletop computing environments and tangible interaction).

Figure 3.12 illustrates the overall research methodology that we have pursued in $L^3D$. Our approach is grounded in Popper's basic assumption that the growth of human knowledge proceeds from problems and from attempts to solve them: "Knowledge does not start from perceptions or observations or the collection of data or facts, but it starts, rather, from problems" (Popper, 1959). In our research in $L^3D$ we have integrated the analysis of existing theories and the exploration of new theories, the development of systems, the engagement in practice, and the evaluation of our efforts in formative and summative assessments. The upward spiral in Figure 3.12 indicates these different activities influenced each other mutually and allowed us to make progress in the advancement of each of them. Depending on the different projects, the starting activity could be any of the four activities: sometimes we started with an assessment of existing theories or artifacts and developed new systems and new practices, while at other times we engaged in theoretically grounded system building efforts. The EDC's experience over time represents a combination of these activities looking at problems to understand the impacts in them.

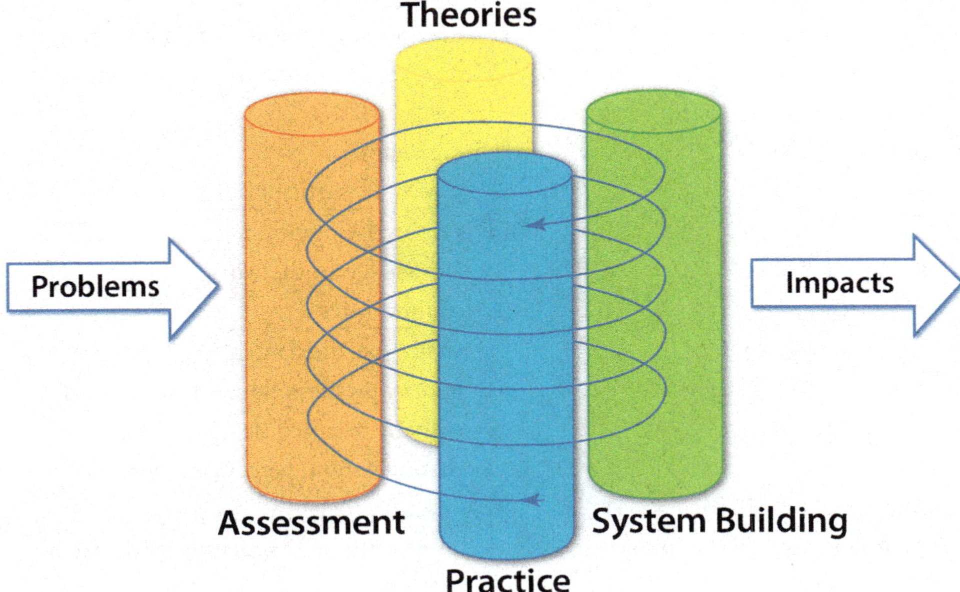


Figure 3.12: $L^3D$'s research methodology: an integrated view.

Another way to characterize our research methodology is that we tried to analyze "how things are" by collecting data, doing experiments and studies, and identifying analogies and success models. Being interested not only in interpreting existing worlds but in design, the EDC investigated "how things could and should be" in collaborative design and decision making.

### The Framework for the EDC Provided by L³D's Intellectual Identity

Table 3.1 provides an overview of the research foci that we have developed and that contributed to the "intellectual identity" of L³D. Many of the concepts mentioned in Table 3.1 are discussed in more detail in specific sections throughout of the book.

Table 3.1: Description of L³D research foci in contrast to alternative approaches

| Alternative Focus | L³D Focus |
| --- | --- |
| Artificial Intelligence (AI) | Intelligence Augmentation (IA) |
|   replacement |   empowerment |
|   emulate |   complement |
| Instructionist Learning | Constructionist Learning |
|   learning about |   learning to be |
|   learning when the answer is known |   learning when the answer is not known |
| Design for Users | Design for Participants and Designers |
|   complete systems |   seeds |
|   user-centered design |   meta-design |
|   access |   informed participation |
| Human Mind | Distributed Cognition |
|   knowledge in the head |   knowledge in the world |
|   individuals |   communities |
| General-purpose Environments | Domain-specific Systems |
|   human-computer interaction |   human problem domain interaction |
|   programming languages |   domain-oriented design environments |
|   universal |   customization, personalization |
| Gift-wrapping with New Media | Co-evolution |
|   adding technology to existing processes |   reinventing new processes and new organizations |
| Desktop | Ubiquitous Computing |
|   physical or digital |   cyber-physical systems |
|   desktops and laptops |   tabletop and mobile computing |

### Unique Contribution of the EDC to the Research Foci of $L^3D$

The EDC has contributed to the $L^3D$ research foci summarized in Table 3.1 moving from individual task orientation to support for coping with complex design problems.

Most of the pressing and important problems in today's world can be characterized and classified by some of the following attributes:

- problems of a *magnitude* which individuals and even large teams cannot solve and require the contribution of all interested citizens (Bennis and Biederman, 1997);

- problems of a *systemic nature* requiring the collaboration of many different minds from a variety of backgrounds—illustrated by the growing importance of application domain knowledge for most software systems and the fact that this knowledge is held by end-users and domain experts rather than by software developers who suffer from a "thin spread of application domain knowledge" (Curtis et al., 1988); and

- problems modeling *changing and unique worlds* supported by open and evolvable systems based on fluctuating and conflicting requirements—illustrated by the emerging mismatches between evolving worlds and the systems which model these world (Fischer et al., 2001).

These problems are complex, open-ended, and ill-defined (Rittel and Webber, 1984; Simon, 1996), requiring:

- contributions of many minds, particularly from the people who "own" problems and are directly affected by them (Ehn, 1989);

- the integration of problem framing and problem solving, where the understanding of the problem co-evolves with the activity of designing a solution (Schön, 1983);

- collaboration among people from different disciplines and educational levels (Clark and Brennan, 1991);

- asynchronous communication supported by design rationale between different designers because the artifacts and systems evolve over long time periods (Moran and Carroll, 1996); and

- intelligent use of technologies and resources that support collective knowledge construction where multiple people contribute to a shared knowledge representation (Arias et al., 2001).

## 3.4   THE EDC: A SOCIO-TECHNICAL ENVIRONMENT

The vision of the Center for LifeLong Learning and Design (L$^3$D) is focused on activities to establish the scientific foundations for the envisionment, design, development, and assessment of *socio-technical environments* (Fischer and Herrmann, 2011; Mumford, 1987; Trist, 1981) that serve as amplifiers of human capabilities and that will bring transformative improvements in the ways people live, learn, work, and collaborate (Engelbart, 1995).

The design of socio-technical environments complies with the need of integrating two different types of structures and processes: (1) *technical systems* that are engineered to provide anticipatable and reliable interactions between users and systems and (2) *social systems* that are contingent in their interactions and a subject of evolution. The EDC as a socio-technical environment is focused on objectives, techniques and processes to allow users to act as active contributors, designers, and decision makers. In doing so, it does not provide fixed solutions but a framework within which *all stakeholders* can contribute and it addresses the fundamental challenge that one of the major roles of new media is not to deliver predigested information to individuals, but to provide the opportunity and resources for social debate and discussion.

The EDC is an integrated human-computer system grounded in the physical world. It shifts the emphasis away from the computer screen as the focal point and creates an immersive environment overcoming the limitations of disembodied rationality (Dourish, 2001) in which stakeholders as users can incrementally create a *shared understanding* through their participation in collaborative design and decision-making processes.

The EDC research explored and contributed to the following design requirements for socio-technical environments supporting collaborative design and decision making:

- support for *cultures of participation* (Fischer, 2011) that put the owners of problems in charge and give them control of how technical systems are used and which functionality is underlying the usage;

- mechanisms to support adaptation and evolution at use time with *meta-design* (Fischer and Giaccardi, 2006) by offering functionality for tailorability, customization, and user-driven adaptability;

- developments based on the *seeding, evolutionary growth*, and *reseeding* model (Fischer et al., 2001), in which the seed is "underdesigned" (Brand, 1995) at design time by representing basic structures (e.g., in accordance with relevant standards) but it leaves space and options for the development of concrete details at use time;

- *creating a common design workspace* in which any member of the community can engage in actions and reflections in a seamless yet coherent way, and that ensures the continuity of cycles of action and reflection (Schön, 1983);

- *increasing visibility and interpretability* of any member's action so as to create an experiential mode in other members and trigger their reflection in action as well as on action;

- *intertwining individual reflection and collective reflection* so that the reflection of each member can be channeled back into the common design workspace to influence subsequent design actions, enabling members to become sources of backtalk.

Some specific developments of the EDC contributing to a socio-technical environment framework are as follows.

- *Collaborative design and decision making*: The tabletop computing environment encourages face-to-face collaboration: (1) when working with the system, people are situated around the table, facing each other to facilitate communication; and (2) they cooperatively build and negotiate a common model of their individual mental models (Arias et al., 2001).

- *Shared understanding and common ground*: Participants cooperatively build and negotiate a common model of their individual mental models. Physical objects serve as anchors for communication about and reflection on the represented concepts.

- *Design as an argumentative, evolving process:*: The EDC engages participants in dealing with a set of possible worlds effectively by exploring design alternatives, and by nurturing a design dialog.

- *Creating externalizations*: The contributions of the participants and the emerging design (1) are captured within the EDC by a set of external memory structures recording the design process and the design rationale; these externalizations represent low-cost, modifiable models that assist stakeholders in creating shared understanding by engaging in a "conversation with the materials"; (2) allow the collaborative and incremental creation of boundary objects that serve as objects for mutual understanding for all participating stakeholders; and (3) support that the tacit knowledge of participants is made explicit (Arias and Fischer, 2000).

- *Supporting simulations and visualizations*: This will allow participants to engage in "what-if" games and to replace anticipation of the consequences of their assumptions and design decisions by analysis (Suchman, 1987).

- *Integrating computational critics*: They can act as "virtual stakeholders;" they are triggered by breakdowns (e.g., based on design conflicts) and they link action and reflection by making argumentation relevant to the task at hand.

- *Making evolution a "first-class design activity"*: Support for end-user development and meta-design allows participants to capture important information not anticipated at system design time, encourages a culture of participation, and addresses the open-ended nature of problems.

## 3.5    CONCLUSIONS

The *research activities and developments* behind the EDC presented in the chapter demonstrate the value of interdisciplinary work as reflected by merging the outcomes of (1) the CoPlan environment from urban and regional planning and (2) DODEs from computer and cognitive sciences. The EDC inherited important different aspects from CoPlan and DODEs:

- *design requirements* derived from a domain inspired environment for urban design and planning;

- *the linkage of action and reflection spaces* to support reflection-in-action and reflection-on-action;

- *face-to-face interaction* as an important setting in participatory decision making toward the resolution of wicked problems;

- *tangible interfaces* to facilitate the interactive participation between players and the tabletop environment;

- *computational simulation* as a powerful means for understanding complex systems;

- *critiquing* as a mechanism to link construction and argumentation ;

- the power gained through *domain orientation* by supporting interaction at the level of the problem domain and not only on a computational level; and

- the importance of putting owners of problems in charge by supporting *end-user modifiability*.

The chapter also described the value gained from the synergistic relationship between the overall $L^3D$ research agenda and the EDC, i.e., how the EDC's development *influenced* and *was influenced by* such agenda. The developments from physical to digital media attained through the integration of these paradigms, along with the advancements to our research agenda, demonstrate the value of interdisciplinary collaborations in the creation of innovative systems to support and advance developments and knowledge in the area of human-centered informatics.

# CHAPTER 4

# Contributions of the EDC to Human-Centered Informatics

The EDC as a *socio-technical environment* (Fischer and Herrmann, 2011) provides a research platform for exploring innovative approaches in design, creativity, and learning—three important domains of human-centered informatics that are described in this chapter. The topics discussed in the three sections are not mutually exclusive but are highly interrelated between themselves and with the EDC, as indicated in Figure 4.1. The knowledge to understand, frame, and solve complex design problems does not already exist, but is constructed and evolves during the solution or resolution processes of these problems. By incorporating a number of innovative technologies, including: (1) tabletop computing; (2) the integration of physical and computational components supporting new interaction techniques; and (3) an open architecture, the EDC supports design, creativity, and learning by all participants.

The EDC as a socio-technical environment is therefore not only significant as a technical achievement in computer science (specifically in tabletop computing), but as an example of principled analyses of helping humans to cope with complex systemic problems requiring collaborative design (Arias et al., 2001). To accomplish good work in human-centered informatics, it is not sufficient to know *how* to build systems—one must also be prepared to discover *which systems are worth building* and *on which principled design strategies these systems should be based*.

The EDC combines theory and technologies as discussed throughout this book. As *theorists and analysts*, we address *why*. As *system builders*, we address *how* by using technologies to create instrumental versions of our theories.

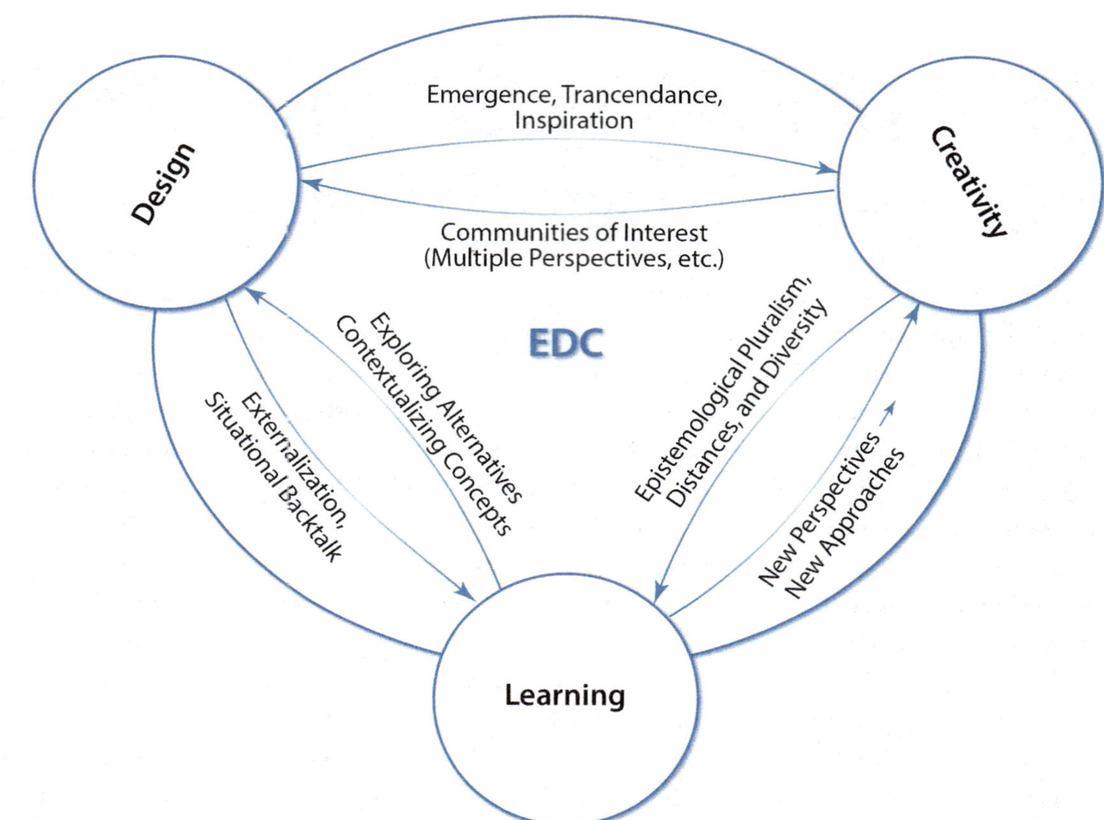


Figure 4.1: The relationship of the EDC to design, creativity, and learning.

## 4.1   EDC AND DESIGN

Design is a ubiquitous, everyday activity in which consciously or subconsciously many people engage. It is not restricted to any specific discipline, such as art or architecture, but design is a broad human activity pursuing the question "how things ought to be" (as compared to the natural sciences that studies "how things are") (Simon, 1996).

The possibilities and the practice of design are a function of the media with which we design (Postman, 1985). In this section, we will describe the mutual influence (1) how design theories and methodologies have influenced the development and evolution of the EDC and (2) how our work with the EDC has deepened our understanding of design.

Important aspects and affordances of design supported by the EDC are: (1) dealing with a *set of possible worlds* effectively (i.e., exploring design alternatives) to account for design as an argumentative process, for which the goal is not to prove a point but to create an environment for design dialogs; (2) creating *low-cost modifiable models* that help us to create shared understanding, have a conversation with the materials, and replace anticipation (of the consequences of our assumptions) by analysis; and (3) using the domain orientation to bring tasks to the forefront and support *human problem-domain communication.*

### 4.1.1　THEORETICAL FRAMEWORKS FOR DESIGN

The theoretical framework underlying the EDC was influenced by a number of design theorists including:

- Herbert Simon (1996), specifically his ideas about: (1) that design problems have no optimal solutions but "satisficing" should be used as a criteria to judge design solutions; and (2) the importance of external representation for incorporating an *emerging design* in a set of external memory structures (including the recording of the design process and the design rationale);

- Donald Schön (1983), specifically his ideas about: (1) linking action and reflection thereby supporting "reflection-in-action" and "reflection-on-action"; and (2) designers creating situations that "talk back" to them;

- Horst Rittel (Rittel, 1984; Rittel and Webber, 1984), specifically his ideas about: (1) *wicked problems* creating the necessity to integrate problem framing and problem solving; and (2) using the *symmetry of ignorance* as a source of power for mutual learning by providing all stakeholders with means to express their ideas and their concerns;

- Christopher Alexander (1964), specifically his characterization of *unselfconscious cultures of design* to describe the importance of design-in-use. In unselfconscious design, breakdown and correction occur side by side; there is no formal set of rules describing how to repair breakdowns, since the breakdowns were not anticipated. Instead, the knowledge to repair breakdowns comes from the knowledge of the participants, who are best able to recognize a lack of fit, and how the artifact should be changed to improve its fit to the environment; and

- Bill Curtis and his colleagues (1988), specifically their identification of three problems in software design: (1) *the thin spread of application domain knowledge among media designers*; (2) *fluctuating and conflicting* (making it impossible to have complete specifications because requirements fluctuate over time and conflict with each other; and (3) *communication and coordination breakdowns* among participants who have different knowledge backgrounds.

Based on the contributions by these authors and numerous other researchers, design approaches can be differentiated along the following dimensions.

- *Technical rationality* (Taylor, 1967) is based on the assumptions that: (1) design is a highly structured process of rational decision-making, and (2) analysis and synthesis can be considered as independent processes. This approach is adequate when requirements can be known and formulated in a precise manner. It is challenged by the growing evidence that system requirements are not so much analytically specifiable as they are collaboratively evolved through an iterative process of consultation between users and software developers (CSTB, 1990).

- *Participatory design* (Ehn, 1989) is based on the assumptions that: (1) participants want to take control of their lives (the quote in Section 1.1 from the President's Council on Sustainable Development); (2) design processes have an argumentative structure in which design decisions are made by considering issues from several alternative positions; and (3) participants (as owners of problems) are able to articulate what they want. The limitations of this approach come from insisting on total participation and neglecting expertise possessed by well-informed and skilled designers (Rittel, 1984). Moreover, because new requirements emerge throughout the existence of an artifact, they cannot be completely identified at design time (Henderson and Kyng, 1991).

- *Design conjectures approaches* (Popper, 1965) (and closely related approaches such as "libertarian paternalism" (Thaler and Sunstein, 2009)) are based on the assumptions that: (1) participants with design expertise develop design conjectures at design time and initial objects to think with, (2) these conjectures need be open to refutation and rejection by the people for whom they are made, and (3) not all stakeholders have equal design expertise; each of them has a particular expertise, but is ignorant of other areas.

## 4.1.2    DESIGN METHODOLOGIES

In all design processes two basic phases can be differentiated: *design time* and *use time* (Figures 4.2 and 4.3). Most established design methodologies are primarily related to design time: system developers (with or without user participation) create environments and tools for the world as *imagined* by them to anticipate users' needs and objectives. They engage in formal and intentional design activities targeted towards the creation of artifacts or systems as imagined. They engage in planning activities guided by the predicted needs of future user populations and design *potential environments* (Gans, 1991).

At *use time*, users' activities are shaped by a world as *experienced* and planning is enriched by situated actions (Suchman, 1987). But because their needs, objectives, and situational contexts may be different from what has been anticipated at design time, systems often requires modifications to fit the users' needs (Henderson and Kyng, 1991).

The need to empower participants as designers and active contributors is not a luxury but a necessity. Computational systems modeling some particular "world" are never complete but they must evolve over time because (1) the world changes and new requirements emerge and (2) skilled domain professionals change their work practices over time and therefore their understanding, needs, and use of a system will be different requiring modifications to support new practices.

The following *design methodologies* established in computer science (Ye and Fischer, 2007) can be differentiated with respect to which stakeholders are present at design and use time, which information do they take into account, and which activities do they carry out.

- *Professional Design:* Early digital artifacts were developed by computer science professionals without too much concerns about users (Taylor, 1967). This was an adequate design methodology at the time, because the users were also computer professionals and the designers lived in the same conceptual worlds as the users.

- *User-Centered Design:* As digital artifacts became more ubiquitous and users were not only computer professionals but came from other disciplines, user-centered design (Norman and Draper, 1986) complemented professional design. Designers (with the help of ethnographers) studied different user communities and derived design criteria characterizing the respective worlds.

- *Participatory design:* The people affected by a design should have a say in the design process. Participatory design (Binder et al., 2011) involves users (or user representatives) more deeply in the process as co-designers at design time by empowering them to propose and generate design alternatives themselves (Figure 4.2). Participatory design can be characterized as "design for use before use" in Binder et al., (2011) and supports diverse ways of thinking, planning, and acting by making work, technologies, and social institutions more responsive to human needs and competencies. It requires the social inclusion and active participation of the users. Participatory design has focused on system development at design time by bringing developers and users together to envision the contexts of use.

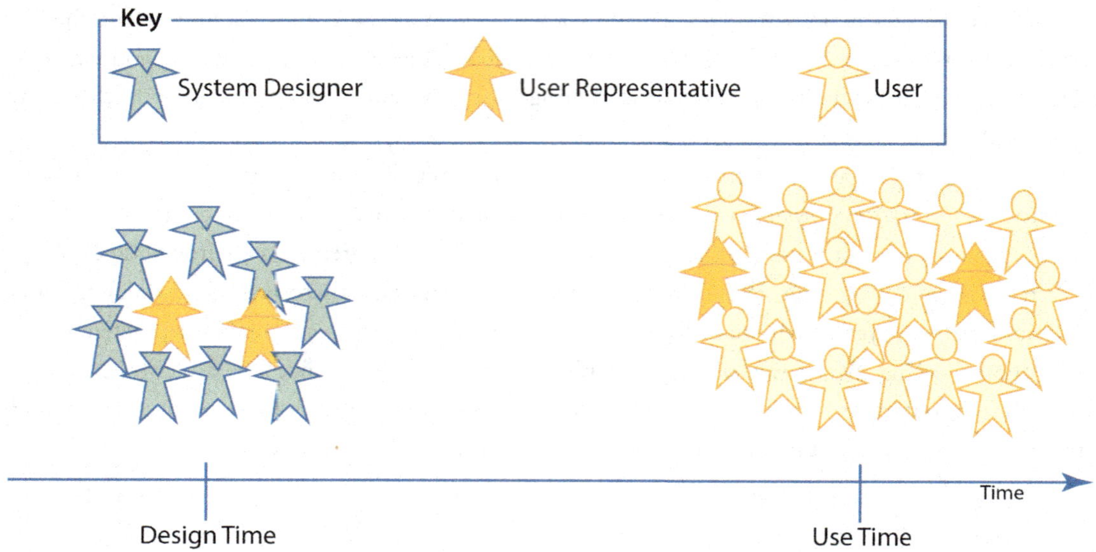


Figure 4.2: Design and use time: roles and involvements in participatory design.

The three design methodologies described above focused primarily on activities and processes taking place at design time in the systems' original development, and have given little emphasis and provided few mechanisms to support systems as living entities that can be evolved by their users over time.

## Meta-Design

Despite the best efforts at design time, systems need to be evolvable to fit new needs, account for changing tasks, deal with a great variety of subjects and contexts, and incorporate new technologies.

Meta-design (Fischer and Giaccardi, 2006) provides the enabling conditions for putting owners of problems in charge by defining the technical and social conditions for broad participation in design activities. It addresses the challenges of fostering new mindsets, new sources of creativity, and cultural changes to create foundations for innovative societies.

Meta-design is an emerging conceptual framework aimed at defining and creating socio-technical environments as living entities. It extends existing design methodologies focused on the development of a system at design time by allowing users to become co-designers at use time. Meta-design (Figure 4.3) can be characterized as "design for design after design" (Binder et al., 2011) and is grounded in the basic assumption that future uses and problems cannot be completely anticipated at design time, when a system is developed (Suchman, 1987; Winograd and Flores, 1986). At use time, users will discover mismatches between their needs and the support that an existing system can provide for them. Meta-design *extends boundaries* by supporting users as active contributors ("users-as-designers") who can transcend the functionality and content of existing systems. By facilitating these possibilities, *control* is distributed among all stakeholders in the design process.

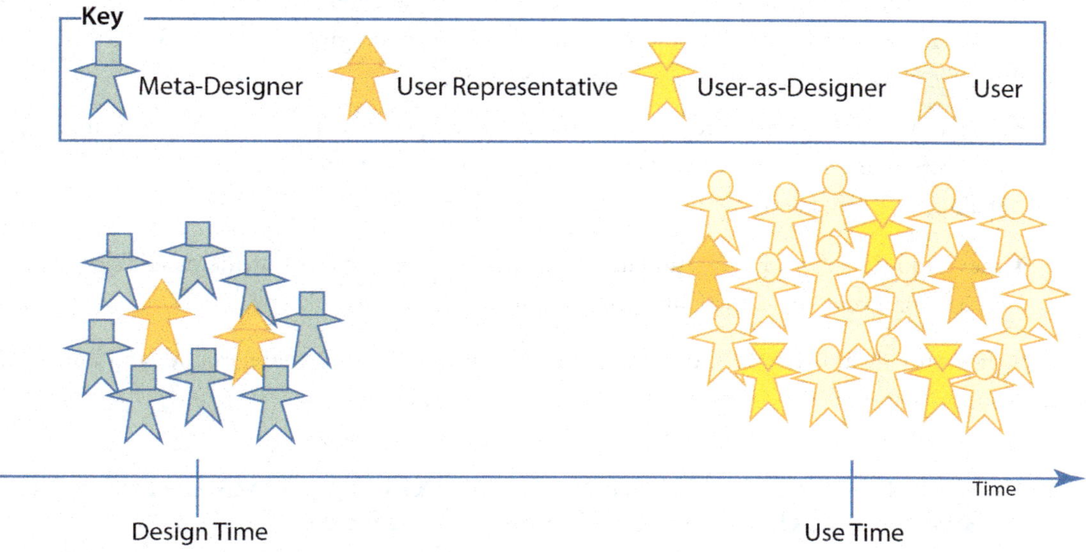


Figure 4.3: Design and use time: roles and involvements in meta-design.

A fundamental objective of meta-design is to establish a basis for the creation of socio-technical systems that empower all stakeholders being actively engaged in the *continuous development* of specific solutions rather than restricting them to prescribed ways of interacting with the technical system or with its users. Meta-design is not only focused on technological aspects but also on the development of appropriate organizational processes and structures representing the context of the system. Organizational structures and processes evolve by the activities, routines, and decisions of people and meta-designers need to develop frameworks allowing users to evolve the design of technical systems and the development of appropriate organizational structures and procedures. In this context, integral EDC notions such as DODEs, end-user modifiability, and reflection-in-action are an instantiation of meta-design contributing to the evolution of systems to fit changing human needs.

## Collaborative Design

Design projects may take place over many years, with initial design followed by extended periods of evolution and redesign. To account for this objective, design artifacts typically are not designed once and for all, but instead they evolve over long periods of time (Fischer et al., 1992). In such long-term design processes, designers may extend or modify artifacts designed by people they actually have never met. This has been the case with the design of the EDC and the evolution of its architecture (Chapter 6) through its applications in different domains (Chapters 5 and 7).

Based on the fact that a "group has no head," the externalization of tacit knowledge (Polanyi, 1966) is one of the most important objectives in collaborative design (Reeves, 1993). Externalizations (Bruner, 1996) support design in the following ways:

- they cause us to move from a vague mental conceptualization of an idea to a more concrete representations of it thereby creating situational back-talk (Schön, 1983) by making thoughts and intentions more accessible to reflection;

- they produce a record and rationale of our mental efforts that is outside people's heads rather than vaguely in their internal memory; and

- they provide a means for others to interact with, react to, negotiate around, and build upon ideas.

### 4.1.3    DIFFERENTIATING DESIGN COMMUNITIES: COMMUNITIES OF PRACTICE AND COMMUNITIES OF INTEREST

Design communities are social structures that enable groups of people to share knowledge and resources in support of collaborative design. Different communities grow around different types of design practices. In our research, we have:

- differentiated two kinds of design communities, *communities of practice* (CoPs) (Wenger, 1998) and *communities of interest* (CoIs) (Fischer, 2001a);

- compared them in order to understand the respective strengths and weaknesses; and

- developed different socio-technical environments supporting CoPs and CoIs, e.g.: (1) DODEs for individuals from specific CoPs, and (2) the EDC for CoIs working together in specific application domains.

#### Communities of Practice (CoPs)

Communities of Practice (CoPs) consist of practitioners who work as a community in a certain domain undertaking similar work. Learning within a CoP takes the form of *legitimate peripheral participation* (LPP) (Lave and Wenger, 1991), which is a type of apprenticeship model in which newcomers enter the community from the periphery and move toward the center as they become more knowledgeable. *Open source communities* (Raymond and Young, 2001), consisting of people who share an interest in the production and use of a software system, exemplify many characteristics of CoPs. The members participate according to their own interests and their own skills. As their skills grow in their interactions, they may move beyond their initial roles and take more responsibility. As a result, products evolve, and people and their knowledge grow as well (Ye et al., 2004) as illustrated with the EDC. Sustained engagement and collaboration lead to boundaries that are based on shared histories of learning and create discontinuities between participants and non-participants. Highly developed knowledge systems (including conceptual frameworks, technical systems, and human organizations) are biased toward efficient communication *within* the community at the expense of acting as barriers to communication with outsiders—boundaries that are empowering to the insiders are often barriers to outsiders and newcomers to the group.

### Communities of Interest (CoIs)

Communities of Interest (CoIs) are defined by their collective concern with the resolution of a particular problem and bring stakeholders together from different CoPs. CoIs can be thought of as "communities of communities." Examples of CoIs are: (1) a team interested in software development that includes software designers, users, marketing specialists, psychologists, and programmers; (2) a group of citizens and experts interested in urban planning; and (3) a group of interactive artists comprising people with very different backgrounds and expertise (e.g., visual artists, musicians, performers, designers, architects, computer scientists). These developments are illustrated with the different case studies (Figure 5.1) described in this book.

Table 4.1 characterizes and differentiates CoPs and CoIs along a number of dimensions. The point of comparing and contrasting CoPs and CoIs is not to pigeonhole groups into either category, but rather to identify patterns of practice and helpful technologies. People can participate in more than one community, or one community can exhibit attributes of both a CoI and a CoP. Our $L^3D$ center (Section 3.3) represents an example: it has many of the characteristics of a CoP (having developed its own stories, terminology, and artifacts), but by actively engaging with people from outside the $L^3D$ community (e.g., other colleges on campus, people from industry, international visitors, and so forth), it also has many of the characteristics of a CoI. Communities do not have to be strictly either CoPs or CoIs; they can integrate aspects of both forms of communities, and may shift over time as the nature of the concerned problems change.

Table 4.1: Differentiating communities of practice and communities of interest

| Dimensions | CoPs | CoIs |
|---|---|---|
| **nature of problems** | embedded in one domain | extend over multiple domains |
| **knowledge development** | refinement of one knowledge system; new ideas coming from within the practice | synthesis and mutual learning through the integration of multiple knowledge systems |
| **major objectives** | codified knowledge, domain coverage | shared understanding, making all voices heard |
| **weaknesses** | group-think | lack of a mutual awareness |
| **strengths** | shared ontologies | diversity; more creativity potential |
| **people** | beginners and experts; apprentices and masters | stakeholders (owners of problems) from different domains |
| **learning** | legitimate peripheral participation | informed participation |

Both forms of communities exhibit strengths and weaknesses. CoPs are biased toward efficient communications with the same kind of people by taking advantage of a shared background. The existence of an accepted, well-established center of expertise and a clear path of learning toward this center allows the differentiation of members into novices, intermediates, and experts. This distinction makes these attributes viable concepts associated with people, and provides the foundation for legitimate peripheral participation as a workable learning strategy. The barriers imposed by CoPs are that *group think* (Janis, 1972) can suppress exposure to and acceptance of outside ideas; the more someone is at home in a CoP, the more that person forgets the strange and contingent nature of categories from the outside.

A reason for our interests in CoIs associated with the EDC's design and development is the fact that the strength of CoIs is their potential for supporting *creativity* because different backgrounds and different perspectives can lead to new insights (Bennis and Biederman, 1997; Campbell, 1969). CoIs have great potential to be more innovative and more transforming than a single CoP by exploiting the *symmetry of ignorance* (Rittel, 1984) as a source of social creativity. A fundamental barrier for CoIs might be that the participants fail to create common ground and shared understanding (Clark and Brennan, 1991; Resnick et al., 1991). This barrier is particularly challenging because CoIs often are more temporary than CoPs: they come together in the context of a specific project and dissolve after particular objectives are met or the project has ended.

### 4.1.4   THE IMPORTANCE OF BOUNDARY OBJECTS FOR DESIGN COMMUNITIES

"If a lion could speak, we could not understand him."—Wittgenstein

*Boundary objects* (Bowker and Star, 2000; Star, 1989; Wenger, 1998) are externalizations of ideas that are used to communicate and facilitate shared understandings across spatial, temporal, conceptual, or technological gaps. In design communities, boundary objects help to establish a shared context for communication by providing referential anchoring (Clark and Brennan, 1991). Boundary objects can be pointed to and named, helping stakeholders make sure they are talking about the same thing. Grounding communication with external representations helps to identify breakdowns and serves as a resource for repairing them.

In CoPs, boundary objects represent the domain concepts and ontologies that both define and reflect the shared practice. They might take the form of documents, terminology, stories, rules, and unspoken norms. For example, the boundary objects in a community of researchers include research papers, dissertations, and a conceptual framework that encompasses the individuals and work done within the community. In this sense the EDC is a socio-technical environment that supports the communication and construction of boundary objects (Arias and Fischer, 2000) in order to attain shared understandings through informed compromises of members within and between CoPs and CoIs.

In CoIs, boundary objects support communication across the boundaries of different knowledge systems, helping people from different backgrounds and perspectives to communicate and to build common ground (Figure 4.4).

Boundary objects allow different knowledge systems to communicate by providing a shared reference that is meaningful within both systems. Computational support for CoIs must therefore enable mutual learning through the creation, discussion, and refinement of boundary objects that allow the knowledge systems of different CoPs to interact. In this sense, the interaction between multiple knowledge systems is a means to turn the *asymmetry of ignorance* (Rittel, 1984) into a resource for learning and *social creativity* (Fischer, 2000b).

Boundaries are the locus of the production of new knowledge and innovative insights and ideas. They are where the unexpected can be expected, where innovative and unorthodox solutions are found, where serendipity is likely, and where old ideas find new life. The diversity of CoIs may cause difficulties, but it also may provide unique opportunities for knowledge creation and sharing (Arias et al., 2001).

Importantly, boundary objects should be conceptualized as evolving artifacts that become understandable and meaningful as they are used, discussed, and refined (Ostwald, 1996). For this reason, boundary objects should be conceptualized as reminders that trigger knowledge, or as conversation pieces that ground shared understanding, rather than as containers of knowledge. The *interaction* around a boundary object is what creates and communicates knowledge, not the object itself.

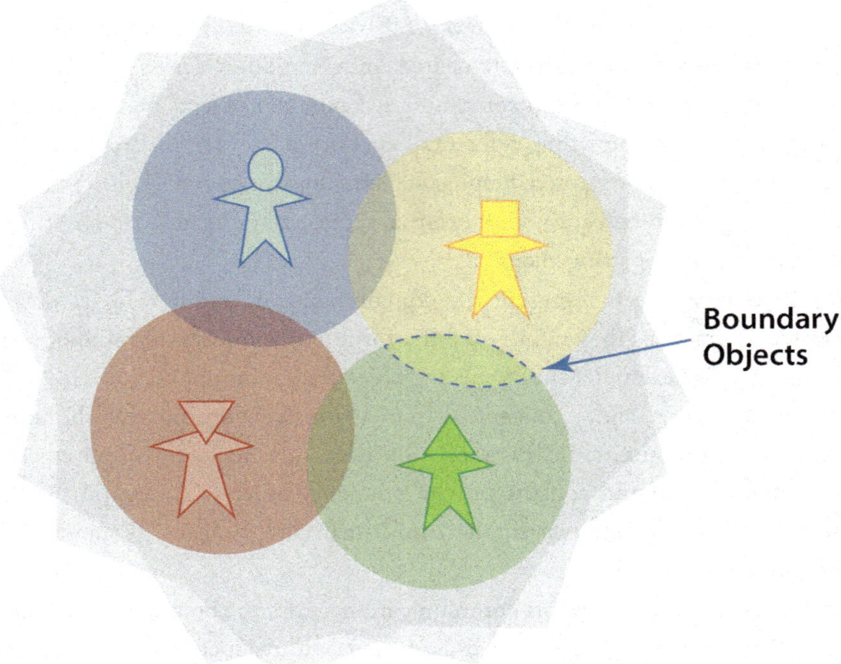


Figure 4.4: Boundary objects as bridges between CoPs. Boundary objects should be meaningful within the conceptual knowledge systems of at least two communities of practice. The meaning need not be the same—in fact, the differences in meaning are what lead to the creation of new knowledge.

Boundary objects perform a brokering role involving translation, coordination and alignment between the perspectives of specific CoPs. The efficiency of the boundary objects in attaining these functions is contingent on the nature of the constituencies (e.g., their respective level of competency, motivation, and experience). Boundary objects as described, can serve two major purposes: (1) they can serve as objects to support the interaction and collaboration between different communities of practice; and (2) they can serve the interaction between users and (computational) environments. In this later case one can argue that they serve the interaction between the users and the designers (being present "virtually" through the system created by them).

Humans serving as knowledge brokers can play important roles to bridge boundaries that exist across or within communities. For example, within design communities that develop around complex software systems, members who are interested and inclined to learn about the technologies may develop into *power-users* (also known as "local developers" and "gardeners" (Nardi, 1993)) who are able to make modifications and customizations. By making needed changes to a system on behalf of the community, or by teaching others how to do so, power-users help others to transcend the boundary that exists between using a system as it is and modifying it.

### The EDC as a Boundary Object and Boundary Objects in the EDC

The EDC functions as a boundary object to create shared understanding between different CoPs coming together as CoIs. This overarching function emerges from its internal support functionality over use-time. In the EDC, designs function as communication artifacts around which stakeholders from different CoPs, coming together as a CoI in the context of a specific problem, can negotiate their contributions, their positions, and their alignments. Action space objects are domain-oriented—they represent objects in the problem domain in terms of both visual appearance and behavior within the simulations. These objects and their behaviors are meaningful to all stakeholders who have familiarity with the problem domain. However, the precise meanings of the objects and the implications of these meanings for design decisions for each stakeholder may not be shared initially among them but constructed between them over use-time. The objects serve as boundary objects by providing a common starting ground for stakeholders to identify and explore the differences in their understandings and to build new understandings that bridge the boundaries (Table 4.2).

For example, in the domain of transportation planning (illustrated with the scenario presented in Chapter 2), stakeholders include transportation engineers and neighborhood residents who will work together to improve the design of bus routes in their neighborhood. In the action space, they use domain objects, such as buses, bus stops, neighborhoods, and streets to explore different facets of the problem. An engineer might think of a bus stop in terms of its capacity to serve a certain size of neighborhood, whereas residents might think of bus stops in terms of its convenience to their houses, or maybe in terms of its after-dark safety. The bus stop object in the EDC is a boundary object for engineers and residents to build a shared understanding of the "bus-stop" concept in terms of the importance and implications for the particular design. This process is enhanced by the action space simulation, which helps stakeholders to explore alternatives, and the reflection space, which provides background that informs each perspective.

Table 4.2: EDC support mechanisms for boundary objects

| EDC Support | Description | Contribution to Different Aspects of Boundary Objects |
|---|---|---|
| physical languages (action space) | tangible representations that are manipulated by groups of users | encourages face-to-face collaboration, providing a common language for people to express themselves and making the tacit explicit |
| computational simulations (action space) | models that capture constructions, analyze situations, and display ramifications | allows for users to engage in "what-if" games, provides interactive ways to capture and visualize information |
| information repositories (reflection space) | evolving Web sites that display relevant information and capture feedback | captures knowledge made explicit through interactions around the action space and stores it to inform participants at a later time in the reflection space |
| open evolvable objects and tools (action and reflection space) | supporting meta-design to capture changes and evolve systems when new situations arise | captures important information not anticipated at design time, encourages a culture of participation, addresses the open-ended nature of problems |

A major contribution of the EDC has been to support participatory design, collaborative design, and meta-design in which expertise is distributed among different stakeholders, requiring that stakeholders can assume both the role of designer and user or teacher and learner depending on the specific context. To support mutual learning and shared understanding among different groups of stakeholders, representations such as boundary objects are needed which can be understood by all participants. In this sense, the EDC serves as an socio technical environment that supports through its use the creation of boundary-objects by facilitating opportunities where different "cultures" can meet and make their tacit knowledge or insights explicit (Arias and Fischer, 2000).

Externalizations often serve the purpose to create "situations that talk back to us"(Schön, 1983). This "back-talk" will be severely limited by representations that do not serve as boundary objects. While some of the back-talk will be provided by the design situation itself, this may be insufficient because of our limited ability to notice breakdowns and problematic situations by visual inspection or when careful analysis is limited. In our research over the last decade with the EDC we have developed additional mechanisms to further increase the "back-talk" (Fischer, 1994b): (1)

feedback from human stakeholders involved in the design process; (2) computational critics; and (3) simulation components that illustrate the behavior of an artifact. In providing additional feedback, it is important that the "back-talk" is relevant to the actual design situation and that it is articulated in a way that the designer can understand. Utilizing the asymmetry of knowledge by eliciting what is relevant at the appropriate time varies in its relevancy depending on the context of what is being discussed at a given time.

## 4.1.5    THE SER MODEL: AN EVOLUTIONARY PERSPECTIVE FOR DESIGN

The *seeding-evolutionary growth-reseeding (SER) model* (Fischer et al., 2001) is a process model that provides a framework for understanding: (1) how the EDC as a socio-technical environment and as a platform was built, used, and evolved over extended periods of time; (2) how specific projects were designed using the EDC by various CoPs and CoIs in different domains; and (3) which factors contributed to the evolutionary growth and restructuring and redesign of the EDC.

### An Evolutionary Perspective for Design

We live in a world characterized by evolution in both natural and human-created systems. Biology tells us that complex natural systems are not created all at once but have evolved over time. Evolutionary processes are ubiquitous and critical for the design of socio-technical systems (Basalla, 1988; Simon, 1996) such as the EDC. The driving forces behind the evolution of these systems (the EDC being one prototypical example) is their use in solving real-world problems, the changing assumptions and objectives behind them, and new media available and employed to conceptualize and solve these problems.

Empirical data shows that a substantial portion of the total lifecycle costs of complex systems occur after they are deployed (Computer Science and Technology Board, 1990). These costs occur not primarily for fixing mistakes made during system design, but rather they are devoted to enhancing the system in ways that were not foreseen by the original designers. A considerable portion of these costs is due to the fact that essential information about the system (such as design rationale (Moran and Carroll, 1996)) is not captured during development and must be reconstructed by the designers who must enhance the system. Brooks (1987) argued that *successful* software gets changed because it offers the possibility to evolve. An evolutionary design perspective acknowledges that systems will undergo continual development, and attempts to merge development, maintenance, and enhancement into cycles of an evolutionary process. For these reasons, the SER model can be used to characterize the long-term evolution of successful software systems such as Unix and Microsoft Office and large cities (providing insights about the developmental path of historically grown cities such as London and Paris or "planned cities" such as Brasilia, Canberra, and Abudja (McHarg et al., 1978)).

The SER model (Figure 4.5) describes evolutionary processes at three levels: (1) the EDC framework (details about specific evolutionary changes are described with respect to architecture, hard- and software in Chapter 6); (2) the incremental modeling of application domains (examples provided by the different case studies in Chapter 5); and (3) the development of individual artifacts within specific application domains (as illustrated with the scenario in Chapter 2).

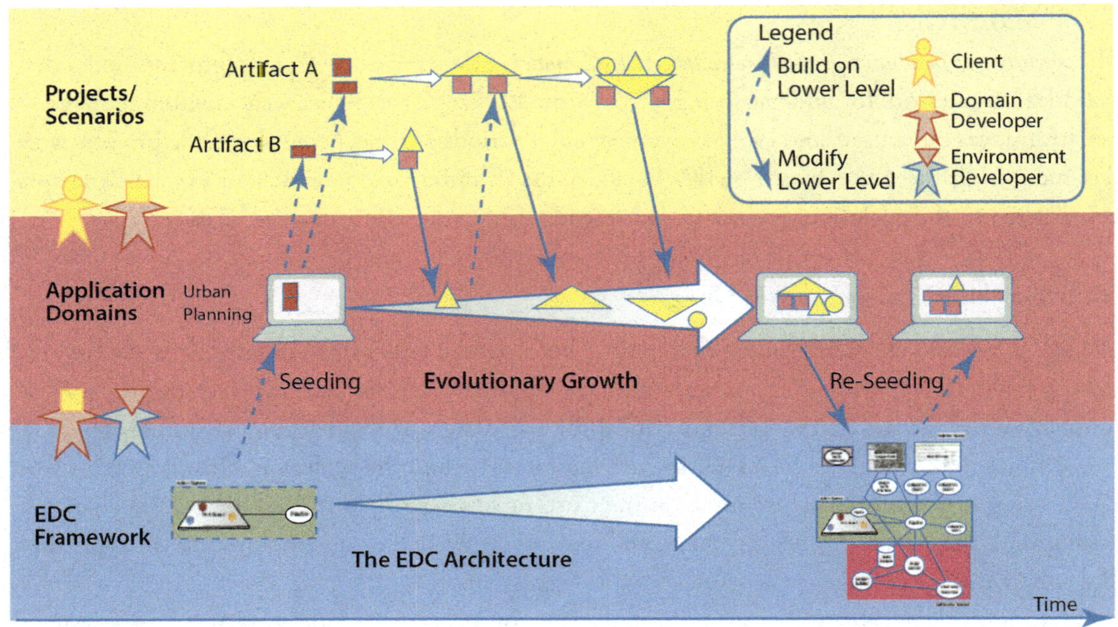


Figure 4.5: A graphical illustration of the SER Model in the context of the EDC.

## The Seeding Phase Using the EDC for Creating Specific Projects

The goal of the seeding phase to create a specific project in a particular domain entails embedding as much domain knowledge as possible into all components of the architecture. All stakeholders must participate: the developers who have the necessary knowledge to customize the EDC platform to a specific application domain and the participants who bring domain knowledge and their objectives to the table.

Rather than expecting participants to articulate precise and complete system requirements prior to seed building, we view *seed building* as knowledge *construction* (in which knowledge structures and access methods are collaboratively designed and built) rather than as knowledge acquisition (in which knowledge is transferred from an expert to a knowledge engineer and finally expressed in formal rules and procedures) (Ostwald, 1996).

From this knowledge construction perspective, design requirements are not so much analytically specified as they are collaboratively evolved through an iterative, mutual learning process to create shared understanding and establish common ground. Requirements are elicited by constructing and evaluating prototypes and other objects that are meaningful within the practice of the participants. The externalizations should facilitate mutual learning among all stakeholders: (1) the role of developers is to make suggestions about how the work practices of participants can be changed and improved using the EDC, and to create prototypes that model these suggestions; and (2) the role of the participants is to critique the suggestions of the developers and to guide them toward a better understanding of the domain.

However, the design knowledge associated with design projects characterized by ill-defined, wicked problems done with the EDC can never be considered as complete. The reason being that each design project addresses a problem that is in some respects unique, and therefore generates new knowledge that can be added to the seed. The seed is therefore explicitly designed to evolve as it is used in projects (Henderson and Kyng, 1991). Rather than being considered as complete, the seed is considered to provide knowledge and examples that can help designers to understand new problems, and to provide a structure to which designers can add new knowledge as new problems are solved. Postulating the objective of a seed emphasizes evolution as the central design concept.

## Evolutionary Growth Phase

The evolutionary growth phase begins when a project has been sufficiently seeded to support design. Evolutionary growth is driven by the needs that arise in the design and redesign of the platform and from individual projects. The EDC and its projects are *open systems* that support participants to incrementally model and evolve artifacts by articulating additional knowledge, analyzing and resolving conflicts, and making decisions. In some instances, developers are not present in the day-to-day use of the EDC, requiring interaction processes and interfaces that allow participants themselves to perform modifications to the system.

Adaptations and extensions are not without cost, and often require expertise that many participants do not have and are not interested to acquire. Collaborative work practices (Nardi, 1993), in which selected members of work groups (often called power users, local developers, or gardeners; e.g., the students mentioned in Section 7.1 were taking up these roles) are willing to acquire a deeper understanding of the EDC to perform incremental changes (providing additional content information and/or modifying the environment itself) play an essential role to bring the SER model alive in the EDC.

**Reseeding Phase**

The reseeding phase is a deliberate effort of revision and coordination of information and functionality to organize, formalize, and generalize knowledge added during the evolutionary growth phases. The need for reseeding becomes apparent when an artifact based on numerous decentralized contributions has evolved to a point that its usefulness and usability suffers from disorganization, or when participants try to undertake actions that are not supported by the existing architecture of the EDC. While numerous reseeding efforts have been undertaken during the 20 years history of the EDC at the hardware and software level (specific examples are provided in Chapter 6), additional desired extensions remain for future research activities (Chapter 9).

## 4.2    EDC AND CREATIVITY

> "You cannot use smoke signals to do philosophy. Its form excludes the content."—Postman (1985, p. 7)

Creativity is a human competency intrinsically related to the activities of design and learning. The understanding and support for creativity has emerged as an important objective for human-centered informatics (National-Research-Council, 2003; Shneiderman, 2002). While creativity is often associated with art, in the context of the EDC we are concerned with the notion of creativity as it is required in everyday work, learning and design practices. This type of creativity is in most cases not *historical*, but *psychological* (Boden, 1991). A resulting product is not necessarily novel or original to a community but is personally or psychologically novel to the individual who produced it. While analyzing outstanding creative people (Gardner, 1995) contributes towards establishing a framework for creativity, understanding creativity in the context of everyday activities is equally important for letting people become more innovative and create better work products.

### 4.2.1    INDIVIDUAL AND SOCIAL CREATIVITY

> "The strength of the wolf is in the pack, and the strength of the pack is in the wolf."—Rudyard Kipling

The power of the unaided individual mind is highly overrated (John-Steiner, 2000). Although creative individuals (Gardner, 1993; Sternberg, 1988) are often thought of as working in isolation, much of our intelligence and creativity results from interaction and collaboration with other individuals (Csikszentmihalyi, 1996). Creative activity stems from the relationship between individuals and their work, as well as from the interactions between individuals. In other words, creativity does not only happen tacitly inside people's heads, but in the interaction between a person's thoughts and a sociocultural context (Engeström, 2001). Situations that support social creativity need to be sufficiently open-ended and complex so that users will encounter *breakdowns* (Schön, 1983). As any professional designer knows, breakdowns—although at times costly and painful—offer unique opportunities for reflection, learning and innovative thinking.

The focus of the EDC on social creativity does not imply that *individual creativity* should be considered irrelevant. As indicated by the quote from Kipling, we believe that there is an "and" rather than a "versus" relationship between individual and social creativity. Social creativity does not necessitate the development of environments in which the interests of the many inevitably supersede those of the individual. Creative individuals, such as movie directors, champions of sports teams, and leading scientists and politicians can make a huge difference, as analyzed and shown by Gardner in exemplary cases (Gardner, 1995). Organizations get their strength to a large extent from the creativity and engagement of their individual members (Fischer et al., 2005). Appropriate socio-technical settings can amplify the creative outcome of a group of people by both augmenting individual creativity and multiplying it, rather than by simply summing up individuals' creativities. We need to understand how individual and social creativity (Fischer et al., 2005) interact with each other as it is explored in the Caretta project (Section 7.2).

From the perspective of human centered informatics, *social creativity* includes the exploration of computer media and technologies to help people work together. It is relevant to design and learning because collaboration plays an increasingly significant role in design projects that require expertise and learning in a wide range of domains. Its value and importance are not only because it can lead to new products and services, but because individuals, organizations, and societies must adapt through innovative thinking to a rapidly changing world if they are to remain competitive (Sternberg, 1999).

Despite the rhetoric of collaboration, the prevailing perspective is still focused on a culture in which people need to distinguish themselves as individuals (Bennis and Biederman, 1997). The EDC brings social creativity alive by:

- allowing participating stakeholders to express themselves by combining different perspectives and generating new understandings, thus avoiding being entrenched in "group think" (Janis, 1972);

- making all voices heard and exploiting the symmetry of ignorance (Fischer, 2000b) as a source for new insights rather than as limitations; these two concepts are specifically important in dealing with complex, systemic problems that require more knowledge than any single person possesses (e.g., in software design, domain experts understand the practice and system designers know the technology); and

- supporting different types of distances and diversity (Table 4.3) in multiple dimensions (Fischer, 2005) and creating understandable boundary objects across different domains (Star, 1989) will allow users to develop common ground and shared understanding.

## 4.2.2    IMPACT OF DISTANCES AND DIVERSITY ON CREATIVITY

Creative activity stems from of the relationship between individuals and their work, and from the interactions between an individual and other human beings. Because complex problems require more knowledge than any single person possesses, it is necessary that all involved stakeholders participate, communicate, collaborate, and learn from each other. *Distances* (across spatial, temporal, and technological dimensions) and *diversity* (bringing stakeholders together from different cultures) are important sources for social creativity.

Table 4.3: Differentiating distances and diversity

| Distances and Diversity | Rationale | Addressed by | Media / Technologies | Challenges |
|---|---|---|---|---|
| **spatial** | participants are unable to meet face-to-face; low local density of people sharing the same interests | computer-mediated communication | e-mail, chat rooms, video conferences | achieve common ground; involve large communities ("the talent pool of the whole world") |
| **temporal** | support long-term, indirect communication and meta-design | design rationale, building on previous work | group memories, reflection spaces | motivate efforts to document design decisions for others |
| **conceptual *within* domains** | shared understanding | communities of practice (CoPs), | domain-oriented design environments | avoid group-think |
| **conceptual *between* domains** | make all voices heard | communities of interest (CoIs); boundary objects | Envisionment and Discovery Collaboratory | establish common ground; integration of diversity |
| **technological** | things (in contrast to humans) are available; complement human abilities | distributed cognition, socio-technical environments; | agents, critics, simulations | formalization; digital fluency |

### 4.2.3    SUPPORTING CREATIVITY WITH THE EDC

In the context of the EDC, we have focused our studies of creativity on design activities with an emphasis on the importance of lifelong learning. The analysis of everyday design practices (Rogoff and Lave, 1984) has shown that knowledge workers and designers have to engage in creative activities in coping with the unforeseen complexities of everyday, real-world tasks.

All media have had an impact on creativity, and creativity has produced new media. In this general view, there is not much new about the impact of the computer. Information technologies have reached a level of sophistication, maturity, cost-effectiveness, and distribution so they are not restricted only to enhancing productivity; they also open up new, creative possibilities through the distribution of knowledge (National-Research-Council, 2003). Looking for its peculiar kind of influence, we will briefly describe unique features of the EDC in supporting creativity.

#### Distributed Cognition: Exploring New Role Distributions Between People and Computers

People think and act in conjunction and partnership with others and with the help of artifacts and tools (Salomon, 1993). Current computer systems deprive people of potential creativity by requiring them to do tasks for manipulating computer systems themselves, not directly relevant to their work domain. To better support creativity, computer systems need to be designed to minimize efforts required to use the systems' functionality not directly relevant to designer's work domains. The EDC is a socio-technical environment that allows people to be engaged in more authentic tasks in their work practices by allowing them to deal with domains, rather than fighting with tools. An important design objective of the EDC is to make computational system invisible and enable participants to communicate with the problem domain rather than with computational tools.

#### Reflection-in-Action: Making Argumentation Serve Design

Schön (1983) describes that design is an iterative process of action and reflection. A designer creates a design move, which creates a design situation talking back to the designer, uncovering dimensions of the design task. Design is not a rule-oriented logical activity but a series of discovering emerging features and arguing about the situations. As such, discussions and arguments about design do not preserve their semantics if isolated from relevant artifacts. Although recording design rationale and design processes are known to play an important role in creative design, such rationale needs to be embedded within the context of design. Action and reflections spaces are tightly integrated in the EDC; examples of this integration are illustrated with (1) dynamically generated analytic views of land use in the reflection space of the corresponding land use constructed by participants in the action space (Figure 2.6), and (2) by providing argumentation about the impact of land topology and vegetation for fire emergencies (Figure 5.10).

### Integration of Problem Framing and Problem Solving

To support creativity, the importance and benefit of articulating goals and problem requirements and creating artifacts helps designers lessen the burden of mental demands in carrying out design activities. Creating externalizations is not a matter of emptying out the mind but of actively reconstructing it, forming new associations, and expressing concepts in linguistic, pictorial, or other explicit representational forms while lessening the cognitive load required for remembering them.

### Emergence: Seeing New Relationships

Emergence as a fundamental aspect of creative design happens when unplanned and unforeseen effects and consequences are recognized. The Walking-Distance example (Figure 2.11) provides a specific example of a visualization based on individual, decentralized actions indicating promising areas for bus stops that no individual had in their head prior to the exercise.

### Critiquing: Signaling Breakdowns and Supporting Contextual Elaboration

Schön's framework is based on the basic cycle of "seeing-drawing-seeing." However, Schön's notion of seeing is "not good enough;" as Rittel pointed out, "buildings do not speak for themselves." Participants in EDC sessions often have insufficient knowledge and experience to fully understand the conversation with the materials of the situation. Critiquing mechanisms (Fischer et al., 1998) serve as "interpreters" that support designers in seeing and understanding the "back talk" of the situation. Critics provide a computational mechanism that allows designers to think about what they are doing while this thinking can still make a difference. They support contextual elaboration by making the information provided relevant to the task at hand and thereby providing opportunities for learning on demand.

### Exploiting the Creativity Potential of Communities of Interest (CoIs)

Following Snow's opinion "The clashing point of two subjects, two disciplines, two cultures ought to produce creative chaos" (Snow, 1993), the EDC is focused on not to reduce heterogeneity and specialization, but to support it, manage it, and integrate it by finding ways to build bridges between local knowledge sources and by exploiting conceptual collisions and breakdowns as sources for innovative thinking. The diverse viewpoints and expertise distributed across the membership of a community are the driving forces to exploit the *creativity potential of CoIs*. The opportunity of exchanging, sharing, and integrating diverse ideas leads to the emergence of new and more creative ideas (Fischer, 2005).

A specific example from land-use exploration that occurred in one of our EDC planning sessions illustrates the interesting conceptual collisions and conflicting opinions that can occur in such settings (Figure 4.6). In collaboratively exploring different land-use schemes, a discussion evolved around the situation that some participants argued that a golf course should be considered as recreational space, whereas others pointed out that because fees are charged for using it, a golf course should be considered as a commercial venture.

Figure 4.6: A conceptual collision: Is a golf course commercial or recreational land use?

Our work with the EDC has demonstrated that more creative solutions to complex wicked problems can emerge from the collective interactions with the environment by heterogeneous CoIs than homogeneous CoPs (Wenger, 1998): the EDC avoids group think (Janis, 1972) by supporting open representations that allow for deeper understanding, experimentation, and possibly refutation and it provides unique opportunities to bring social creativity alive by transcending individual perspectives.

### Empowering Communities with the EDC

The diverse viewpoints and expertise distributed across the membership of a community are the driving forces to explore one of the research questions that we pursued in this context with the EDC: "How can the creativity potential of CoIs be exploited?" The opportunity of exchanging, sharing, and integrating diverse ideas leads to the emergence of new and more creative ideas (Fischer, 2005). However, diversities also can bring barriers: members must be able to create a shared understanding of the concerns spanning their conceptual domains (Resnick et al., 1991) as well as combine and integrate the varied knowledge bases from different people (Engeström, 2001). These skills often do not exist at the beginning of the problem-solving process, but evolve incrementally and collaboratively.

The collaborative design activities supported by the EDC bring together participants from various backgrounds to frame and solve ill-defined, open-ended design problems (Rittel, 1984). Our new developments will explore the closely interrelated requirements of:

- developing *boundary objects* (Star, 1989) that support communication across the boundaries of different knowledge systems, helping people from different backgrounds and perspectives to communicate and build common ground;

- exploiting the *symmetry of ignorance* and *supporting diversity* (Fischer, 2005) among participants as sources of new ideas and insights rather than limitations; and

- supporting *rich ecologies of participation* (Preece and Shneiderman, 2009).

## 4.3    EDC AND LEARNING

### 4.3.1    MULTI-DIMENSIONAL ASPECTS OF LEARNING

Conceptions of *learning* are often of a very narrow nature: it happens in schools, there is a teacher who tells learners what is important and necessary to learn, it is an individual activity, and it is experienced by learners as something they have to do. As the demands for learning undergo a period of profound transformation, there is a need for exploring innovative multi-dimensional aspects of learning. Figure 4.7 provides an overview of the multi-dimensional aspects of learning—and the following section briefly describes the essential issues related to the different aspects of learning.

#### Who Learns: People at Different Stages

Learners may be students in different grades and institutions, persons working in industry, or curious citizens attempting to understand more about the world surrounding them (the later being the primary context for the EDC). Some of the learners may be beginners (and general and standard introductory courses will serve them well) whereas other may have a rich knowledge background and very specific objectives requiring more individualized learning opportunities.

#### Why Learn: Different Objectives

Some people learn because they need to pass a test, fulfill the requirements of a course in school or university, and others learn because they are passionate about some endeavor (Collins and Halverson, 2009). As discussed in Chapters 5 and 7, the primary objective for the participants in the EDC to learn is the collaborative engagement in resolving problems and making decisions in authentic, personally meaningful problems (Arias et al., 1999).

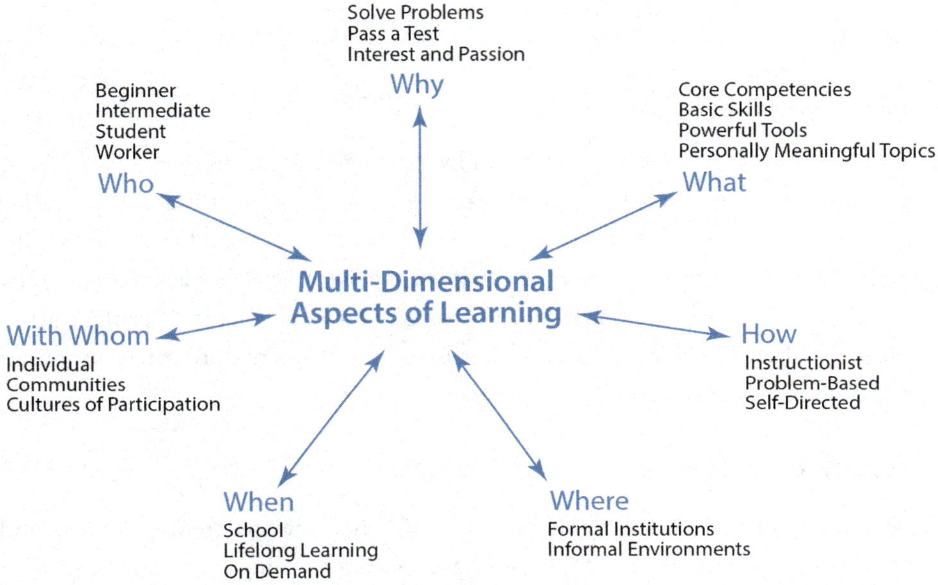


Figure 4.7: Multi-dimensional aspects of learning.

### What to Learn: Problem-specific Knowledge and Acquiring Basic Skills and Core Competencies

In formal learning environments, learning is determined to a large extent by a curriculum. Learners encounter few opportunities to frame problems derived from their own objectives. Problem-specific knowledge should be complemented with learning opportunities to acquire the basic skills and core competencies for the 21st century. Learning opportunities provided by the EDC do not primarily consist of learning and memorizing facts, but are focused on: (1) acquiring and using information relevant to the task at hand; (2) identifying, organizing, planning and allocating resources; (3) collaborating with others; and (4) working with a variety of technologies.

### How to Learn: Learning in Different Ways

Learning in today's world should be conceptualized as an inclusive, social, informal, participatory, and creative lifelong activity. Many problems (specifically design problems) are unique and ill-defined and the knowledge to address them is not "out there" requiring contributions and ideas from all involved stakeholders. Participants in the EDC must be *active contributors* rather than passive consumers and the EDC as a socio-technical environment must foster and support mindsets, tools, and skills that help learners become empowered and willing to actively contribute (Fischer, 2002; von Hippel, 2005).

## Where to Learn: At the Right Places

Historically, schools provided the setting where individuals engaged in learning. Research on everyday cognition demonstrates that the formal learning in schools and the informal learning in practical settings have important differences (National-Research-Council, 2009). What we discover about learning in schools is *insufficient* for a theory of human learning: schools are often focused on individual cognition, on memorization and on learning general facts whereas learning in the EDC should be focused on shared cognition, use of powerful tools and external information sources, and situation-specific competencies (Resnick, 1987).

## When to Learn: At the Right Time

Information overload and the rapid change of our world have created new problems and new challenges for learning and education. People will have to keep learning new knowledge and skills throughout their lifetimes as their lives and jobs keep changing. New approaches are needed to circumvent the unsolvable problems of *coverage* and *obsolescence*. The EDC supports *learning on demand* (Fischer, 1991) as a promising approach as follows: (1) it contextualizes learning by allowing it to be integrated into personally meaningful problems rather than relegating it to a separate phase; (2) it lets learners see for themselves the usefulness of new knowledge for actual problem situations, thereby increasing the motivation for learning new things; and (3) it makes new information relevant to the task at hand, thereby leading to more informed decision making and better artifacts.

## With Whom: Transcending to Individual Human Mind

Systemic problems require more knowledge than any single person possesses because the knowledge relevant to either frame or resolve these problems is usually distributed among stakeholders coming from different disciplines (Fischer and Sugimoto, 2006). The "Renaissance Scholar" (meaning the person who is knowledgeable in all relevant fields) no longer exists (Csikszentmihalyi, 1996). To deal with complex multi-disciplinary problems, people need to use the powerful tools technology provides for finding, analyzing, manipulating, and communicating knowledge bringing different and often controversial points of view together to create a shared understanding among these stakeholders can lead to new insights, ideas, and artifacts. In the past, most computational environments have focused on the needs of individual users. Our research has evolved from empowering Renaissance Scholars in specific domains (e.g., with domain-oriented design environments) to creating shared understanding among "Renaissance Communities" as communities of interest (Fischer, 2013) with the EDC by attempting to bring people with different background knowledge and different value systems together and to overcome the biases and barriers of their separate languages.

## 4.3.2 CONCEPTIONS OF LEARNING EXPLORED AND SUPPORTED BY THE EDC

The EDC attempts to make unique contributions to the different aspects of learning identified in Figure 4.7. We believe with Wenger (1998) that learning cannot be designed, but it can be *designed for* by creating social and technical environments that will facilitate, foster, nurture, and support learning. Some of the specific requirements for learning that we have pursued with the EDC are that: (1) learning should take place in the context of authentic, complex problems (because learners will refuse to quietly listen to someone else's answers to someone else's questions) (Bruner, 1996); and (2) active, self-directed learning should fostered and supported with a focus on mutual dialogs, joint knowledge construction, and constructive dialogs between individual negotiating their differences while creating their shared voice and vision. Three other conceptualization of learning have driven the development of the EDC: (1) "learning to be"; (2) "learning when the answer is not known"; and (3) the integration of working and learning.

### Learning About vs. Learning to Be

*Learning about*, as an objective for learning and education, is focused on the accumulation of intellectual capital realized in a curriculum that stresses the communication of culturally central theories, facts, and skills (Hirsch, 1988). The approach assume that this curriculum is identifiable and structured as a coherent and fine-grained sequence of educational objectives. *Instructionist* approaches can be effective and are often well suited for "learning about" (e.g., learners getting introduced to domains of knowledge that are new to them, e.g., Mathematics 101, Design 101, or Urban Planning 101).

*Learning to be* (Brown, 2005) is focused not as much on teaching about mathematics, design, or urban planning, but on what it means and takes to be a mathematician, a designer, or an urban planner. Important dimensions of *learning to be* include learning by being engaged in personally meaningful problems, teachers engaging in problem-solving activities in front of their students rather than lecturing, fostering communities based on "horizontal" and "vertical" integration (by bringing together individuals coming from different disciplines and including undergraduates, graduates, post-docs, faculty members, and people in industry), and enculturation of learners into communities of practice with legitimate peripheral participation (Lave and Wenger, 1991).

### Learning When the Answer is Known vs. Learning When the Answer is Not Known

In many introductory courses (particularly in disciplines belonging to the natural sciences (Simon, 1996)), the answer to the problems discussed in courses exists and is known by the teacher, and the core challenge is "for learners to learn what the teacher knows." In such settings, lectures based on the transmission model are reasonable and cost-effective strategies

Theorists like Bruner argue that the most important gift of cultural psychology to education is the reformulation of the impoverished conception that "teaching is fitted into a mold in which a single, presumably omniscient teacher explicitly tells or shows presumably unknowing learners something they presumably know nothing about" (Bruner, 1996, p. 20). In settings where *the answer is not known and a "right" answer may not exist* (as it is the case in wicked, ill-defined design problems pursued with the EDC), information is not a commodity to be consumed but is collaboratively designed and constructed, emphasizing innovation, continuous learning, and collaboration as important processes in which workers as stakeholders create new knowledge as they carry out their problem framing and problem solving activities. The role of the omniscient teacher does not exist in such settings: "In important transformations of our personal lives and organizational practices, we must learn new forms of activity which are not there yet. They are literally learned as they are being created. There is no competent teacher. Standard learning theories have little to offer if one wants to understand these processes." (Engeström, 2001, p. 138).

### Integration of Working and Learning

Learning in the EDC is integrated into framing and solving problems rather than being separated and taking place in a classroom. Learning in the EDC can be characterized as follows: participants are engaged in some activity, they experience a breakdown, and they reflect about the breakdown (e.g., the piece of lacking knowledge, the misunderstanding about the consequences of some of their assumptions). Table 4.4 summarizes some of the major differences between learning in schools and learning in the context of the EDC.

Table 4.4: A comparison of different conceptualizations of school learning and lifelong learning

| Dimensions | Learning in School | Learning in the EDC |
|---|---|---|
| **emphasis** | "basic" skills | learning as a fundamental aspect of life |
| **problems** | given; well-defined<br>focus on problem solving | constructed; ill-defined<br>focus on problem framing and problem solving |
| **new topics** | defined by curricula, assigned-to-learn, decontextualized | arise incidentally, need-to-know, on demand, contextualized |
| **structure** | pedagogic or logical structure | interests, problems, work activities; learning often takes places without teaching |
| **cognition** | knowledge in the head;<br>individual cognition;<br>general learning | distributed; use of tools and external information resources; shared cognition; situation-specific competencies |
| **roles** | expert-novice model;<br>teacher and learner = f{person} | reciprocal learning;<br>teacher and learner = f{context} |
| **teachers** | expound subject matter ("sage on the stage") | engage in guided discovery learning ("guide on the side") |
| **learners** | consumers | active participants |
| **mode** | instructionism<br>(knowledge absorption) | design; making; constructionism (knowledge construction) |
| **drawbacks** | decontextualized, not situated | important concepts are not encountered |

## 4.4    CONCLUSIONS

Learning, design, and creativity are three fundamental research concepts where the development of the EDC as a socio-technical environment has played a dual relationship whose outcomes have proven valuable in terms of (a) *technology* supporting the development of *theory* and (b) *theory* supporting the development of *technology*.

Related to design, the EDC has been instrumental in advancing our theoretical contributions in design methodologies; the notion of design communities of both practice and interest; the concept of boundary objects and their importance to design communities; and the instantiation of the SER Model as an evolutionary guide for the EDC and its development (Chapter 6).

In the context of creativity, the EDC applications in real world cases (Chapter 5) and in our exprinces in the classroom (Chapter 7) expanded our understanding of: (1) the concepts of *indi-*

*vidual* and *social creativity*; (2) the notions of *distance* and *diversity* and their impacts on creativity; and (3) the central role played by the EDC's support of creativity in *collaborative learning and design.*

With respect to learning, the EDC has been instrumental in extending our understanding of its multi-dimensional aspects such as: *Who learns?*, *Why?*, and *What do we learn?*, or *How and Where to learn?*; along with the various conceptions of learning such as: *learning about* vs. *learning to be*, or the *integration of working and learning* (Chapter 7).

The contribution of this chapter is that it gives an insight of the theoretical basis for understanding the other chapters of the book individually and in terms of the relationships with each other thereby providing a basis to explore central questions for the advancement of tabletop technologies and their future contributions to human-centered informatics and education.

Grounding our approach in conceptual frameworks defined by design, creativity, and learning empowered us to complement "technology-driven approaches searching for applications" towards the development of socio-technical environments based on tabletop computing and tangible technologies.

CHAPTER 5

# Case Studies in Different Application Domains

Based on our overall approach that our research was not driven by developing new technologies in search of an application, but by creating socio-technical environments to address problems, case studies in different application domains have played an important role (Popper, 1959).

Figure 5.1 provides an overview of the major case studies reported at different places in the book.

Figure 5.1: An overview of the different case studies conducted with the EDC.

This chapter describes three selected case studies in which our research team collaborated with stakeholders from different application domains addressing real-world problems on:

- *campus planning* with a focus on a new research park campus of the University of Colorado (CU) at Boulder in collaboration with the Regents of CU and representatives of the City of Boulder;

- *emergency management* with a focus on creating training and operational environments for making communities more resistant and resilient to wildfires in collaboration with the Boulder County Fire Department; and

- *energy sustainability* with a focus on creating environments exploiting the opportunities of smart grids and smart meters to motivate and support people to engage in environmentally responsible behavior in collaboration with the citizen of Boulder.

For the three problem domains described in this chapter well-defined solutions did not exist requiring that potential solutions had to be actively created by all participants.

## 5.1    CAMPUS PLANNING

Important planning and decisions take place on an ongoing basis between the Regents of the University of Colorado and the Boulder City Council. The importance for an EDC application to support this relationship is that more often than not, it takes place within a context of conflict with a great need of resolution. The university's areas under property law are considered state property. Consequently, in a great number of development issues, campus planning of the University of Colorado does not have to meet the land use, zoning, and building regulations of the city. This point has historically been the source of great conflicts over the years in the relationship between the city and the university. This is particularly so when it comes to campus building heights on campus. The city traditionally regulates building heights to protect the views of its mountain background traditionally considered a major natural amenity of the city. Therefore, this regulation has been a source of conflict since it has direct consequences on the shape, size and construction costs of buildings on campus.

Given these reasons, our collaboration with these two different groups of representatives using the EDC was useful to support sessions which provided the following special opportunities and challenges: (1) both groups are local, making it feasible to bring them together in local face-to-face meetings; (2) the groups represent different constituencies that pursue in many problem situations different objectives leading to numerous conflicts between their objectives and values; and (3) the shared environment provided by the EDC created a focal point for discussion, allowing participants to build common ground and explore possible resolutions to issues impacting both organizations.

The meetings that we conducted provided unique opportunities to evaluate:

- the adequacy of our interaction tools (the members of both of these communities are interested in the problems and not in computational artifacts);

- the enrichment of having a facilitator to guide them through an effective design process; and

- the objective whether conflicts could be turned into productive interactions of different opinions.

Figure 5.2 shows how representatives of the Boulder City Council and the Regents of the University of Colorado gathered around the EDC action space to discuss different perspectives through explorations afforded by computational models related to a design problem of common interest and concern.

Figure 5.2: A design session with representatives of the Boulder City Council and the Regents of the University of Colorado.

The EDC environment developed for the particular case study allowed the exploration of numerous different design alternatives and challenges. Two of them will be briefly described here: (1) "massing" (total square footage) related to different building heights and (2) the impact of building heights on surrounding places and views.

## Exploring Different "Massing" Options

Figure 5.3 shows the arrangement of different building structures eventually to be built in the research park. Assumptions are made by the planners about the heights of different building to be constructed.

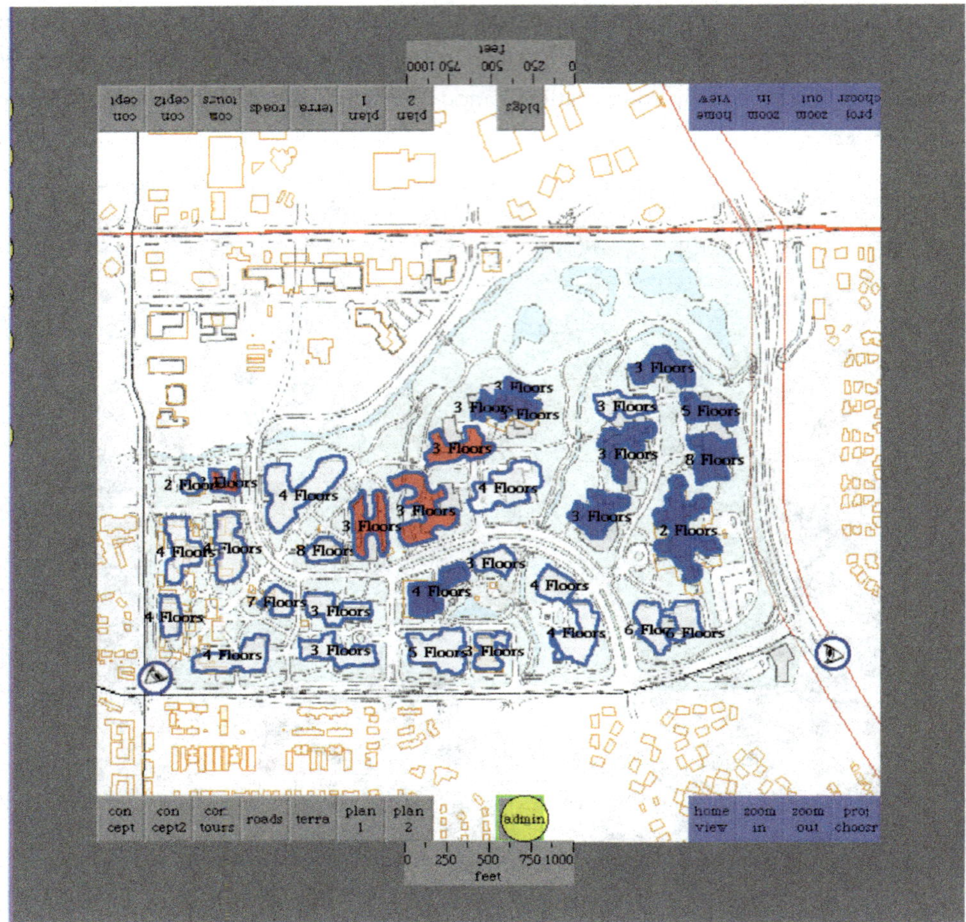


Figure 5.3: Action space representations exploring and visualizing "Projected Building Massing." Supporting interactive exploration of proposed campus development alternatives and the relationships between the shape, floor area, and structure heights of buildings for the campus research park.

Following similar techniques as described in the scenario in Chapter 2 as various choices are made for building heights by the participants in the EDC action space, the resultant total gross square footage for the research park is dynamically computed and represented in the reflection space in a quantitative representation (Figure 5.4).

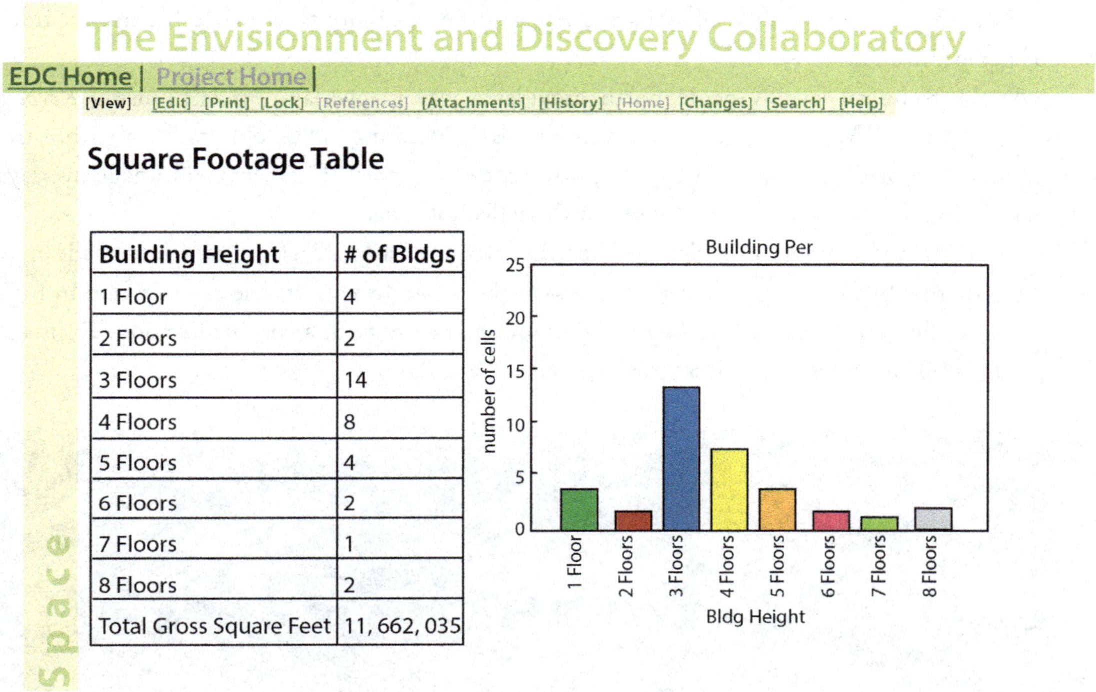

| Building Height | # of Bldgs |
|---|---|
| 1 Floor | 4 |
| 2 Floors | 2 |
| 3 Floors | 14 |
| 4 Floors | 8 |
| 5 Floors | 4 |
| 6 Floors | 2 |
| 7 Floors | 1 |
| 8 Floors | 2 |
| Total Gross Square Feet | 11, 662, 035 |



Figure 5.4: Visualizations of "massing" in the reflection space.

## Visualizing the Impact of Building Heights on Surrounding Places

The EDC allows stakeholders to sketch new buildings, associate a height with them, and analyze their impact on the surroundings (e.g., do they block a neighbor's view of the mountains—one of the most controversial issues in the City of Boulder that has led to extensive rules about height limitations). The ability to change perspective views in urban planning projects is an obvious necessity to understand visual impacts of different development actions. The information visualized in the action space is generally presented in a top-down *plan view* being considered a natural representation among designers and planners. However, not everyone can readily read a plan view and understand its 3D implications. A perspective view can be useful to allow more participants to visualize certain aspects of the situation thereby creating a basis for better informed rational decision making with visualizations.

As explained in Chapter 6, the EDC uses Google Earth in a mash-up approach. A couple of action space tools including (1) the *helicopter* view (providing a view from above) and (2) the *eyeball* view (allowing to "walk through" the simulation at ground level) can be used to control the viewpoint seen in Google Earth, allowing participants the flexibility to visualize the impact from various perspectives.

At the technical level, Google Earth provides a way to overlay objects by using *Keyhole Markup Language* (KML) data through a web link. By generating KML objects from within the simulation and providing access through a lightweight web server, 3D objects and image overlays are relayed to and displayed on the Google Earth Reflection Space.

The sketching support provided by the EDC requires a small effort to create crude new building structure by depicting a floor plan and associate a height with it. The visualization in Figure 5.5 shows the impact that a building of a certain height has from a specific location. To image this in our minds is at best very difficult, if not impossible.

Figure 5.5: The visual impacts of high building shown in Google Earth using a "Helicopter" view.

The crude building structures shown in Figure 5.5 can be compared with *fat-pencil technologies* that are important in early stages of design because they allow designers to focus on the essential aspects of the task in this phase of the process and they minimize the efforts to create them. Fat-pencil technologies can successfully combined with techniques for *incremental formalization* (Shipman, 1993) where additional structure is added over time to model more realistic forms. Figure 5.6 shows a later stage of the design after the crude images are refined to resemble more closely the buildings that will be eventually constructed and their visual impacts. This process is supported in the EDC by allowing designers to import 3D models constructed with SketchUp from the 3D Warehouse (https://3dwarehouse.sketchup.com).

Figure 5.6: Using more realistic buildings from the 3D-Warehouse.

While we have not done any formal assessment studies to evaluate the design sessions done in the context of this case study, the following two quotes illustrate the impression that the EDC left on some of the participants:

> "The EDC would allow us to attract the maximum number of people to development and make improvements that are somewhat timeless in their dimension."—a Professional Campus Planner

"The EDC is an amazing, powerful tool that helps the entire audience to be on the same page and visualize what could be quite complicated drawings or renderings in a very easy format in which everyone 'gets it.'"—a Professional Real-Estate Developer

## 5.2    EMERGENCY MANAGEMENT

"I hear and I forget, I see and I remember, I do and I understand."—Confucius, 450 BC

"Tell me and I forget, Teach me and I remember, Involve me and I will learn."—Benjamin Franklin, 1750

Experiential learning (Dewey, 2009) (often also referred to as learning-by-doing and learning-through-discovery and exploration) is a philosophy and methodology of education that engages learners in direct experiences and focused reflection (and thereby is closely related to reflection-in-action and reflection-on-action (Schön, 1983)).

Experiential learning occurs when carefully chosen experiences are supported by reflection, critical analysis, and actions and are structured to require the learner to take initiative, make decisions and be accountable for results. Experiential learning requires environments that allow learners to be actively engaged in posing questions, investigating different settings, experimenting, solving problems, and assuming responsibility. In the case of *emergency management* there is overwhelming evidence (as indicated by the quotes from Confucius and Franklin above) that people who only read about possible natural disasters (e.g., by studying checklists) are less well prepared when a real disaster occurs compared to people who engaged in experiential learning.

In this case study, the EDC was used to develop a highly interactive and engaging environment for *emergency management education, assessment, and planning* that supports an experiential learning environment and is similar in capabilities to an aircraft flight simulator. By using this approach, emergency management decision makers and managers can "experience" natural and human-made disasters, allowing them to exercise and assess contingency planning and actions and in a fundamentally different way. The specific emergency explored was one dealing with wildland fires, a costly experience in many states of the western U.S.

The specific content knowledge modeled in this case study is focused on wildfires (a major natural hazard in Colorado) and the study is based on a collaboration between $L^3D$ and the COMET program (COMET-Program, 2006) of the University Corporation for Atmospheric Research's (UCAR). Participants gather around the EDC action space to explore wildfire concepts as well as the organizational and communication issues related to wildfire mitigation and response. The action space is linked with a reflection space developed for meteorological education (MetEd; https://www.meted.ucar.edu) on fire behavior and its interaction with weather allowing participants to explore both how wildfires are impacted by weather conditions and how wildfires sometimes create their own weather.

The motivation for participation in the *experiential learning* activities ranges from professional and civic pride to protection of life and property and included learners from various groups including:

- *experienced wildfire managers* who wish to collaborative share, improve upon, or even move beyond current practices (dePaula and Fischer, 2005);

- *new wildfire managers* given responsibilities for which they have limited background but for which they want to prepare themselves to respond appropriately (Fischer, 2000a);

- *citizens* who live in areas highly susceptible to wildfires who want to understand what the community response plan is and what they can do to mitigate risks to their property (Fischer, 2002); and

- *students* at all levels who will use this environment as an important and engaging context for many topics in STEM disciplines.

Using a Geographic Information System (GIS) model of their region, the participants focus on an area that has been the site of several recent wildfires. They begin the self-directed learning activity by describing (in the action space) the area and the facilities and buildings that are of concern, then exploring the GIS data that is provided, including topographical maps, plant fuel inventories, slope and aspect data, and historical data from previous fires (Figure 5.7). As their meeting progresses, a fire simulation is initiated that requires the group to formulate a response plan.

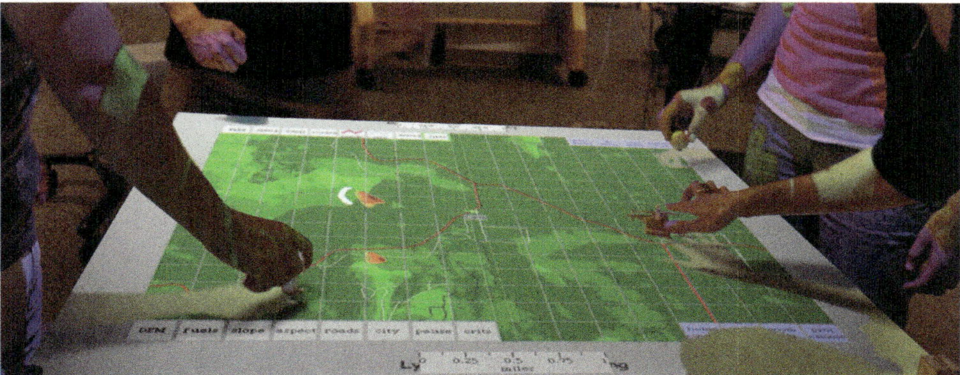

Figure 5.7: The wildfire environment in the action space. This figure shows participants interacting with a digital elevation model (DEM) base map with a road layer in the action space of the EDC, constructing and responding to a fire simulation.

One aspect of this response plan deals with the creation of *emergency fuel breaks*: areas that are cleared of combustible fuels to halt or impede the progress of a fire. Using a tool in the interface, the group specifies the proposed location for a fuel break. Using the task model for the creation of fuel breaks, as well as the placement of buildings on the map specified by the group, the system infers that the placement specified by the group is on a line of travel for the fire that is based only on the wind direction and does not take into account the slope of the terrain in the area of the fire. As a result, the fuel break is too close to the fire given its rate of travel (the fuel break could not be constructed before the fire reaches the site).

Various elements of the natural landscape play in to fire behavior: the elevation, slope, and aspect (the direction the slope faces) all impact the way that fires spread (Figures 5.8a-d). For example, fires spread faster on the uphill side of a fire due to the heating of combustible material by the rising heat of the fire. The fuel complex, represented by the various types of vegetation and their maturity and condition, impact what material is available to burn and how quickly the fire can spread. Other factors, such as wind direction and speed, as well as humidity also play into the behavior of the fire.

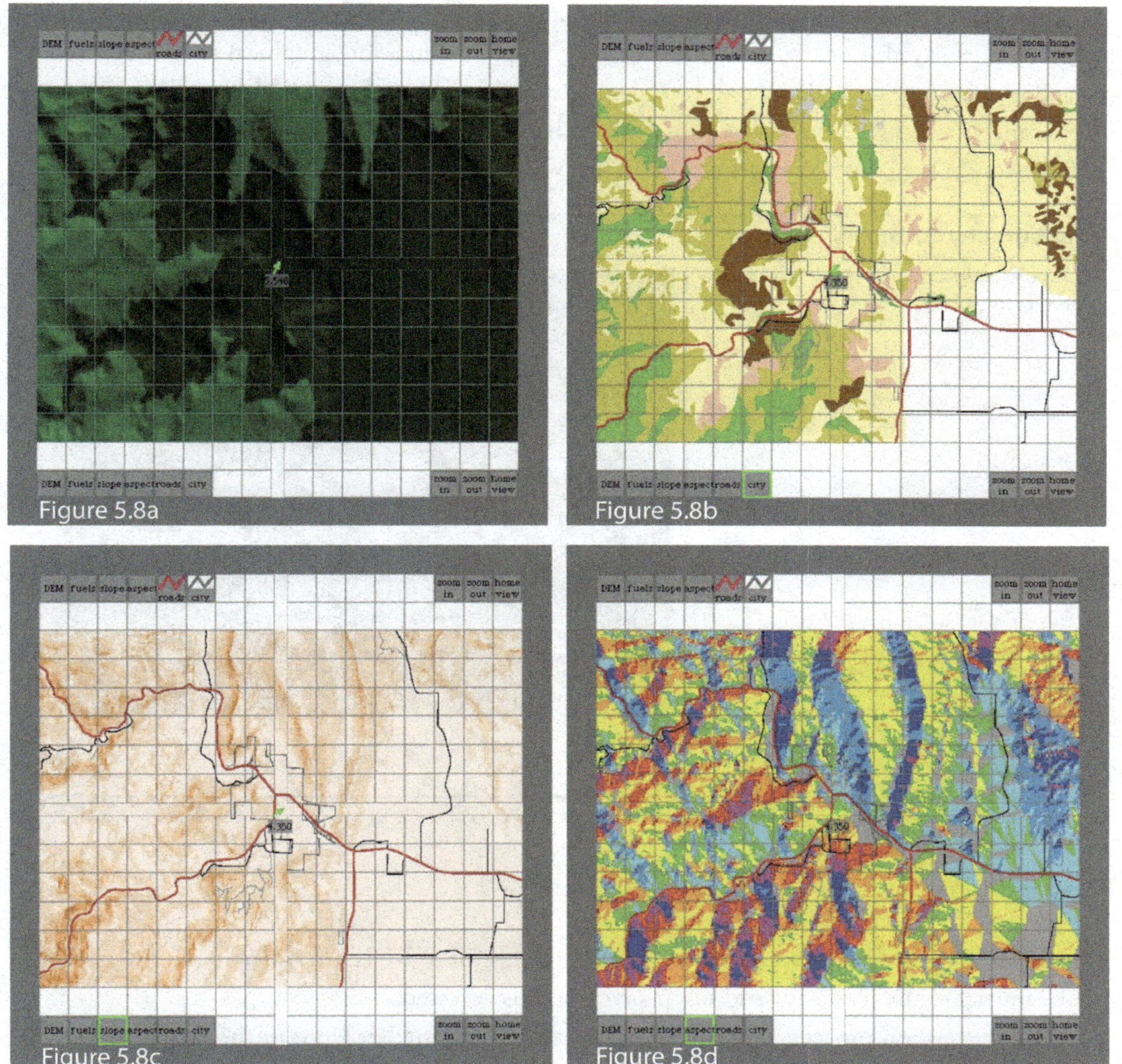



Figure 5.8: Action space with different characteristics of natural systems related to fire behavior. These figures show the various configuration layers in the action space to support risk analysis through understanding the impacts on the behavior of wild fires by: (a) topology; (b) vegetation; (c) slope; and (d) aspect.

As these various layers are explored in the action space, MetEd lessons related to that information are displayed in the reflection space. For example, when a topographical layer is selected in the action space, a lesson related to how topography impacts fire behavior is shown (Figure 5.9). As participants interact with the model surrounding that layer, they can explore the related information in the lesson in the context of their collaborative work.

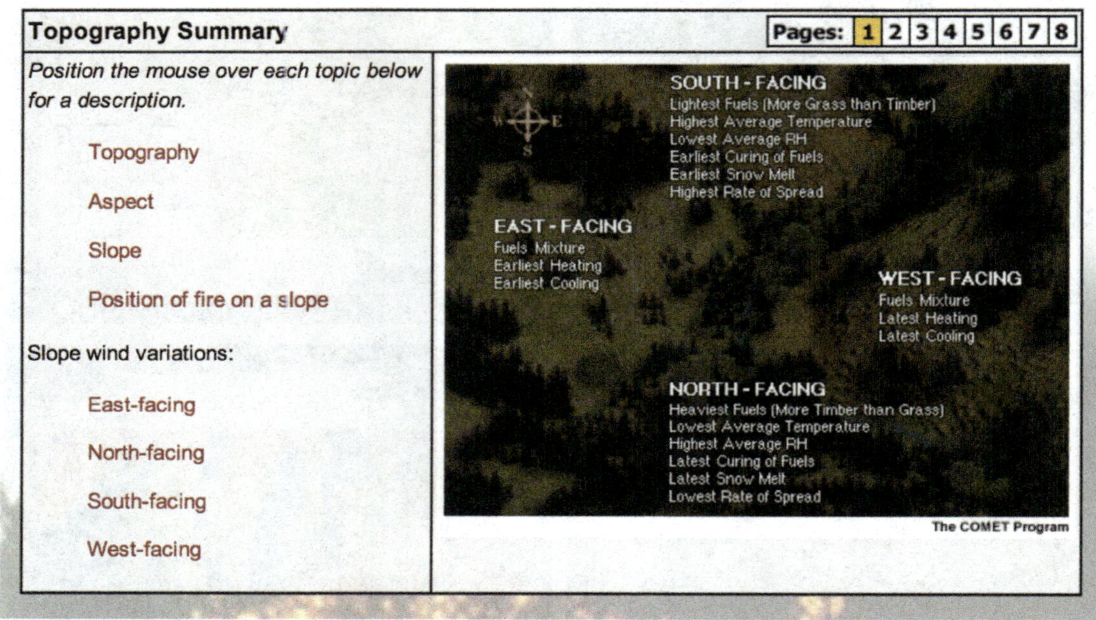


Figure 5.9: A topology lesson in UCAR's MetEd site.

Similarly, when they access the vegetation layer, a set of MetEd lessons on the fuel complex and its impact on fire behavior and fire management is accessed.

As the session proceeds, the participants can start a simulated fire in the action space. The fire model is a coarse-grained one, but is based on the various data layers discussed so far: slope, aspect, vegetation, and wind, giving a broad sense of how a fire might move based on the situation.

A "wind" piece in the action space can be used to change the direction the simulated wind is coming from and its magnitude based on where it is placed on the board: the direction is indicated by the angle to the center of the board; the magnitude, by how far the piece is placed from the center. The arrow in the center of the board indicates the current wind origin direction and the text below the arrow, its magnitude. This allows the participants to explore various situations related to changing weather.

Figure 5.10: Reflection space illustrating the impact of the "fuel complex" on fire behavior in COMET.

## Visualizing Fire Behavior in Perspective View

Whereas professional planners and others who are accustomed to using a 2D "plan view" map have little difficulty in interpreting the maps and layers in the action space, this is not necessarily the case for all participants. An additional Google-Earth-based reflection space is already being used to show the layers in maps to a potential larger audience than what can be comfortably accommodated at the table. By using another piece called a "helicopter" in the action space, participants can take advantage of the capabilities of Google Earth to show 3D perspective views. Placing the helicopter in various locations on the table changes the viewpoint allowing the participants to control what is shown in the Google Earth view. Objects in the simulation can be sent to the Google Earth reflection space as 3D models: for example, the dynamic fire area is shown in a perspective view in Figure 5.11.

Figure 5.11: 3D goggle visualization of fire behavior.

The capabilities of the simulation go beyond simply viewing information. The participants can design interventions and see how those elements might impact the fire's behavior. For example, one strategy used by wildfire managers is to create fire breaks, by clearing terrain of combustible material. In the action space, participants can use the fire-break tool to sketch out the fire break path and the width of the area to be cleared and critics could give feedback on the design of fire break. As the fire simulation proceeds, the effectiveness of the fire break can be understood. If the cleared area is not wide enough, high winds can cause the fire to "jump" the break. An important issue in real situations is how to ensure the safety of residents. In the simulation, wildfire managers can create evacuation plans and then simulate evacuation of residents. Figure 5.12 illustrates how "fire breaks" and "evacuation routes" can be identified in the simulation.

Figure 5.12: Action space visualization of road systems.

The EDC in this case study supports several levels of engagement in experiential learning related to different levels in understanding, motivation, and retention by the participants.

- *Fix-It Level*: At this level the participants can obtain suggestions for alternative placements for fuel breaks (based on the task model) and continue with their exploration without engaging in learning.

- *Reflection Level*: At this level, learning is focused on making information relevant to the task at hand (Fischer et al., 1996). The participants can explore and reflect on how to design fuel breaks. Arguments for the fuel break task model are shown in the reflection space consisting of issues related to the design of fuel breaks as well as additional information on the impacts of wind, slope, aspect, fuel, humidity, stored moisture content, and time of day on fire travel.

- *Contextualized Tutoring Level*: This level allows participants to gain a more coherent understanding of the topic under investigation (and it can be pursued when participants have sufficient time to do so). A contextualized tutorial utilizes a model of the participants' background knowledge and personal profiles, the partially developed construction, and the partially articulated specification created by the participants as part of their self-directed learning activities to identify task-relevant tutoring episodes and contextualize them to the interests and needs of the learners.

Many additional research questions can be pursued in the context of this example how the EDC can be employed to investigate interesting issues related to learning (Section 4.3).

- In what situations and under what conditions is it preferable to employ a *guided discovery approach* (Mayer, 2004) rather than a completely self-directed approach? When is it preferable to guide participants through elements of the problem so that they can have sufficient context to frame the problem adequately?

- How should learning opportunities derived from *breakdowns, impasses, and conceptual collisions* (Fischer, 2000b) be detected and presented to participants?

- How should *user models* (Fischer, 2001b) for background knowledge and learning be created and maintained? How should appropriate background information be presented when the background knowledge of the individuals is different? How should progress in learning be assessed and attributed appropriately?

- How should we allow participants to *articulate their high-level objectives* (e.g., via a specification component (Nakakoji, 1993)) for their specific situation (in addition to the domain model and generic scenario provided as a starting place)?

- How can the contextualized tutoring episodes make use of shared representations that allow participants to create *shared understanding and common ground* (Clark and Brennan, 1991)?

Similar to the case study reported in Section 5.1, we have not done any formal assessment studies to evaluate the design sessions done in the context of this case study. The role of the EDC serving as an *inspirational prototype* was expressed by one of the participants (the Assistant City Manager of Boulder) with her remark: "The EDC would be an outstanding tool to show simulations to the community so that people would know what to do in the event of an emergency." She argued that responders often know what to do in certain emergencies, but the general public is not well enough informed—providing a unique opportunity for the EDC to improve personnel training and education for all citizens.

## 5.3    ENERGY SUSTAINABILITY

Exploring fundamental new possibilities for energy sustainability is a national priority (Ehrhardt-Martinez et al., 2010). Smart grids overlay the electricity distribution grid with information and communications infrastructure that improve management and reliability as well as provide opportunities for new forms of consumer involvement with smart metering and support for tracking energy use.

Energy is not visible and is frequently not a topic of discourse considered important and interesting enough (other than occasional rants when electric bills arrive). Many citizens suffer from "energy illiteracy" (Reeves et al., 2009) and conversations among households in communities are rare. Currently, most perspectives and decision making related to energy use in the consumer arena are focused on the individual or individual households. Whereas the individual household is where the final decisions are made and effected, the broader, collaborative context can provide an opportunity for understanding and motivating individual action.

The case study documented in this section has been part of a large research effort of the $L^3D$ center to contribute to energy sustainability. Our focus to reduce energy consumption through behavior changes complements most other approaches pursued by engineering disciplines that are oriented on novel ways of producing energy, more energy efficient devices, and improved infrastructures for storing and distributing energy. Based on our global research orientation to empower human beings rather than replace them with technology (Table 3.1), our approach is taking advantage of smart grids and smart meters by engaging humans as active decision makers and not merely as passive consumers requiring new levels of human understanding and involvement (Fischer, 2011).

An important part of our overall development was pursued by Holger Dick in his Ph.D. thesis (Dick, 2013). He developed the socio-technical energy feedback system EMPIRE (Empowering People in Reducing Energy Consumption), evaluated it in experimental studies via Amazon Mechanical Turk, and deployed it to University of Colorado students (Dick et al., 2012). He was able to show that systems based on individual empowerment approaches were effective in motivating people to save some energy but that more substantial savings could potentially be achieved by complementing the individual support with environments that would nurture and support communities. Social environments influencing people's behavior should be influenced by paying attention to: (1) *public commitment* (committing publicly to something increases the likelihood of actually following up on it; (2) *social norms* (behavioral standards that have been established in a community from which community members do not want to deviate); and (3) *social proof* (observing other people's actions and behavior and inferring from them which actions or behaviors are recommendable) (Cialdini, 2009).

The extensions to EMPIRE pursued with the EDC are a specific instance of the developments described in Chapter 3 that complement the support for individual designers with domain-oriented environments (DODEs) with the support of design communities with the EDC. Building on our experiences and insights from our work in supporting cultures of participation (Fischer, 2011), the EDC was used to design and implement a suite of tools allowing the community of EMPIRE participants to share and become aware of people's energy improvements, their insights, their behaviors, and their consumption.

These tools represent the foundation for a *supportive social* combine behavioral techniques (Ariely, 2010) with human-centered design to allow citizens to explore the *broader, collaborative context* to understand and modify their own energy consumption behavior. The project goes beyond simply exchanging tips and information on energy usage (as many free and independent websites and messaging boards do already), and beyond showing individual energy usage (as it was done in early systems such as Google PowerMeter and Microsoft Hohm that are not available anymore). These tools were targeted to make citizens aware how their consumption behavior at the individual level impacts energy resources when these impacts are viewed as the aggregate behavior of a larger population. The design was driven by the objectives to: (1) help citizens collaboratively understand which kind of behaviors are or are not sustainable; and (2) overcome a sense of futility at the individual level by understanding that what "we do as individuals can make a difference." Illustrating the results of aggregate behavior allows people to see the impacts of their individual choices at a broader scale, and by supporting multiple perspectives and diverse opinions, new opportunities and approaches to sustainable energy behavior can be explored.

Figure 5.13 provides an overview of the EDC developments for this topic area allowing participants to explore data and simulations for gaining a better understanding of the interaction between their individual energy choices and the overall behavior of their neighborhood's energy use.

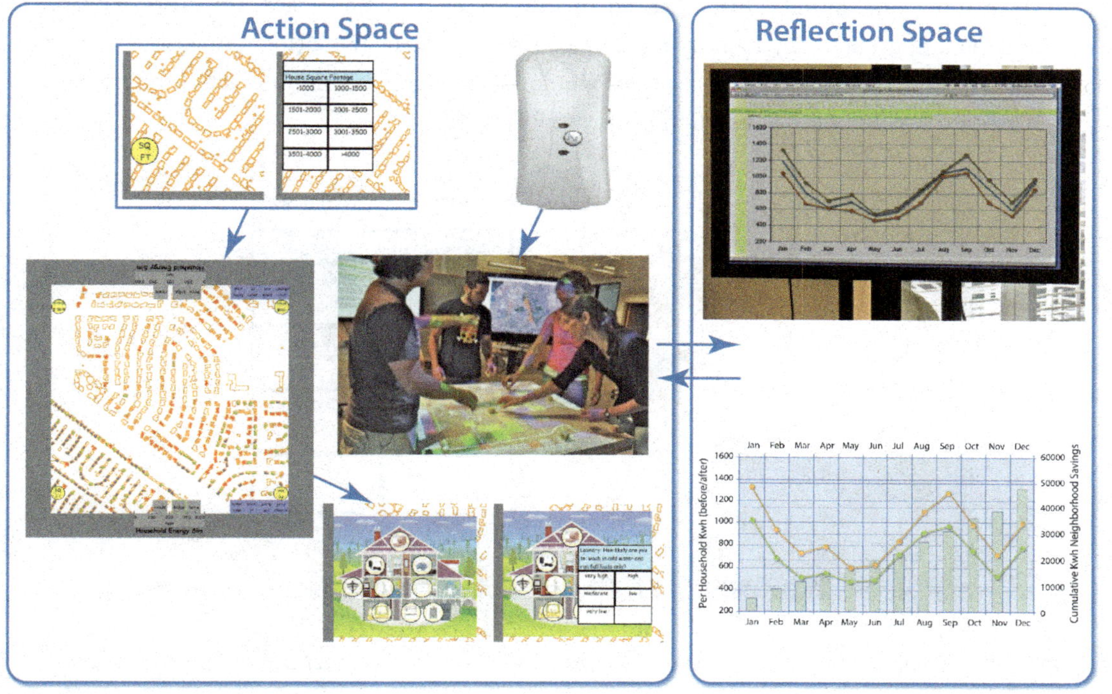


Figure 5.13: Overview of developments for the EDC supporting energy sustainability projects.

Before engaging in the collaborative design session, participants will have analyzed their own individual energy consumption using home energy monitors (Figure 5.14; information from the monitors (the device shown on the left) is sent to a server and from there it is displayed on a laptop or smart phone) and uploaded this information into the EDC using EMPIRE.

Figure 5.14: Energy monitors (smart meters): providing detailed data for consumers insight.

As an additional initial activity, participants (in the EDC action space) can create a profile of their individual households by identifying characteristics of their home (including: square footage, household size, degree of insulation, types of windows and doors) using interaction points around the surface of the EDC tabletop system (Figure 5.15).

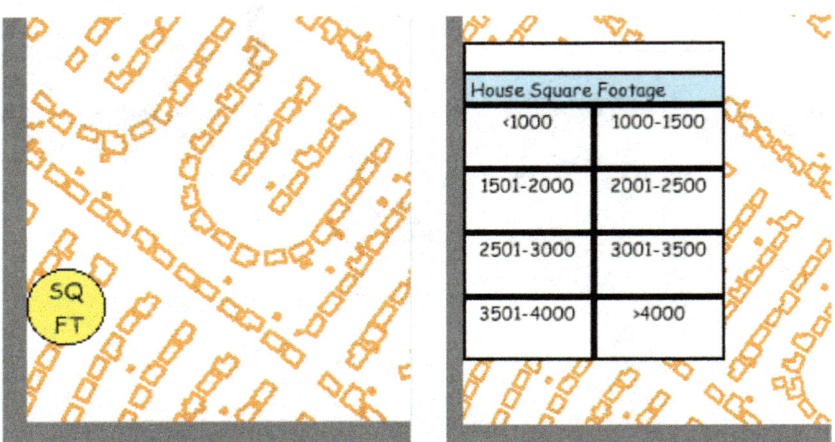


Figure 5.15: Participants creating profiles in the EDC of their specific energy-relevant parameters.

As the participants specify their individual profiles, the map of homes in their neighborhood is color-coded indicating what households match each participant's profile (Figure 5.16). This process is helpful in identifying commonalities, allowing cohorts to become apparent based on energy consumption levels, and understanding the spatial distribution of the energy demands.

Once the household profiles are established in the system, the EDC is able to create another visualization allowing participants to compare their individual consumption with others (Figure 5.17) and discuss and reflect upon the underlying behavior leading to very different usage of energy.

After the analysis of existing consumption patterns and behavior, the collaborative design session proceeds by exploring new opportunities and ideas how to reduce energy consumption. The participants take turns (this can be done individually, by pairing up with others with similar profiles, or by discussing each situation as a whole group) to engage in the following activities.

1. They work together to devise strategies for their situation (as related to their profiles) to save energy by changing schedules and reducing use. A model of a house with various tips for energy use is part of the initial seed, and by selecting areas of or objects within the house some initial choices are provided to guide the discussion.

2. As specific choices are made in the context of a given household, participants can then see the calculated results of the changes in energy outcomes for this house (a) reflected

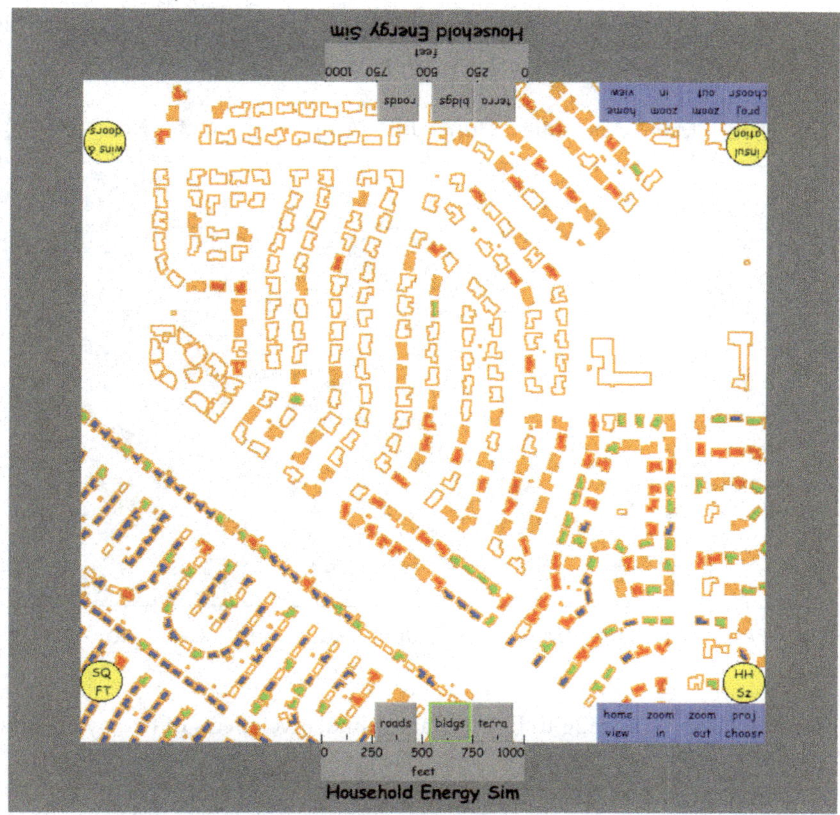


Figure 5.16: The action space: a system-generated map of the neighborhood.

Figure 5.17: Comparisons of outcomes of the collaborative design activities for saving energy.

in the usage graph, (b) aggregated over similar houses, and (c) the impact this would create on overall use of energy in the community.

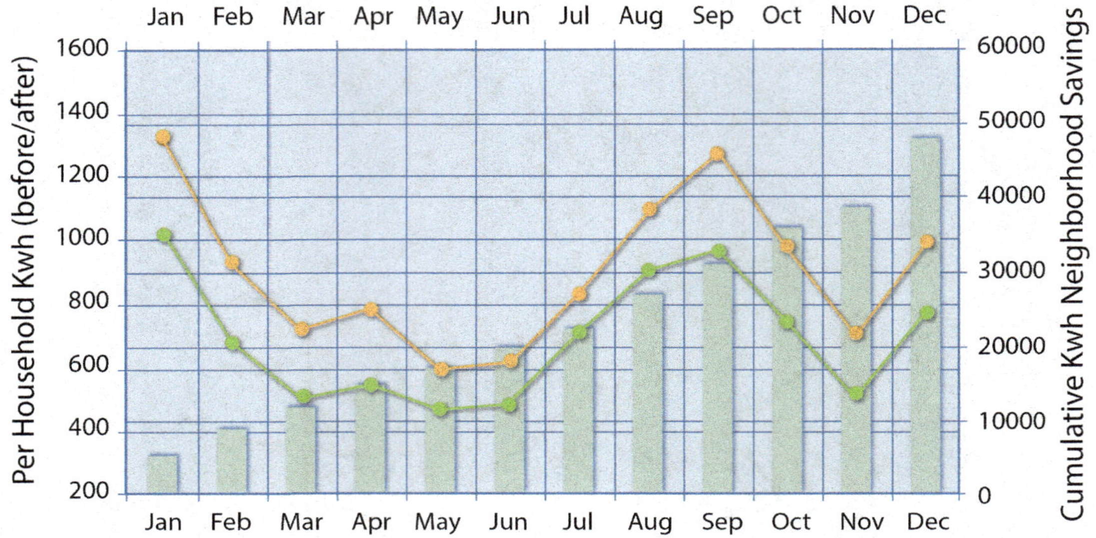


Figure 5.18: Reflection space showing differences and cumulative effects of energy choices.

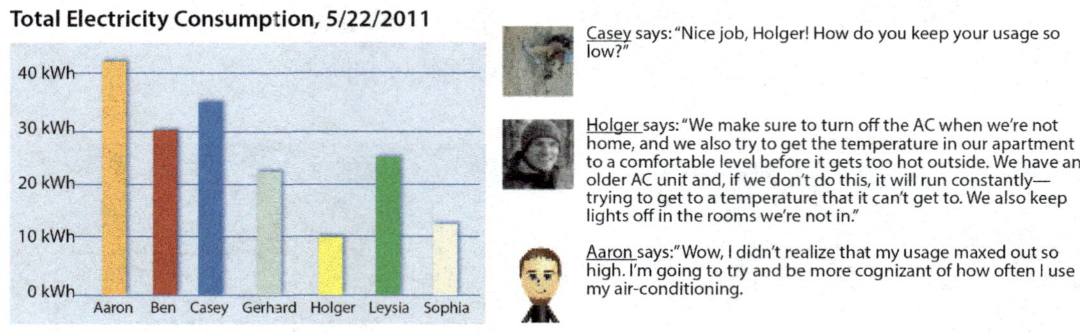


Figure 5.19: Reflection space comparing consumption of neighbors with embedded discussion.

As a final step, the profiles, decisions, and data generated during the design session are uploaded in the Boulder Community Wiki for Energy Sustainability (Figure 5.20) where the results can be shared with others, be retained for future design sessions, and applicable and desirable suggestions being implemented in their daily lives. Neighborhood households are contacted through the neighborhood association's mailing list and encouraged to follow the activities of the participants. If participants allow it, data can be shown to feed back the participants how they are doing in relation to the goals they have set for themselves. Comments can be made on how the community is progressing toward a more collective sustainable energy behavior.

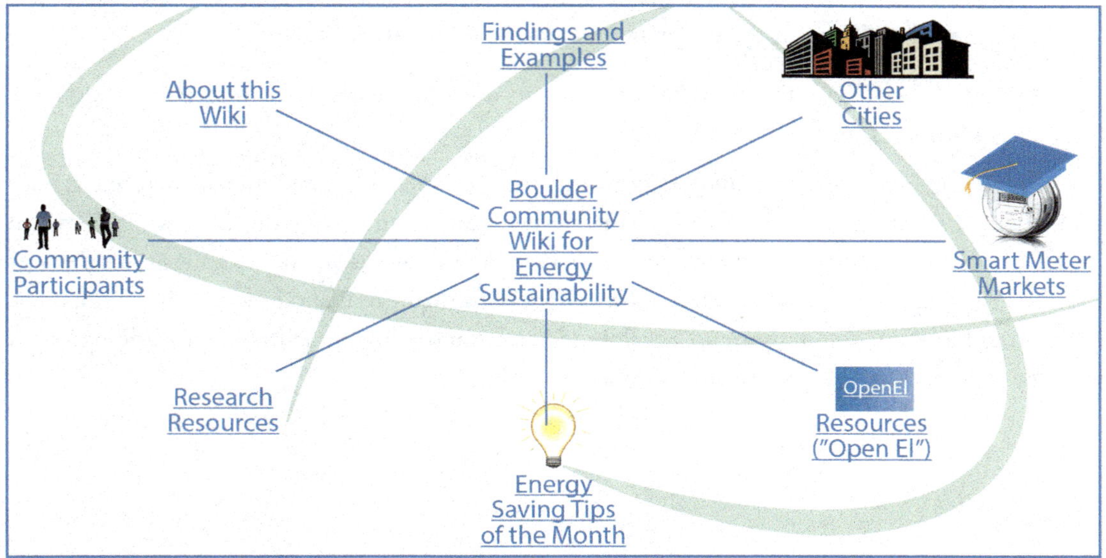


Figure 5.20: Reflection space and the community wiki for energy.

This case study explored the applicability of the EDC to the challenging problem that our current lifestyle is not sustainable and human energy consumption causes global warming. Governments, industry, and environmental groups are undertaking major efforts to reduce energy consumption, largely resulting in systems that, although technically innovative, are static and closed, viewing citizens as a passive consumer. To reduce energy consumption to sustainable levels, technological innovations and policy changes are not sufficient but changes in human behavior at the individual and the community level are necessary.

## 5.4    CONCLUSIONS

Based on the content introduced in Chapters 2, 3, and 4 to form a baseline understanding of how the EDC works, and how it was created from a practical and a theoretical perspective, this chapter presented three selected real-world cases of the EDC's application domains: (1) *campus planning* in collaboration with CU Boulder and the City of Boulder; (2) *emergency management* with a focus on creating training and operational environments to cope with wildfires; and (3) *energy sustainability* to motivate and support citizen to engage in environmentally responsible behavior.

The three case studies enhanced our understanding about the notion of "domain" and its mutually reinforcing relationship with the EDC:

- EDC → Domain: the EDC's functionality and developments helped all stakeholders to extend and deepen the understanding of the domains; and

- Domain → EDC: the demands of different domain created new interesting design requirements for the EDC.

Exploring innovative technologies in the context of human-centered informatics, one cannot think about it divorced from the domain as it has been demonstrated by the EDC's "fit" between the EDC's functionality and the application to the three domains in this chapter and others as described in Chapter 7. Therefore, *domain knowledge*, both theoretical and practical, is a fundamental building block for the design and development of support functionality when thinking about building socio-technical environments such as the EDC.

# CHAPTER 6

# The Evolving Design of the EDC

The primary forces driving the efforts described in this book are support for broader forms of participation and inclusiveness in design and decision-making processes. These were the major considerations that continued to push our iterative development and evolutionary design processes forward using our theory, system building, practice, assessment methodology (Figure 3.12) and following our seeding, evolutionary growth, reseeding (SER) model (Figure 4.5).

Figure 6.1 provides an overview of different evolutionary stages of the EDC discussed in detail in this chapter.

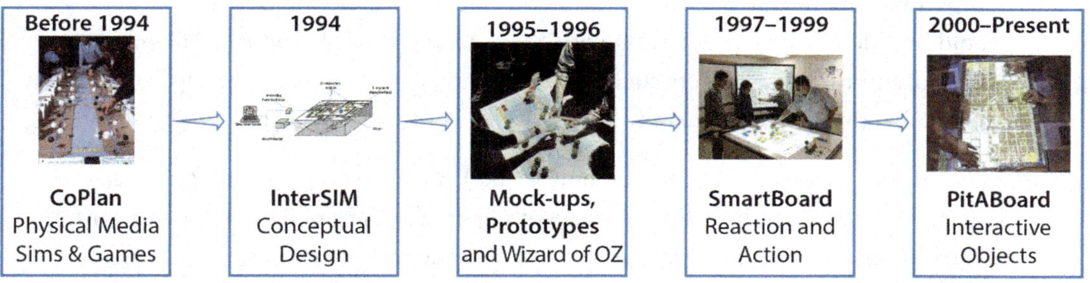


Figure 6.1: Timeline of different phases of the EDC developments.

## 6.1 HARDWARE DEVELOPMENTS SUPPORTING FACE-TO-FACE INTERACTION WITH COMPUTATIONAL MODELS

At the beginning of this research effort around 1995, little work had been done in the area that is now known as "tabletop" computing (Dillenbourg and Evans, 2011; Müller-Tomfelde and Fjeld, 2012), which led us to develop designs and prototypes supporting our approach to design, creativity, and learning (Figure 4.1).

### 6.1.1 INTERSIM: THE ORIGINAL DESIGN FOR THE EDC

Inspired and based on the SimLab's CoPlan physical modeling system described in Section 3.1.1, we developed a design for the **Inter**active **Sim**ulation Workstation (Intersim) with the goal of developing a tabletop computational environment to meet the following requirements.

- Based on the experience using physical media in the Cole Neighborhood experience (Chapter 3), the Intersim should represent an interactive integration of the computer on the side into the tabletop workstation by combining the presentation of the computer simulation with the physical models.

- As an important prerequisite for conflict resolution, the station should be mounted on a table that the participants could sit or stand around, thereby supporting direct, face-to-face communication between the participants, as is possible as with the previous 3D physical simulation models (Figure 3.2).

- The station should have a means of tracking position and identity of multiple physical simulation pieces simultaneously. These physical simulation pieces would represent a language of objects and would become a tangible interface (Hornecker, 2011) allowing participants to interact directly with the simulation. The objects of the language would be able to carry information with them, taking it or placing it from and on the tabletop, and the same objects could be adapted to support descriptive, evaluative and prescriptive thinking on demand (Figure 3.3).

- In addition, cursor-based (pen- or mouse-like) devices should support interactions that do not map directly to the language of objects for the simulation (e.g., to control simulation parameters, modify spatial views and query supporting spatial data).

- The station should allow base maps for the setting being simulated to be shown along with visualizations of related spatial data.

The Intersim station was designed as a rear-projection system with an integrated transparent/translucent interaction panel (Arias, 1995b). In its initial conception, the image from a workstation screen would be projected onto the interaction panel from underneath (Figure 6.2). The interaction panel would use a radio frequency induction mechanism to cause miniature antennae embedded in interactors to emit a signal, each with a unique signature. The interaction controller could then triangulate on these signatures and provide location and identity information for each interactor. These interactors could then be embedded in physical elements used in the simulation or used as cursor manipulators (similar to a mouse or drawing pen). Users would be able to place and move the 3D pieces of the simulation language, or interact with other aspects using cursor manipulators. Rather than a single locus of control as in most systems designed to support only a single-user interaction, multiple, simultaneous interactions would be supported.

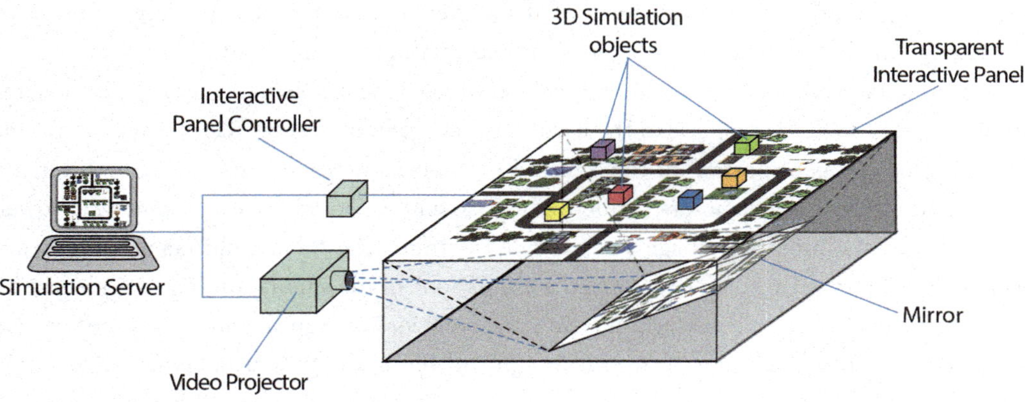


Figure 6.2: The initial architecture of the Intersim workstation.

### Interaction in the Intersim

Control of the simulation space was to be by manipulation of the 3D pieces on the Intersim station. As the users would also use the pieces to facilitate person-to-person communication regarding complex real-world situations during the simulation, it should be straightforward for them to interact with the simulation system in much the same way as in the physical media simulation-games. However, a major difference would be when making locational decisions: the Intersim should allow to evaluate various alternatives simply by moving pieces on the board and evaluating the visualization of simulation results displayed on the board interactively and on demand. The objective was to create a completely new way in human-computer interaction through a new socio-technical environment (Section 3.4).

Although the details of the Intersim design were never fully realized, the requirement and goals continued to be guiding principles throughout the development of the EDC.

### 6.1.2   "WIZARD-OF-OZ" EXPERIMENTS

Early work focused on drawing out various issues of the design using Wizard-of-Oz approaches and utilized an initial version of the Agensheets programming language (Repenning, 2014). Sessions with potential user communities explored where to focus our development efforts and work out some specific questions. For example, our assumption was that rear (bottom-up) projection on the horizontal surface would be a necessary aspect of the design, yet it would increase the complexity of the design. We built a bottom-up projection table as well as a front (top-down) projection setup (Figure 6.3). In working with subject groups, we found that whereas the bottom-up setting avoided shadows due to hand and body occlusion, this setup suffered greater light loss, requiring dimmer room lighting and creating a form of "halo effect" where the objects placed on the table were not as visible due to the (relatively) brighter rear lighting behind them.

In the top-down setup, the shadows produced were not as problematic as originally assumed. Certainly shadows were problematic in the usual vertical, front-projection setup, where one's whole body would block a major portion of the screen; in the horizontal setup, most shadows were only transient hand and arm movements. While the top-down version still needed somewhat lowered ambient lighting, the projected image also provided illumination for the objects and avoided the "halo effect." In addition, in some situations the animations in the simulation (e.g., raindrops) were hidden underneath the objects in rear projection, but were visible atop the objects in the top-down case. This led us to pay less attention to this design constraint and gave us a better understanding of some of the trade offs faced.

Figure 6.3: The Intersim "Wizard-of-Oz" setup. Utilizing an initial version of AgentSheets and top-down projection.

## 6.1.3   SMART BOARDS: INTEGRATING TOUCH AND PROJECTION TYPES

To move beyond the initial Wizard-of-Oz approach, we acquired SmartTech Smart Boards—a rear-projection version for the vertical reflection space and a front-projection version for the horizontal action space. In addition to both types of projection, the hardware supported touch functionality in both the action and reflection spaces. In terms of software, we continued to use the AgentSheets programming language. Through this setup, the EDC gained the capability to provide the physical objects of the language (Lego blocks at this time) with computational behavior and simulation capabilities, e.g., simulating the bus icon running and programming its behavior to stop at a bus stop (Figure 6.11).

Several scenarios were developed and tested using this setup providing insights into important aspects and limitations of the around-the-table interactions.

There was considerable engagement and interaction, both with the computational simulation and across the table with other participants—there was a tendency to use the simulation and the physical pieces to "talk through to" others and to emphasize certain points. The focus tended to be on the problem being discussed, with particular perspectives being revealed by different participants and often uncovered in the process. This observation encouraged us to continue our efforts.

However, the limitations sometimes caused breakdowns in the interaction that distracted from the focus on the problem being discussed. The major limitation turned out to be that the technology only supported *single touches by only one player* at a time. If there was more than one touch, the location reported by the device was at a point representing the average of the two touch locations. While this limitation was not as problematic in the vertical setup of the reflection space (with usually no more than two users making turn taking straightforward), the horizontal table with multiple players facilitated many situations in which more than one person wanted to draw or move at the same time as another player and the simultaneous actions caused problems.

This limitation was further compounded by the fact that the software substrate being used was designed for single-user interaction and used a moded-interaction paradigm. This meant for the user that in addition to being careful to take turns, attention needed to be paid to having the correct mode (draw, place, delete, move) selected when turns were switched. Although this often caused interaction breakdowns, it was interesting to see forms of *group awareness* (Gutwin and Greenberg, 1998) arising around this situation with users often intervening for each other when an action was about to occur in the wrong mode.

Figure 6.4: The initial version of the EDC using Smart Boards. Integrating Smart Boards for the action and reflection spaces with overhead and rear-view projection and utilizing AgentSheets to support interactivity in the action space of the Lego Blocks as the language of objects.

## 6.1.4   EDC-PITA BOARD

To overcome these limitations of the earlier EDC, the "Participate-in-the-Action (PitA)"-Board was developed using technology created for electronic chessboards (by DGT Projects (DGT, 2015)) allowing several objects (with embedded transponders) to be tracked simultaneously thereby each object of the language then be given a particular form of behavior by the software simulation.

The PitA-Board is composed of four DGT Projects chessboards linked together and placed in a custom-made table (Figure 6.5b). Each of the chess pieces contains an RF circuit with a unique signature that allows for 15 different unique inputs per context, and any number of pieces with the same signature. The board resolution is limited to the chessboard-square size of the grid, but provides an advantage over the earlier version of the EDC with support for simultaneous input to the simulation by various users. Similarly to the earlier version above, an overhead projector linked to the PitA simulation server provides the players with visual feedback on the board, and outlines the grid that a piece may be placed into.

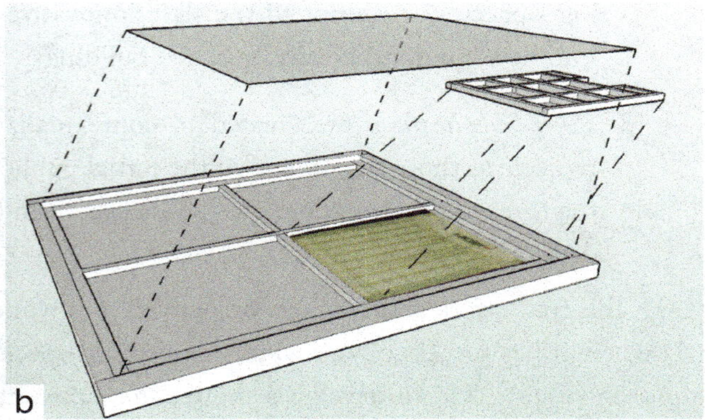

Figure 6.5: The PitA-Board: (a) an early 2-board prototype of the PitA-Board using overhead projection and showing simultaneous parallel interactions by multiple stakeholders around the table; and (b) underside view of the PitA-Board construction linking four DGT chessboards.

Related to the EDC functionality, we have explored integrating other aspects of hardware developments. For example, to support the integration between personal and shared information spaces, we experimented with using PDAs and Smart Phones (this was further pursued in the Caretta project; see Section 7.2.1). Utilizing WiFi connections users can interact with information from the shared information space or contribute information from their personal information to the shared space of the EDC-PitA board.

## 6.2    SOFTWARE ARCHITECTURE AND EVOLUTION

### Driving the Development of the EDC Forward

Just as the hardware evolved as described in the previous section, the EDC's software development evolved, starting with the initial concerns behind the merger of the two paradigms described in Chapter 3, and using a theory-based framework consisting of three layers:

1. a *domain-independent architecture* for an integrated physical/computational environment that supports collaborative design by linking action and reflection spaces and by creating new possibilities for multi-modal interaction, contextualization of information, and open, evolvable systems;

2. *application domains* that instantiate the domain-independent architecture for specific classes of real problems. This layer includes application domains such as, among others, (1) locational decision problems in Urban-Planning or (2) the creation of Learn-

ing-Spaces, an attempt to translate innovative approaches to learning and teaching into new computationally enriched buildings;

3. *specific applications* are created to contextualize the application domain to specific projects as those mentioned in the initial public transportation scenario of Chapter 2, the three application domains of Chapter 5, and the EDC role in the various inspired development of Chapter 7.

This framework and architecture parallels our work integrating CoPlan and DODEs (Figure 3.1) where it has successfully provided application-specific support (Chapter 5) and used the SER approach (Figure 4.5) to develop a more generalized domain-independent architecture to use in other domains and applications (Figure 6.6).

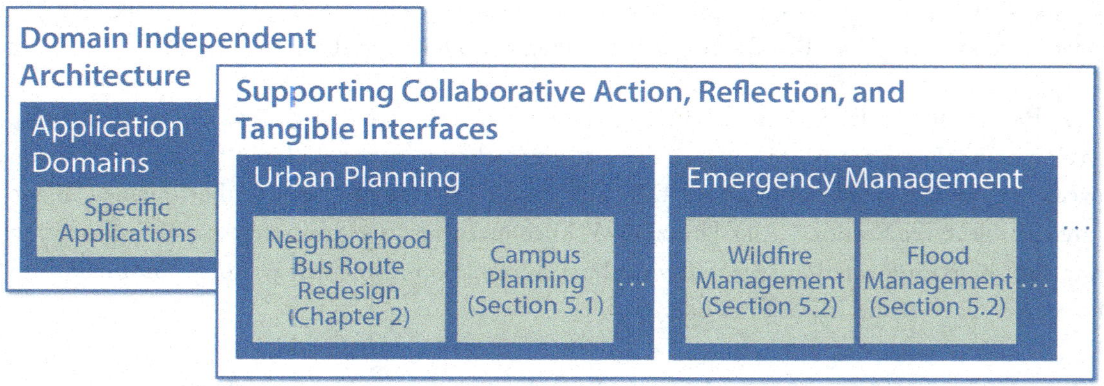


Figure 6.6: Overview architecture of EDC.

## 6.2.1  EARLY SOFTWARE EFFORTS USING AGENTSHEETS

Early versions of the EDC environment (in the Wizard-of-Oz version and the Smart Board version) were based on AgentSheets simulation system, which allowed us to prototype several scenarios quickly with their respective simulation behaviors.

The focus of this effort was based on our assessment of SimCity (http://www.simcity.com) and exploring question: "why were these systems not used in urban planning?" The primary reason that we found in discussions with urban planners was that planning addresses *open-ended problems* in a real world context and that SimCity represented a *closed system*: it did not allow the introduction of elements into the simulation that were not part of SimCity's designers' conception of the problem. This made such systems difficult to use in ill-structured design settings, where framing the problem is part of the problem-solving process (Rittel, 1984).

*AgentSheets* (Repenning, 2014) is an open-ended, agent-based, visual programming environment. Users can quickly create a language of agents that interact with their environment, which itself is a grid of other agents, e.g., the bus agent behaves over the grid with the road agents such as turns and "T" intersection (Figure 6.7; the screen image is drawn from the example "Mr. Roger's Sustainable Neighborhood"; see Section 7.1.2).

Figure 6.7: An AgentSheets worksheet simulation.

Visual AgenTalk (VAT) (Repenning and Sumner, 1995) supports agent-based graphical rewrite rules in Agentsheets and thereby allow users to drag and drop language components onto rule composition windows to create object behavior through a set of "if-then" rules. For example, in Figure 6.8, a rule is being created to allow the navigation character to move along the roads on any game board.

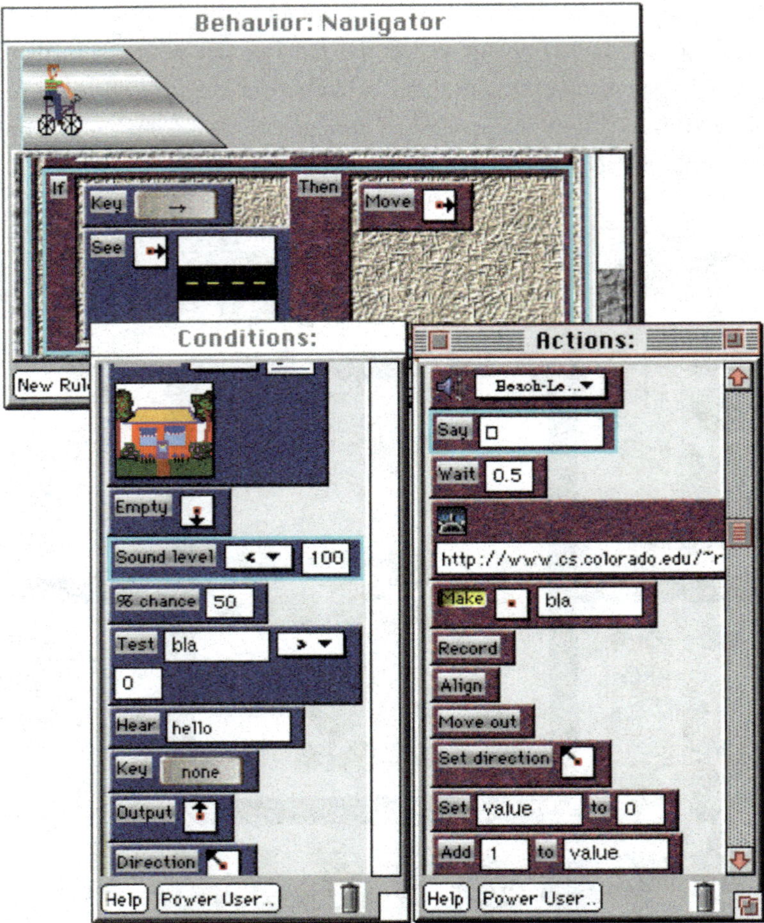


Figure 6.8: The Navigator object: giving the object its navigation behavior with Visual AgentTalk to move along the roads in the action space.

Using drag-and-drop interaction, VAT "if-then rules" composed of conditions and actions can be created to describe the behavior of the agents in the simulations (Figure 6.8). VAT provided a useful substrate for early efforts with the EDC for developing some use scenarios with the Smart Board version of the EDC. It allowed users of the EDC to construct a legend of agents with their respective behaviors, e.g., a bus icon that could run along bus route. Along with the interactive functionality of the Smart Board (the ability to draw on top of streets to identify the user's preferred path between an origin and a destination), a bus route simulation could be created in the action space.

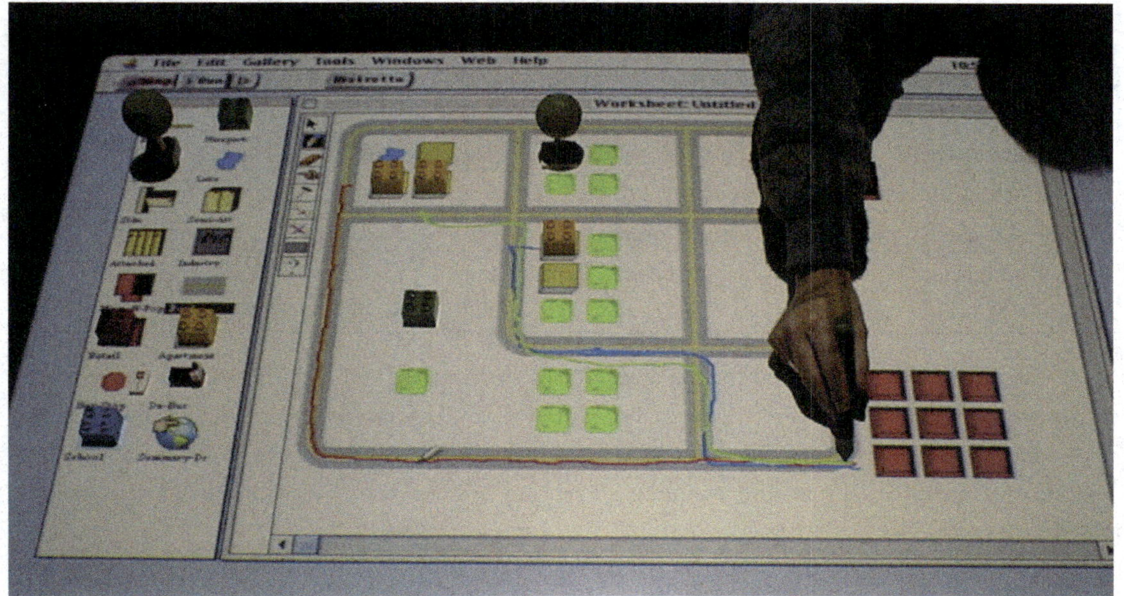

Figure 6.9: Using AgentSheets in an early EDC urban planning application. A version of the EDC showing the legend of objects with their respective behaviors on the left side and a user drawing where the bus route should go in a specific setting in the action space.

## 6.2.2   THE SQUEAK-BASED VERSION OF THE EDC

As the EDC's architecture evolution moved towards the new generation of hardware (the Pi-tA-Board version mentioned in the previous section; see Figure 6.1), we decided to utilize Squeak (a Smalltalk media environment; http://squeak.org) instead of AgentSheets for further development. Table 6.1 summarizes some of the implications of this change that was primarily motivated that Squeak is a completely open-source substrate with large user and developer communities. The E-Toys component of Squeak (http://www.squeakland.org) seemed to be a good starting point to support end-user extension in the future, although our initial efforts have not made use of this capability of Squeak.

Table 6.2 compares the differences between AgentSheets and Squeak along a set of functional characteristics and implementation substrates that represented reasons behind this shift from the EDC's earlier version to the system architecture of the EDC-PitA.

**Table 6.1:** Functionality support comparison of old and new EDC architectures

|  | EDC/AgentSheets | EDC/Squeak |
|---|---|---|
| Physical Recognition | Smart Board (touch screen) | PITA-Board (Passive Sensor) |
| Simulation Engine | AgentSheets | Squeak |
| Visualization Engine | AgentSheets | Squeak, GIS |
| Action Mapper | Custom Java system | XML communication |
| Hypermedia Server | Custom CGIs (Python, Perl) | Swiki (Wiki software substrate) |
| Content Server | File System | Swiki Database, GIS |

The use of Squeak allowed for the rapid development of a graphical interface, hardware drivers, network connections, and relatively easy creation of simulations (such that real-world situations can be modeled by simply defining a few objects and their relationships to each other). In addition, Squeak runs on a virtual machine, enabling almost any system to run any one of the PitA servers and clients.

**Table 6.2:** Comparison of AgentSheets and Squeak implementation substrates

| Features and Activities | AgentSheets | Squeak |
|---|---|---|
| Language substrate | Lisp | Smalltalk |
| Source code available | No | Yes |
| Is written in itself | No | Yes |
| Supported platforms | Mac | Mac, PC, Unix, others |
| Comprehensive documentation | Yes | No |
| Access language substrate directly from simulation | No | Yes |
| Simulation | Grid-based | Non-grid based |
| End-user simulation programming | Yes | Yes |
| Strongly moded interaction | Yes | No |
| End-user programming | Rule-based | Imperative |
| Integrated end-user programming help | Yes | No |
| Expressiveness of end-user programming | Very High | Moderate |
| Family of related simulation objects | Yes | No |
| Simulation primitives fixed | Yes | No |
| Stand-alone content | Java Applet | Browser Plug-In |
| Maintains version information for code | No | Yes |
| Maintains author information | No | Yes |
| Simulation language extensible | No | Yes |
| Networking support | Limited | Extensive |

Table 6.2 compares the differences between AgentSheets and Squeak along a set of functional characteristics and implementation substrates that represented reasons behind this shift from the EDC's earlier version to the system architecture of the EDC-PitA.

## 6.2.3  THE CURRENT EDC SYSTEM ARCHITECTURE

Over years of development, we have evolved an integrative architecture combining a variety of components. Table 6.2 shows the current array of components and their interrelationships at a high level of the EDC-PitA's three computational areas.

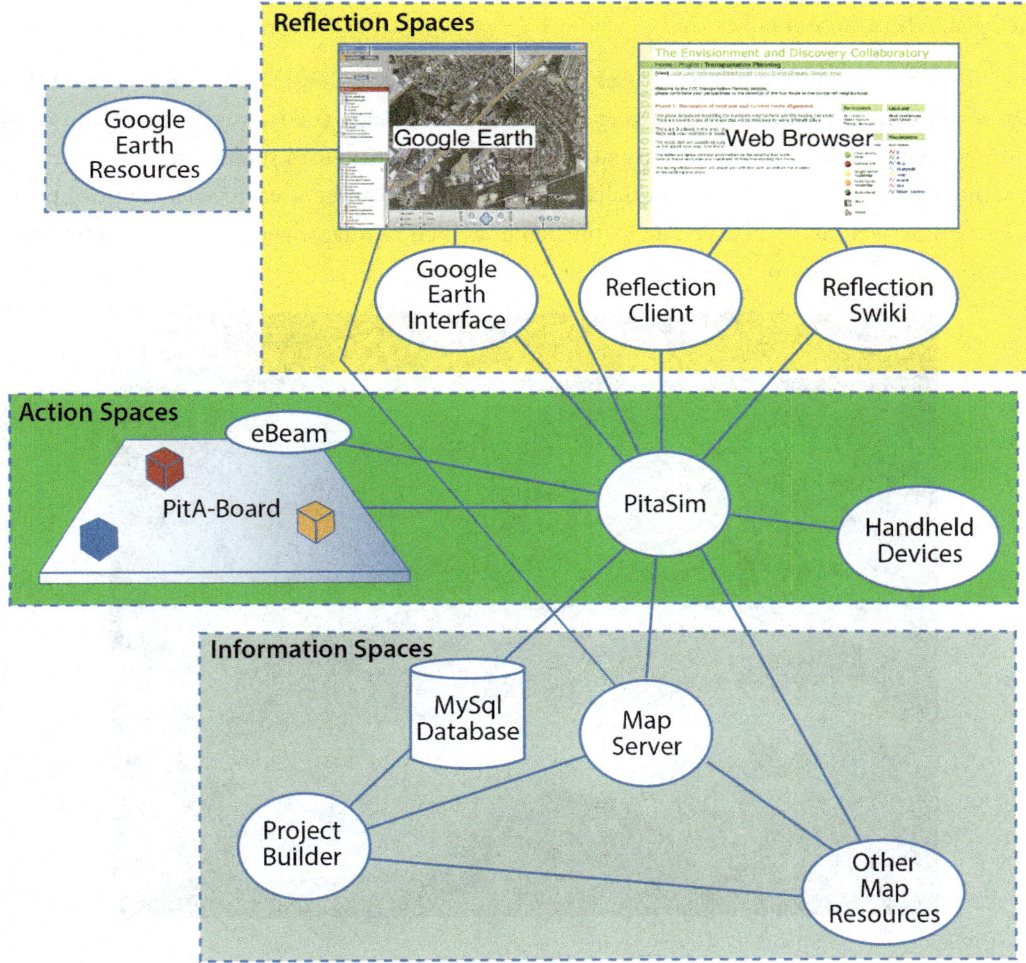


Figure 6.10: Current high-level EDC system architecture: the architecture composed of the reflection, action, and information spaces.

This high-level architecture describes support in three broad areas: action spaces, reflection spaces, and information spaces (Schön, 1983). *Action spaces* are areas where stakeholders can construct designs and interact with the simulations; *reflection spaces* are those areas where argumentation, visualizations, and other information displays are presented to support the action space activities; and the first two are in turn supported by *information spaces*, such as GIS databases, Google Earth data, and live GPS data. While we distinguish between the reflection and action spaces, the line between the two is somewhat arbitrary: there can certainly be reflection activities that go on within the action spaces as well as design actions that can take place in reflection spaces.

## Action Space Developments

Utilizing the PitA-Board hardware for user interactions, scenarios, and simulations were built for applications in various domains and settings (Chapter 5). Utilizing the language of programmable physical pieces, the stakeholders can navigate through various activities interacting with the horizontal action space (Figure 6.10). A specialized "Admin" piece can be used to select various phases of the session as well as special resources on-demand such as map overlays by interacting with "command squares" along opposite edges of the interaction space.

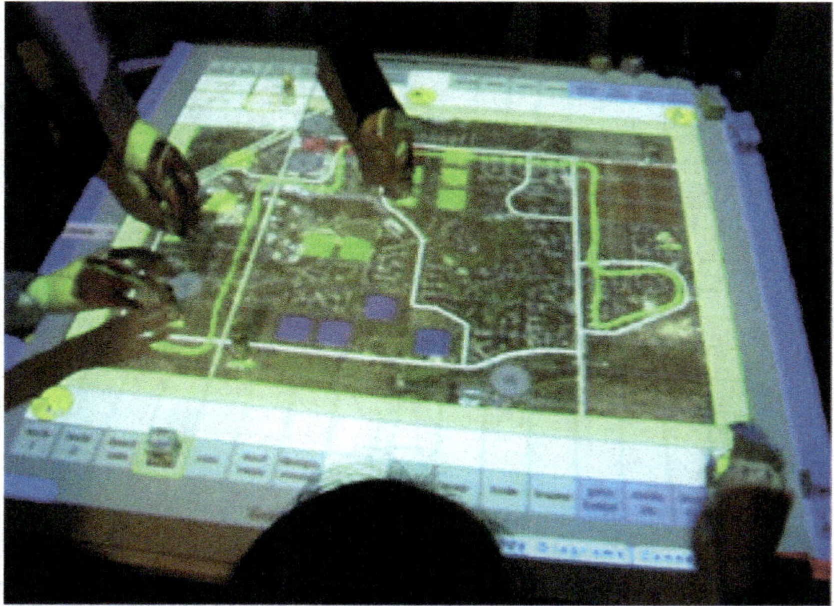

Figure 6.11: Stakeholders around the PitA-Board. Participants can interact with action space through the physical pieces, which represent objects in the simulation or can be used to perform actions using programmed border squares along the edges.

Utilizing the multiple "points of control" provided by the PitA-Board supported tangible interactions (Hornecker, 2011) more closely tuned to the type of domain object being represented. For example, some interactions that might be useful in the domain of transportation are (Eden, 2002):

- *placing ("rubber stamp") behavior:* placement of a physical piece creates a virtual representation that remains when the physical piece is removed and then can be used to place items with known fixed locations, e.g., a house, store, or school, a land use, or a bus stop, thereby supporting user in the description of the setting being discussed;

- *tracking behavior:* the virtual representation follows the physical piece representing an individual moving through the space or an object whose location is subject to change, e.g., a bus along a bus route;

- *drawing behavior:* a piece can be used to trace out a series of points that make up the object being created, e.g., a road, a bus route (Figure 6.12);

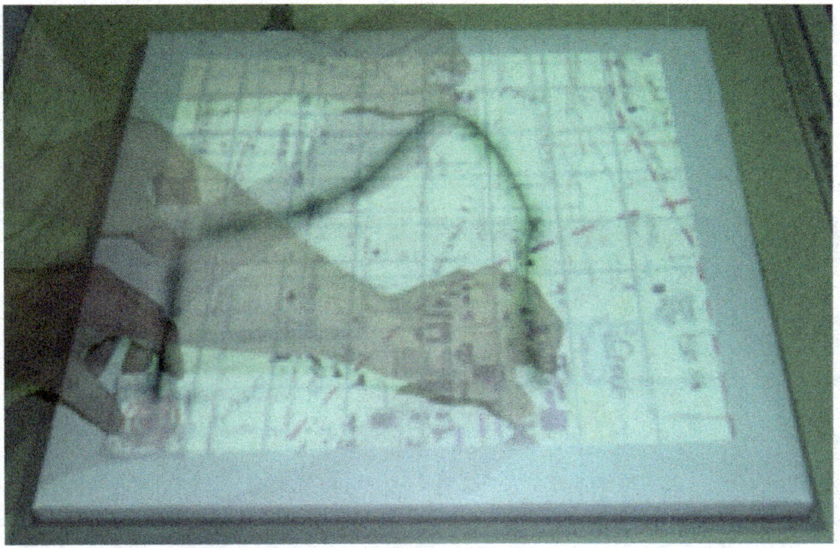

Figure 6.12: Using pieces to "draw" a path. This multiple-exposure photo shows the user tracing out a bus route using a bus-route-drawing object.

- *launching behavior (placing a dynamic item):* the physical piece indicates the initial location of an object that has dynamic behavior—if appropriate, the virtual object begins its dynamic behavior from that point, e.g., the behavior of a bus along a created bus route based on real-time GPS information;

- *erasing behavior:* in addition to the interaction attached to domain-grounded objects, there will still be the need for interaction pieces that support control or inspection of the environment. For example, by having some virtual representations that no longer have corresponding physical pieces (such as a "placed" object in the action space) implies virtual representations need to be removed when they are no longer needed requiring an "eraser" piece; and

- *examining behavior:* a magnifying glass is useful in some contexts to examine the attributes of an object obtained in a previous interaction and that a user wants to review.

These developments create affordances that are more natural to the situation being modeled and the design process being supported by the technology. The interaction mechanisms described above were based on observations collecting over time when users were interacting with the EDC.

## Sketching Support

The earlier use of SmartBoards supported sketching and interactions with simulations. This sketching functionality (except for a very coarse-grained ability shown in Figure 6.12) was lost when we initially moved to the PitA-Board interface. After conducting a few tests of the new interface, several of the participants who had been involved with testing the previous system indicated that the sketching feature was useful and should be re-incorporated into EDC-PitA.

Figure 6.13: The PitA-Board with sketch pen showing overlaid sketches.

In order to add sketching to the new system, an eBeam electronic pen system (http://www-w.e-beam.com/) was employed. This system tracks the movements of a special pen on the surface of the action space and sends the results to an attached computer. Currently, the system uses a single pen provides a different form of collaboration than the concurrent interaction supported by the PitA-Board. Rather than allowing multiple users to make changes at will, the single-pen interface forces *single-linear* rather than multiple-parallel interactions in the action space thereby supporting a single participant to be in charge of making the changes at a given time. This mode of interaction results in turn taking wherein users are able to focus on their ideas with undivided attention, and then pass control to other users who may add to or modify existing sketches. While there is value to single-linear interaction, multiple-parallel sketching support by incorporating the use of multiple pens should be further explored.

The sketching interface involves a set of layers that store the currently displayed sketches from a session, a library of saved sketches, and controls for color and height selection, new layer creation, and other utility functions. Currently, displayed layers may be stacked upon each other on the display with the top layer allowing new objects to be sketched. Each sketch layer may be "set aside" or saved into the library for later reuse. The user may also select to change the pen to an eraser and the height attribute is used in creating 3D visualizations (Figure 5.4).

Sketches made in a layer can also be converted into an actual object in the simulation. By pressing the "make object" button and selecting a line or filled object from the sketch, the object is then imported to the simulation and can be used as an object (e.g., a road, a bus route, a land-use area—depending on the context) within the simulation.

## Reflection Space Developments

The initial implementation of a *reflection space* was simply information placed on web pages that were triggered by certain actions in the action space. To effect the navigation to various web pages, a separate client was implemented that connects to the simulation through a standard network communications protocol link. As a certain point in the simulation is reached, or a particular piece in the language of objects is used, the reflection space will provide pertinent information (Fischer et al., 1996). This information can either be pre-stored by an expert in the field, or can be fetched in real time from the web. The idea of the space is to provide useful information to the simulation participants *on-demand* (Fischer, 1991) so that they may "reflect" upon the action that they just performed. The space may also be used to keep statistics and technical data support about the simulation such as average bus stop wait time per passenger and percent of land used for particular applications (Figure 2.6).

**Information Space Developments**

Whereas the earlier efforts had focused on openness at the behavioral level (e.g., with the support of AgentSheets VisualAgenTalk), interaction with urban planners pointed out that there was another area that many systems kept somewhat closed: the ability to draw on *rich sources of data* that urban planners bring to bear on a planning situation. The focus of much of the work in EDC-PitA became how to allow these resources to be brought into the simulations and used on-demand in design sessions.

This effort took on several facets. The first explored how to utilize open protocols to access and *incorporate GIS data*. The second focused on how to allow design scenario facilitators to integrate and specify interaction for specific projects. The third focused on how to develop ways to utilize various existing tools to support visualization within the environment.

**Incorporating GIS data using Mapserver.** Initial efforts at bringing in various types of data entailed one-off efforts to bring in specific map images or GIS datasets for specific purposes. However, this was often time intensive and not something that could easily scale to general application of the EDC to planning situations. The OpenGIS effort had begun to develop open protocols such as Web Mapping Service (WMS), Web Feature Service (WFS), and later, Web Coverage Service (WCS) to provide an open, standardized way to access GIS data across the Web. Utilizing the University of Minnesota's open-source Mapserver software for our server, we extended some prototype Squeak developments to support WMS and incorporated mechanism to allow scenario programmers to easily incorporate arbitrary maps and features into the simulations.

The incorporated maps are simply images and serve as base and data-layer maps for scenarios, but they did not provide any data to the simulation. Using a WFS query, feature data (such as points, lines, polylines, etc.) can be accessed as XML data, which can then be utilized as simulation objects rather than simply as base maps or background images. For example, bus route data can be pulled down for the specific area, displayed over the base map, and then a simulated bus object can follow the lines (based on the points that make up the lines) to simulate the bus moving through a neighborhood.

## 6.2.4    THE PROJECT BUILDER: A COMPONENT SUPPORTING META-DESIGN

A *meta-design perspective* (Section 4.1.2) requires that a system be open to extension by the users of the system. To allow projects to be developed without requiring the EDC's designers to program within the Squeak Smalltalk programming environment, we created a web-based application supporting the specification of resources and interactions to be used in an EDC session, thus allowing the projects to be designed and tested in a distributed fashion. The initial version of the *Project Builder* (Figure 6.14) allows (1) participants to define projects; (2) upload or link to resources (e.g., maps, icons, WMS data); (3) define action-space interaction behavior; and (4) specify the different phases of projects.

The initial version of Project Builder serves as an administrative interface; in order to use it, a basic understanding of the workings of the system is needed. Based on use tests with urban-planning students, future developments should create an interface that is more oriented toward building a design scenario, stepping users through a series of wizards guiding the process, rather than using a complex interface to specify the necessary components.

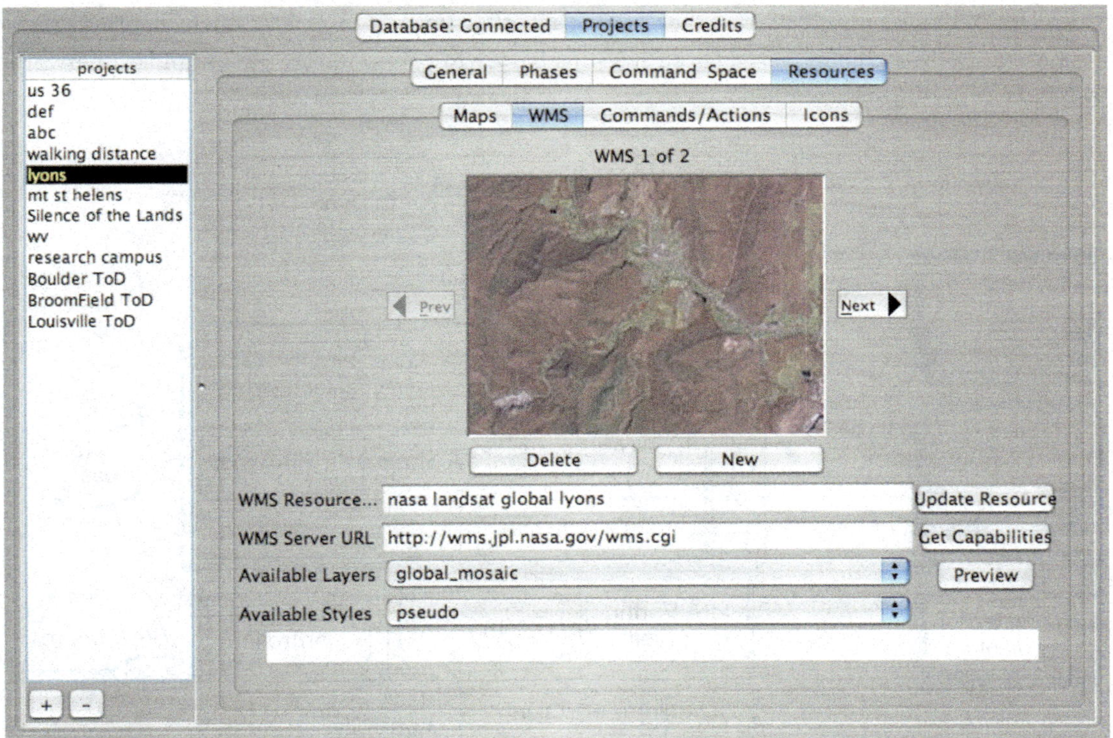


Figure 6.14: Initial version of the EDC Project Builder. To support the evolution of the EDC by users, the Project Builder interface supports the inclusion of GIS and data resources, as well as the specification of the interaction behavior of the EDC within a given project.

## 6.2.5   DETAILS OF THE SOFTWARE IMPLEMENTATION

Figure 6.15 provides a more detailed description (with a brief discussion of these details) of the architecture and components of the EDC software implementation architecture.

The central element of the architecture is the PitA-Core, which handles the primary dynamic simulation component (PitA-Sim), the interface to the user interaction (PitA-Interact), the dynamic interface to the Reflection Spaces (PitA-DynaFlection), the Geographic Information System module (PitA-GIS), and the component that can generate three-dimensional models in the form of Keyhole Markup Language (KML) streams (PitA-KML Generator). In addition, PitA-Core includes a "PitA-Bus" communication component that provides a "pluggable" means of allowing various components of the system to communicate.

Figure 6.15 shows that PitA-Bus clients can either be within the same Squeak image (Local PitA-Bus Components) or they can be in other images, including ones on other hosts (Remote PitA-Bus Clients), using the PitA-Bus Server to communicate via a standard network protocol connection.

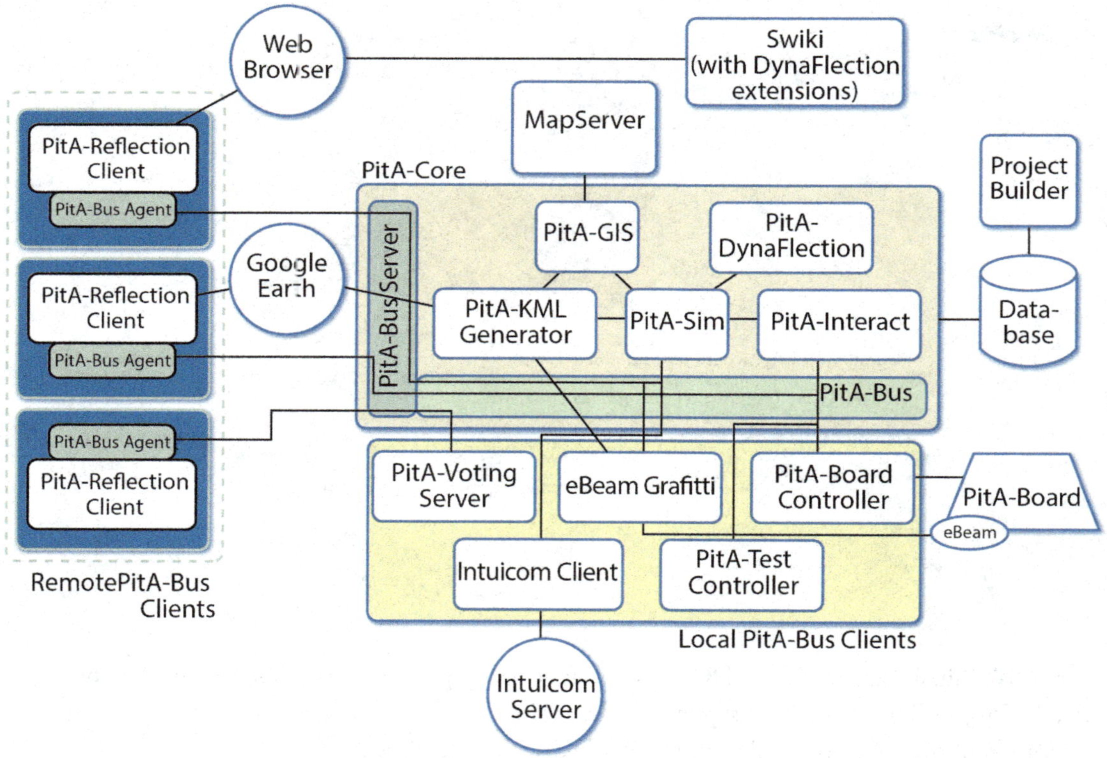


Figure 6.15: Overview of the architecture of the software components of the EDC.

The architecture provides flexibility in deployment, allowing components to run locally or remotely as needed. By including a PitA-Bus client agent along with the client code in a minimal Squeak image, the remote component can receive messages that are of interest to it by specifying filters when it establishes its connection to the server. In addition, the PitA-Bus was extended and used for opportunistic design: for example, using Mash-Up approaches to tie into Google Earth using their open APIs to overlay data and control the view.

## 6.3   CONCLUSION

Although far from perfect, the EDC architecture has provided a flexible way to *rapidly prototype and deploy the innovative approaches* portrayed in the book. The guidance provided by the SER model (Section 4.1.5) inspired a great deal of the effort to use a flexible, open, and inclusive design allowing us to use the EDC to work with students to explore new ideas and new projects with a reasonable effort. The use of components such as Mapserver and Google Earth, has extended the repertoire of design elements to create new applications.

The flexibility of the architecture has been demonstrated in efforts to quickly adapt it to other environments. For example, with some small additional effort (using foreign function interfaces to quickly link to appropriate libraries), the EDC was adapted for use with DiamondTouch Table (Figure 7.13 and Section 9.1).

It is our hope that elements of our experience will serve as a small contribution and continued inspiration to new developments as new efforts and new technologies become available, such as those discussed in Chapter 9, that can be used to provide an enriched environment to support design, creativity, and learning. Based on our experience with the architectural development of the EDC we have come to the realization that the integration and evolution of hardware and software should be done in a mutually beneficial relationship: one cannot be understood without an understanding of the other. Together with the notion of the SER model, this perspective has been useful in the evolution of the architecture driven by observing the limitations of existing versions. Developments such as: (1) users around the table wanted to participate in parallel rather than sequentially; (2) sketching is indispensable; (3) visualization support is needed (e.g., impacts of building heights shown in Figure 5.4); and (4) integration of existing systems (such as GIS and Google Earth) are critical for creating new situated versions of the EDC with a reasonable effort.

CHAPTER 7

# EDC-Inspired Developments

"A primary contribution of this work was to lay a foundation for much work cited in this article and continuing to this day."—Dillenbourg and Evans, (2011, p. 495)

Previous chapters have provided an illustrative scenario of how the EDC works, the merging of two research paradigms and their respective research development activities that led us to create the EDC, its contributions to human-centered informatics, some case studies of different real-world domain applications, and the evolution of its hardware and software architecture. This chapter focuses on developments to evolve the EDC by applying it to new situations, particularly related to teaching, learning, and research and on developments by others that have been inspired by the EDC: (1) *Caretta*, integrating personal and shared spaces (Sugimoto et al., 2004), and (2) *Silence of the Lands*, studying, supporting, and fostering community soundscapes (Giaccardi, 2007). The third part of the chapter presents selected conclusions gained from these experiences.

## 7.1 INNOVATIONS IN THE CLASSROOM: TEACHING, LEARNING, AND RESEARCH

### Introductory Observations

Various conceptions of learning, including its multi-dimensional nature as described in Section 4.3 have been explored and supported by EDC innovations. These conceptions should not be viewed in isolation but rather integrated with the notions of design and creativity when thinking about innovation in human-centered informatics. In the context of learning and design, a slogan that we have used is that the EDC has supported many in *learning to design* and in *designing to learn through research*. This duality inspired our students and collaborators at all levels (undergraduates, graduates, visiting scientists) in learning, researching, and designing in new and creative ways, and at the same time outcomes of the use of the EDC in these activities have inspired us in its further development and evolution.

From this point of view our learning experiences in academic courses and research settings at $L^3D$ and the SimLab, we found inspirations in both directions:

- inspirations stemming from the EDC influencing human-centered informatics; and

- insights grounded in human-centered informatics inspiring new developments based on the EDC platform.

Extending these observations, we need to keep in mind that the EDC's evolution, as described in Chapter 6, does not only come from the high level conceptual notions of design, creativity, and learning described in Chapters 3 and 4, nor from real world applications described in Chapter 5, but from our learning and research experiences with the EDC in the classroom. This is especially true for the initial creative actions and the numerous evolutionary developments that contributed to the design of the EDC's innovative functionality. People who contributed to the development of the EDC over the years can be placed in three categories:

1. *developers* or *meta-designers* in architecture and tabletop computing, domains expertise, and hard/software development;

2. *participants* in EDC authentic planning and design sessions such as policy groups, city and urban planners, community and neighborhood representatives; and

3. *students* and *faculty* engaged with the EDC in learning contexts, particularly those in computer science, city planning, and environmental design.

### 7.1.1  THE EDC INSPIRED DEVELOPMENTS: TEACHING, LEARNING, AND RESEARCH

While all the above-mentioned three categories of people have made significant contributions to the evolution from the InterSim to the EDC (as introduced and described in Sections 3.1.1 and 6.1.1, respectively), it is the third category where the most useful engagements in terms of EDC development (domain, hardware, software) as well as inspirations by the EDC can be attributed. In an interesting way, we could say that these research and learning experiences were in fact our experimentation-in-action that helped us test the ideas as seeds behind the EDC design, as well as to develop, implement, and evolve those ideas into learning and design innovations (Robinson et al., 1997).

Over the years, the list of EDC inspired applications from interdisciplinary learning and research experiences of individuals at the Center for LifeLong Learning and Design (L$^3$D) in Computer Science, the Program of Environmental Design in the College of Architecture and Planning (ENVD), the Institute of Cognitive Science (ICS) and other departments is not only varied but extensive. In return, these projects lead to numerous extensions and developments for the EDC mentioned in Chapter 6.

Table 7.1 includes a selected sample of these innovative activities developed by our undergraduates, graduates, and Ph.D. students and by visiting scientists to the L$^3$D center. Two of the projects from the Table 7.1 (indicated in bold face) that represent the inspirational duality mentioned will be described in detail in the following sections of this chapter.

Table 7.1: A sample of selected EDC learning and research applications

| Description of Project | Unique Contribution |
|---|---|
| **Mr. Roger's Sustainable Neighborhood: Initial effort from a physical shared space to a computational game on networked personal computers (Example 1)** | Provided evidence that 'public gestures' are an important advantage of tabletops, because they allow a smooth coordination among actors (Figures 7.2 and 7.6) |
| *INTERSIM:* Initial tabletop computational version integrating Hardware and Agent-Sheets Software Development | First effort in the development from physical to computational interactive tabletop games and simulations to support learning and design. Explorations in top-down and rear-view projection and interactivity |
| *Creating an Interactive Language:* Making Physical Objects Computational with Crickets, Lego Blocks and AgentSheets | Initial efforts towards the development of tangible interphases to support interactive table top simulations and games through a language of objects |
| *The EDC's Initial Version:* Integration of Agentsheets Lego Blocks and SmartBoards | First integrated version of an interactive Action Space linked to a Reflection Space using Smart Boards (Figure 7.1) |
| *Wayfinding for the Blind:* Creating cognitive maps of campus | Initial efforts integrating outputs of the Action Space with Brail printers to research urban cognition of the blind for campus planning |
| *3D Simulation Capabilities:* The EDC's Seeding, Evolution and Re-seeding from various application experiences: (1) Footprints Sustainability Game; (2) Making Hazard Resistant Communities; and (3) Flood Management Game | Initial integration of GIS capabilities for interactive visualization of planning and design information between the Action and Reflection Spaces. |
| ***Managing Urban Dynamics and Environmental Impacts on Climate Change (example-2)*** | Integration of the functionality to utilize NASA's satellite remote sensing information with census data and visualize it using GIS (Figure 7.8) |
| *Decision Support for Wicked Problems:* Integrating Virtual stakeholders in the EDC | Developments based on critics to construct virtual stakeholders and obtain performance and prescriptive knowledge in planning in the absence of members of critical coalitions |

Throughout our applications of the EDC from its inception in teaching, learning, and research activities in the classroom we found that it was of value for us to continue to use the physical media paradigm in conjunction with EDC developments. The reliance on physical mock-ups in the classroom and laboratory experiences facilitated many instances of innovative thinking that concluded in the development and evolution of various aspects of the EDC's architecture discussed in Chapter 6. The Mr. Roger's Sustainable Neighborhood example from Table 1 has been selected for description in greater depth for this very reason. The approach of the "cardboard mock-up first" and "the subsequent computational development later" was valuable not only in various aspects of learning such as "learning by doing," "learning to design and designing to learn," but also in "learning to research and researching to learn." In addition, the approach provided many inspirations that led to the evolution of the EDC's functionality presented in Chapter 6, which in turn supported subsequent classroom applications. For example, the development of languages of objects (Section 3.1) in the "cardboard mock-ups" developed in the classroom provided the inspiration for interactivity support in the Action Space using Lego Blocks as a tactile interphase in an integrated manner with AgentSheets programing, as was the case in the EDC's initial SmartBoard version (Table 7.1 and Figure 6.4).

The EDC has inspired and supported various types of learning including collaborative learning, self-directed learning, learning on demand, and contextualized learning (Section 4.3). Likewise, we learn through observations or from actual sources, such as the distributed tacit knowledge of others; artifacts created and embedded in the environment; sources of either data or information of various types, such as real or digital libraries, historic or real-time databases; and from our own trial-and-error experiences. How to capture and support these types of learning and sources of knowledge has been the EDC's quest for innovation beyond just a tabletop technology.

Additionally, several research ideas have been inspired and motivated by various aspects of the EDC's functionality to support collaborative research, specifically with a focus on topics such as resource management or hazards management in efforts such as those with the National Center for Atmospheric Research (NCAR) in trying to create hazard resistant communities (Harriss and Arias, 2004). The following sections present two selected examples in learning and research inspired by that the EDC.

## 7.1.2  EXAMPLE 1: MR. ROGERS SUSTAINABLE NEIGHBORHOOD

Mr. Roger's Sustainable Neighborhood was an experience that explored in a classroom setting various notions about learning, such as vertical integration of learning levels, or collaborative and interactive learning introduced in Chapter 4. In addition, at the domain level, the focus of this experience was to explore how information technological development could contribute in making communities sustainable and hazard resistant. This simulation game was designed to teach about complex issues of sustainability at the basic planning unit of the neighborhood. Two versions were developed, the physical board game version or the "physical game" (Figure 7.1) and the computational version of "Mr. Roger's" (Figure 7.4) where among others, the initial explorations in distributed interactions of players was pursued utilizing the World Wide Web (WWW) (Perrone et al., 1996).

Physical board games and the construction of physical models have been shown to be a valuable vehicle for issues of collaboration and conflict resolution, as mentioned in Chapter 3. Also in the classroom, the educational and communicative benefits of the construction of simulation games as models for the real world has been demonstrated by us and others (Arias et al., 1997a; Kafai, 1995). The act of constructing a model promotes contextualized learning about the system being modeled (e.g., a public transportation system), and provides an object or artifact that can be shared, talked about or even argued over, and modified in the service of problem resolution and shared understanding (Arias et al., 1997b).

The explorations in the classroom were carried out at the SimLab and L$^3$D under the auspices of the University Corporation for Atmospheric Research in Boulder, Colorado (UCAR), in conjunction with the Boulder County Healthy Communities Initiative (BCHCI), one of many statewide and nationwide Healthy Communities initiative efforts at the time, whose central goal was to increase citizen awareness of, education about, and participation in decisions pertaining to the myriad issues of sustainability and hazards management.

From the technological perspective, this experience exploited the relationship between physical media and EDC development (Arias et al., 1997a) and allowed us to explore the following objectives:

- moving from a physical to a tangible digital interface in order to support distributed interactivity and collaboration;

- developing new functionality for the action and reflection space through understanding the physical media limitations, e.g., modifiability, expandability, and application adaptability for multiple domains which are central to extending simulation capabilities of these decision-support tools;

- moving EDC interaction from *face-to-face interaction around-the-tabletop* to a collaborative version supporting *one-person-one-computer distributed participation* utilizing the WWW; and

- exploring end-user modifiability—a capacity for creating behavior for new objects and changing the behavior of exiting objects in a tangible interphase to support different types of domain applications for games or simulations, e.g., from hazards management to sustainability of public transportation.

These initial efforts in the Mr. Roger's experience contributed the inspiration for other ideas which we explored in reseeding the functionality of the action and reflection spaces.

## Mr. Roger's Journey from Physical to Digital: A Basis for EDC Functionality

Despite the strengths mentioned above, physical media by its nature have inherent limitations as mentioned in Chapter 3. For example, the use of a physical board games is, limited to one location, and their lack of domain application adaptability is a challenge.

In other experiences with physical media the issue of user modifiability within a game or simulation proved to be very desirable, yet very difficult to attain. Thus, the flexibility of the the physical language interface as well as the management and storage of information, either *created for* or *created by* the physical game sessions were also challenges that Mr. Roger's tried to address by posing the following questions.

- Can we bring the benefits of situation-based physical games to a computational medium?

- Can we add the new benefits of the World Wide Web—while preserving the accessibility and usefulness of the games?

- Can we construct the capacity to have modifiability for end-users to gain adaptability of both the tangible interface as well as domain application flexibility for the action and reflection spaces?

Mr. Roger's Sustainable Neighborhood and its journey from physical board game to a computational version started by using the *Visual AgenTalk* (VAT) visual language (Repenning and Sumner, 1995) and the AgentSheets-based educational system WebQuest. This became the initial development experience of the EDC in the classroom about a computational game designed to teach complex issues of sustainability and advance thinking towards the construction of healthy communities.

## An Initial Useful Phase in Seeding and Reseeding

In Mr. Roger's experience, the physical simulation-game board (Figure 7.1) became useful as an initial phase in the seeding, evolution, reseeding process (SER) described in Section 4.1. This approach provided us with great flexibility for rapid testing of various attributes and relationships associated with the usefulness and usability of the physical media before moving into programming the EDC's functionality to support interactive participation "around the table." Thus an important outcome of this classroom experience was that it provided us with an initial process utilizing the physical media as a means to mock-up creative ideas that would be later programmed and introduced to enhance the EDC's functionality.

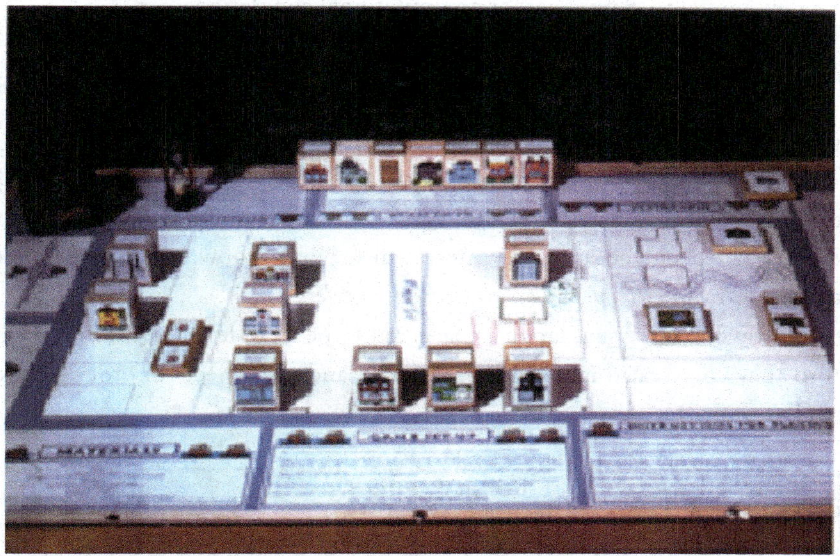

Figure 7.1: Mr. Roger's Sustainable Neighborhood. The physical media version of a tabletop and blocks representing the interactive language of objects to simulate various situations for users to interact on the board.

### Translating Mr. Roger's from the *Physical* to the *Digital*

Over a second design laboratory experience the computational version of Mr. Rogers was constructed. Physical board games are principally "domain specific." In this second experience, three central objectives were explored in the translation of the physical board game to a computational platform:

1. *End-user modifiability:* adding and changing behavior of the language of objects.

2. *Extending an application domain:* adding simulation and interaction to Mr. Roger's Neighborhood language of object to address various domain concerns, from public transportation to real estate and open space access and preservation.

3. *Distributed interaction:* linking web-based situations in the game with relevant information on the WWW.

A basic challenge was the implementation of a visual modeling language that would allow end-users to employ to recreate a situation from the physical game in the computational version, or build a specific new model to support other computational simulations.

### End-user Modifiability: Adding and Changing Behavior of the Language of Objects

In translating the physical game language of objects to explore flexibility in the design of tangible interfaces for the EDC, we sought to find a computational language that could provide the same scaffolding, thereby making a computer-based game modifiable and accessible to the many types of users. This was carried out because our interest in exploring how tabletop technologies could support the transition from *citizen-players* to *citizen-modelers*.

A first step was for the visual language selected to be flexible enough to put into the hands of the players so they could customize the game board and the objects in order to resemble their neighborhood (Figure 7.2).

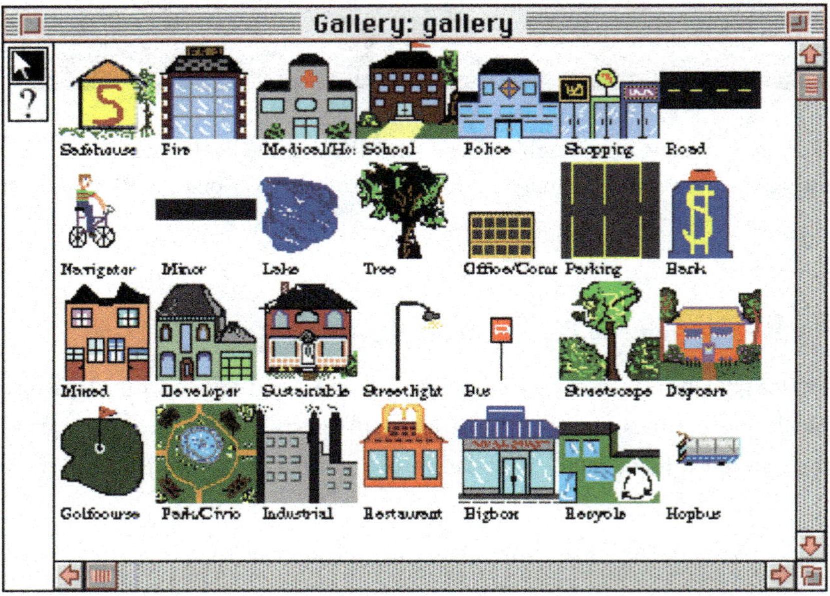


Figure 7.2: A digital language of objects: the language was designed to aid users in describing their neighborhood, evaluating its problems and prescribing actions to attain neighborhood sustainability.

Second, the undergraduates working on the implementation were not computer programmers. Therefore the language of implementation needed to be simple enough for them to become proficient and create the necessary functionality for the purposed of the game participants, while keeping in mind the original goals for the system mentioned above.

### Extending an Application Domain: Adding Simulation and Interaction to the Hop in Mr. Roger's Neighborhood

Finally, we explored the idea of an extension of the application domain of Mr. Roger's Neighborhood to include public transportation as another aspect central to an understanding of urban sustainability, e.g., energy and air quality. Again using VAT, a public transportation simulation was created, loosely modeled after an existing bus system in Boulder where HOP buses serve a route that connects the university campus to the downtown and various commercial areas and residential neighborhoods along the route. A HOP bus depiction was added to the gallery of objects, and it was given behavior (Figure 7.3). Later on, this idea lead to the EDC's capability to integrate real-time data for applications such as the one presented in Chapter 2's Bus Stop Scenario.

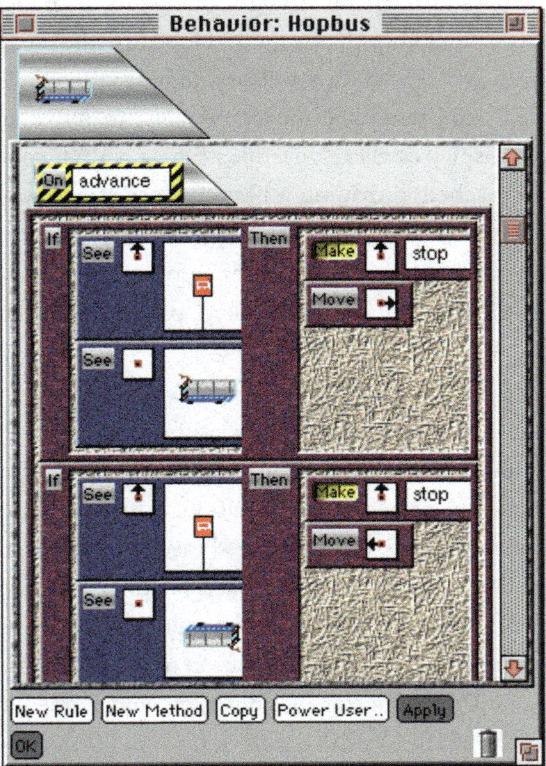


Figure 7.3: Adapting Mr. Roger's to new application domains. Adding a portion of the HOP bus simulation to address sustainability and public transportation.

A bus route loop was added to the game, and the HOP bus was programmed to stop at bus stops along the route, picking up passengers (Figure 7.4). This simulation program was very straightforward to achieve in VAT (Figure 7.3). It became a *seed* whose value was that it pointed the way to other EDC developments and applications such as the Bus Stop scenario in Chapter 2.

### Distributed Interaction: Linking Web-based Situations

Based on the translation of the physical game elements (gameboard, language of objects, interaction rules, and protocols), a version of Mr. Rogers Sustainable Neighborhood using the WebQuest (Perrone et al., 1996) was constructed as a simulation game environment which allowed us to explore for the first time *distributed collaborative participation* over the WWW. In this manner WebQuest allowed middle and high school students to create educational simulation games that use the WWW as a research resource in their social studies' courses.

In the physical game, situation cards were placed on the board at certain landmark locations, and were turned over when moves in the game brought players to these locations. In the computational game, questions about sustainability that were developed by the creators of Mr. Roger's were turned into HTML web pages and placed on a website dedicated to the game As the distributed participants in the web-based game used the navigator piece to move around the virtual game board, they would trigger the display of these questions (using a VAT command for opening web pages) when a landmark was reached, providing a participatory stimulus and integration of these *sustainability situations* into Mr. Rogers Sustainable Neighborhood (Figure 7.4).

The construction of these web pages allowed for information related to the trade-offs that were underlying the sustainability questions to be linked, providing a means to explore the topic in greater depth.

Conclusions and Implications. Experiences such as Mr. Roger's created in interdisciplinary collaborations with student in planning research and design studio courses at the SimLab of the College of Environmental Design, provided a fruitful source of creative ideas as development seeds for the EDC. For example, Mr. Roger's became a very useful initial teaching model in helping us to continue in our classroom experiences the use of physical media as pre-digital programming mockups, and thus an effective seeding and reseeding approach for the EDC's developments and evolution described in Chapter 6. The implications of these experiences extended to later international collaborations such as the enhancement of public education on urban sustainable development with the University of Costa Rica and the Ministry of Education, and funded by the Costa Rica-USA (CRUSA) Foundation for 2008–2010.

Figure 7.4: Mr. Roger's on the web. A step towards linking *face-to-face* participation around the EDC with a distributed *one-individual/one computer* participation.

### 7.1.3   EXAMPLE-2: MANAGING URBAN DYNAMICS AND ITS ENVIRONMENTAL IMPACTS ON CLIMATE CHANGE

Understanding Earth systems is a problem domain relevant to NASA and requires a vast array of resources including detailed observations of the Earth, distributed and diverse data and information archives, powerful simulation and analysis tools, increasingly realistic models, knowledge holdings, and collaboration environments. Access of this vast array of data, information and knowledge is currently limited to a small audience of specialists. A lack of technologies that can translate basic scientific knowledge to those stakeholders who face these problems limits its potential value towards the resolution of complex problems such as understanding the impact of changing climate in urban regions, or the impacts of urbanization dynamics on global climate change.

A core research issue related to this domain was: *How can existing environmental case studies be linked with remote-sensing information to create a rich learning, research and planning tool?*

The focus for this research effort was the development of an interactive planning framework utilizing several types of remote sensing data integrated with *in-situ* information, as a new type of collaborative "human-centered computing" technology for Earth system research, education, and planning. The framework's aim was not only to bring together people around the EDC (scientist, students, planners, community residents, etc.), but to support them in their interactions with the action and reflection spaces with a seamless management of integrated content information: remote sensing data of various types, historical/political information, environmental case studies, and user contributions to the problem space (Figure 7.7). The thesis of this approach was that: (1) this integration of "seed information" is important and most relevant, yet typically neglected when addressing complex problems; and (2) the EDC's use of novel techniques for informed participation with such content integration, would address in an innovative manner the existing need to begin to start explaining better the relationships related to dynamics of urban form and urbanization to the concern of local and global climate change. In this manner, this became an example illustrating the mutually beneficial synergy between the enhancement of the EDC's functionality and that of the application.

The central question to be tested in the proposed research was then: Does the integration of diverse sources of information (remote sensing, *in-situ* case studies, and historical data) through a collaborative technology and in the context of a design activity, improve people's ability to: (a) better understand the interrelationships between diverse sources of information when addressing the mitigation of environmental impacts associated with urban dynamics? or (b) utilize these information sources to enhance participatory planning in addressing urban dynamics?

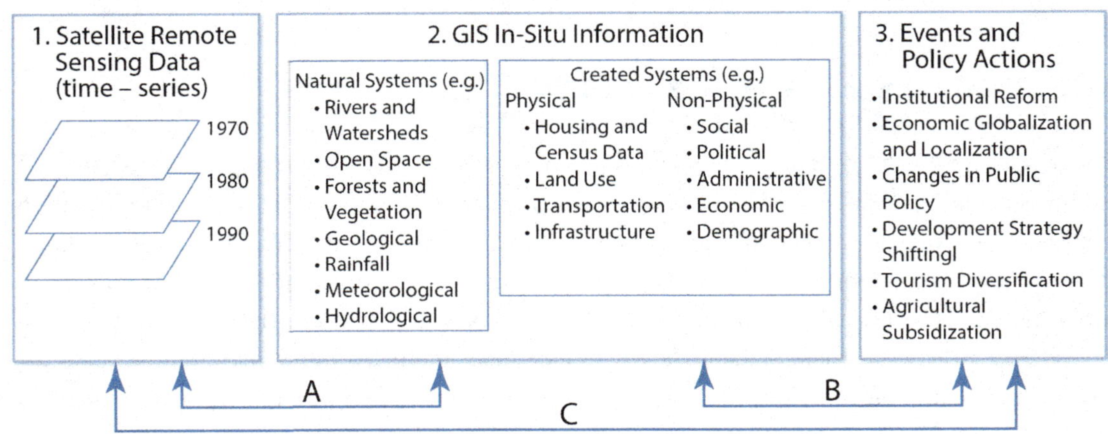


Figure 7.5: Framework for the integration of satellite and *in-situ* information. This integration supports 3 types of interactive relationships in planning for urban dynamics in the EDC—denoted by the A, B, and C arrows.

In order to address the diverse information and user needs, it is desirable to support collaborative design tasks, where stakeholders with different backgrounds collaborate to solve problems of mutual interest. This required the EDC's functionality of the action and reflection spaces to support users through the 3 types of relationships (shown by the arrows in Figure 7.5) in the framework in order be able to frame problems, present information to users in appropriate forms, and capture contributions of users on urban dynamics and environmental change. Therefore the EDC could be seeded with the necessary functionality to support seamlessly the three relationships of the framework (Figure 7.6).

1. Remote sensing data and GIS data plays a complementary role in calibrating the urban form change and in examining the growth tendency in a temporal sense as well substantive issues such as urban growth boundaries, urban density, urban size, spatial urban expansion axis, etc.;

2. Big events and urban policies (at the various levels of government (local, state and federal) as an important input behind impacts on physical and non-physical systems; and

3. Through users around the EDC could explore and examine possible impacts of great events and policies on changing urban form and growth pattern in a temporal sense.

These developments would allow NASA's remote sensing information become useful and usable in enhancing environmental planning and urban growth management in two fundamental ways. First, remote sensing information is an important source of data for the creation of simulation models, and for on-demand information that is critical to solving environmental problems. Translating this data to forms that non-experts can use it for their own problems is an important challenge, both technical and social. Second, geo-referenced remote sensing information can serve as an integrator of diverse sources of *in situ* information and in this manner also create new complementary synergies to enhance the EDC's content.

Figure 7.6: Integrating remote sensing and GIS in the EDC action and reflection spaces.

Visualization of geographic information became a powerful way to establish context in a planning or management process, as well as to anchor other sources of information in the EDC (Figure 7.7). Traditionally, historical, political, and case study data is not directly linked to geographic information. Using geo-referenced data from remote sensing can help synthesize these diverse forms into a more coherent whole and begin to discover possible hidden relationships between them, urban dynamics and climate change. Figure 7.7 illustrates this capability to support an understanding of the impacts of urban dynamics utilizing longitudinal land use and satellite data integrated to explore impacts over time.

Figure 7.7: Back to the future: integrated satellite time-fata for visualization of urban dynamics. Visualizing land-use changes as location impacts of DIA (Denver's International Airport): (a) 1999 Dynamic Window over 1975 satellite data and (b) 1975 Dynamic Window over 1999 satellite data.

Two research topics pursued from utilizing the EDC in this project were:

- attaining "hazard resilient communities" through a better understanding of the environmental impacts (climate change and air quality) of urbanization dynamics (growth and change of urban characteristics) in order for communities to collaboratively design mitigation strategies; and

- training of emergency managers to increase the capacity of the human resource system as a more comprehensive way to insure having "hazard-resistant communities" in the event of information or physical infrastructure breakdowns.

As mentioned previously in this and other chapters, the evolution of the EDC has been incremental, with EDC developments inspiring subsequent applications and in turn other EDC developments. Mr. Roger's Sustainable Neighborhood is an application looking into distributed participation (both synchronous and asynchronous). Such functionality became integral not only in looking at "risk analysis" applications, such as the example on urban dynamics and environmental impacts and inspired us in other research applications exploring the contributions of interactive decision-support technologies in the construction of *hazard resistant and resilient communities* under the Wildland Fires Initiative of the National Center for Atmospheric Research (Harriss and Arias, 2004).

## 7.2    EDC-INSPIRED DEVELOPMENTS BY OTHERS

This section presents two examples of developments by others that were inspired by the EDC: (1) the *Caretta* system extending the EDC by intertwining individual and collective action and reflection (Sugimoto et al., 2004); and (2) the *Community of Soundscapes* (CoS) system incorporating sound in an innovative manner in order for community members to capture and share their sonic experiences and produce an acoustic map using the EDC that changes over time according to people's perceptions and interpretations of their auditory environmental settings (Giaccardi, 2007).

### 7.2.1    CARETTA: INTEGRATING PERSONAL AND SHARED SPACES

Design by a community has both individual and social aspects (Bennis and Biederman, 1997; Fischer et al., 2005). *Individual* design activity inspires and drives collective design activity, and *collective* design activity provides the distributed intelligence context that cultivates and triggers further individual activity (Erickson, 2006). Design by a community does not necessarily require that all members always participate in design activities with the same engagement at the same place and the same time (Nardi, 1993). Depending on the nature of the task, some actions and reflections are better done individually, whereas others are better done collectively. The challenge is to provide multiple devices and interaction spaces that can sustain the continuity of action and reflection from the individual to the collective and vice versa (Fischer et al., 2005).

In open-ended systemic problems (such as urban planning tasks) all the stakeholders want to devise their "best" ideas and need to discus and negotiate with each other to create mutually agreeable design plans. Individual reflections and group discussions often happen in parallel: some participants individually try to come up with their own ideas, and other participants collectively evaluate existing plans. Therefore, collaborative urban planning tasks are processes that require the smooth integration of individual and social creativity; individual creativity drives social creativity, and social creativity triggers further individual creativity.

Caretta uses the inspiration of the EDC to intertwine and integrate personal and shared computational environments for participants. It allows pretesting a solution in one's own private space (some kind of personal digital assistant (PDA)) before applying it to the tabletop avoiding making publicly visible the errors made by a participant. The EDC being focused on collaborative design and decision-making does not support the integration of participants' individual and collective activities.

Caretta was designed to overcome this shortcoming. It provides participants with personal spaces for individual reflections, a shared space for group discussions, and intuitive transition methods between these spaces. Caretta supports users in open-ended urban planning tasks, in which all participating stakeholders want to devise their "best" idea. To reach shared understanding and to make decision, the stakeholders need to discuss and negotiate their ideas and objectives. In actual group work situations, individual reflections and group discussions often happen in parallel: some participants individually try to come up with their own ideas, and other participants collectively evaluate existing plans.

The technological architecture underlying Caretta integrates a multiple-input SensingBoard (Sugimoto et al., 2002) used for the participants' shared space, and PDAs used for individual participants' personal spaces (as shown in Figure 7.8).

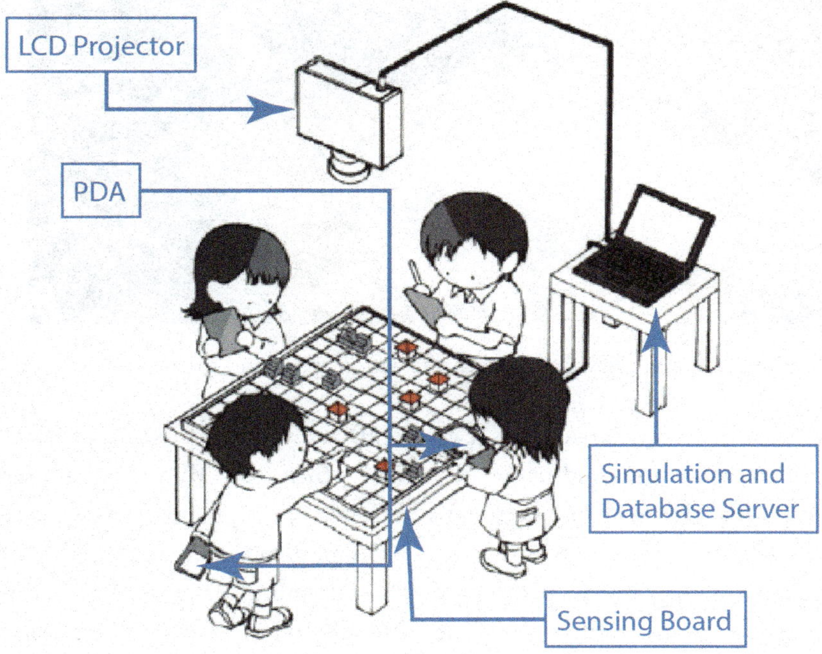


Figure 7.8: The architecture of Caretta.

Users of Caretta can discuss and negotiate with each other in the *shared space* by manipulating physical objects, each of which is enhanced by a radio frequency (RF) tag for rapid object recognition. An augmented reality technology for overlaying virtual graphics onto the shared space through a liquid crystal display (LCD) projector creates an immersive collaborative environment that enhances interactions and mutual awareness among users.

The *personal space* of Caretta works for individual users' actions and reflections because they can freely examine their ideas without being disturbed by other users. Providing each user with a personal space enhances the diversity of individual users' activities: based on their knowledge and experiences, users can externalize and elaborate their own ideas, which can lead to individual creativity.

Figure 7.9: Caretta in use. Players interacting with the action space and their PDAs.

Providing users with the *shared* space (Figure 7.9) allows them to share physical boundary objects and enhances interactions and negotiations with other users. By providing users with intuitive transition methods between the personal and shared spaces, Caretta allows users to easily copy the current situation on the shared space (e.g., a design plan shared and discussed by a group of users) to individual users' personal spaces, and display design plans devised by individual users on their personal space onto the shared space. Therefore, Caretta can support users seamlessly conducting their tasks in both spaces, and enhance collaborative problem-solving processes that require individual and social creativity.

## User Studies in the Context of Caretta

The Caretta user studies (Fischer and Sugimoto, 2006) demonstrated that there is an "and" and not a "versus" relationship between individual and social creativity. In Caretta, individual and social creativity are mutually augmented: users' individual work on their personal space is augmented by their group work on the shared space, and vice versa. Some of the specific insights gained by the user studies are:

- by working in their personal spaces, users were not disturbed by others and could concentrate on their own individual reflection. However in these settings, users did not always conduct their individual activities separately: they were loosely coupled because they worked to find a suitable design plan for the same town from individually different viewpoints. This enhanced the diversity of design plans devised by individual users, and increased the possibility of finding more creative solutions;

- by allowing users to simultaneously manipulate boundary objects in the shared space, Caretta enhanced interactions among users and raised the level of their engagement and awareness; and

- by using the intuitive transition methods, users working in their personal spaces could easily return to the shared space, and vice versa. For example, a user who devised a design plan on his personal space could immediately make his design plan appear in the shared space. The plan shared and reviewed by all users became a trigger for activating group discussions. It was subsequently modified by and augmented with other plans devised by other users on their own personal spaces, and finally accepted by the users as their group plan. Some users actually copied a plan discussed in the shared space to their personal spaces, individually examined it, and proposed the modified plan in the shared space. By reviewing design plans proposed by others, users did not have to examine similar plans repeatedly indicating that the features of Caretta effectively worked to support not only individuals but also social creative planning processes.

CarettaKids (Yamaguchi et al., 2009), an extension to Caretta developed in collaboration with schoolteachers for use in schools, was evaluated with video analysis of the students interactions and pre and post tests and it provided evidence for the following points.

- Students who used CarettaKids presented the simulation results and rules for object arrangement that they had worked out individually in their respective personal space, by using CarettaKids' function of projecting object arrangements and simulation results from a PDA onto a sensing board (Figure 7.10) (Fischer et al., 2005).

- Many of the students who used CarettaKids examined individually generated ideas collaboratively in the shared space. The patterns for these collaborative examinations were: (a) induce a rule for object arrangement from object arrangements devised in personal spaces; (b) deduce a new object arrangement from the rules discovered in the personal spaces; and (c) refine the rules discovered in the personal spaces through group discussion.

- Students who used CarettaKids not only considered important planning concepts such as residential area, industrial area, and forest area, but also understood relations between these factors, thereby deepening their understanding of city planning by taking environmental and financial aspects into consideration.

Figure 7.10: Japanese school children using CarettaKids. Participating school children interacting with the action space as their collective environment and the PDAs as their personal environments.

These studies provided evidence that the degree to which students deepen their understanding was affected by the presence or absence of collaborative examination of individually generated ideas in the shared space (Yamaguchi et al., 2009).

### Co-creation and Cross Fertilization between the EDC and Caretta

The developers of the EDC and Caretta were co-located during a post-doctoral visit of Masanori Sugimoto in L$^3$D and participated in extensive discussions regarding some of the early mock-ups and prototypes of the EDC, including ideas for future directions and requirements. After this visit, *separate parallel efforts* continued, resulting in two separate systems that share many similarities, such as the use of mechanisms to track physical pieces supporting interaction with a computational model.

## 7.2.2  COMMUNITY OF SOUNDSCAPES (COS)

Another development inspired in part by the EDC was the *Community of Soundscapes* (CoS) project that integrating sound to "help communities cultivate a better understanding of sounds and their impacts on experiencing the world around us" (Giaccardi, 2007).

CoS is a socio-technical environment that uses ambient sounds to promote the active role of local communities in the interpretation and management of the lands in which they live. CoS enables community members to capture and share their sonic experiences and produce an acoustic map that changes over time according to people's perceptions and interpretations of their environmental settings. CoS is based on a combination of different technologies including:

- *a sound camera* (i.e., a digital recording device outfitted with ad hoc GPS mapping software); and

- *a public web application* for collaborative mapping called TheSilence.org (www.the-silence.org), which is based on a MapServer engine and is integrated with satellite images and other relevant information via OpenLayers.

Whereas geographical position, time, and date are entered automatically through the Sound Camera, the web application enables participants to add and manage multiple descriptions of the sounds they hear, giving voice to a broad repertoire of experiences and interpretations.

The EDC served as an inspiration for parts of CoS by helping communities cultivate a better understanding of sounds and their impact on experiencing the world around them. Grounded on a conceptual framework based on social creativity, informed participation, and meta-design, the participatory project originally entitled "The Silence of the Lands" promoted a design approach aimed at creating socio-technical infrastructures in which new forms of collaborative design can take place. The project aimed at enabling: (a) the *collaborative creation and exploration* of the soundscape of natural parks and protected areas, contributing to an enhancement of people's imagination and sensitivity to sounds; and (b) the *negotiation* of the understanding and preservation of natural quiet through processes of participation and collaborative design in which local communities play an important role.

The CoS project brought together artists, musicians, interaction designers, software developers, and community experts in order to engage the local communities in both producing and nominating the *audio objects* that would be used to compose the soundscape, and negotiating their experience and understanding of natural quiet in a tangible manner (i.e., by dealing directly with the sounds rather than simply talking about the problem). Ambient sounds, once recorded and made available, worked as a means of translation of the various, individual perspectives and enabled different people to communicate and coordinate their different knowledge and perspectives by acting as "conversation pieces" (Arias et al. 2001).

The overall architecture of CoS includes multiple components as shown in Figure 7.11.

- *Handheld devices* with embedded GPS receivers are used to enable users to record ambient sounds and map them onto terrestrial coordinates. These data allow tracking the positions that users take in a park when collecting an audio object. Data is sent from the handheld device to the server through a wireless connection. The wireless connection is important because it simplifies the uploading and allows participants to interact with other people. In this way, participants are able to experiment "active behaviors" motivating them to explore their environment.

- A *web server* is the core of the system. It enables receiving and storing the sounds collected and nominated by the people, and allows interaction with them through a website and a connected interactive table. The website supports users' personal exploration and reflection, whereas on the table the interaction allows sounds to be manipulated as "conversation pieces" through a set of actions associated with physical objects.

- The *interactive table* is the place that links the physical and the virtual world; it is where the sounds are located and displayed on a geo-referenced map. Computer-generated images associated with the soundscape are projected on the table, while users interact with sounds through physical objects capable of interpreting their actions by means of embedded sensors (Figure 7.12).

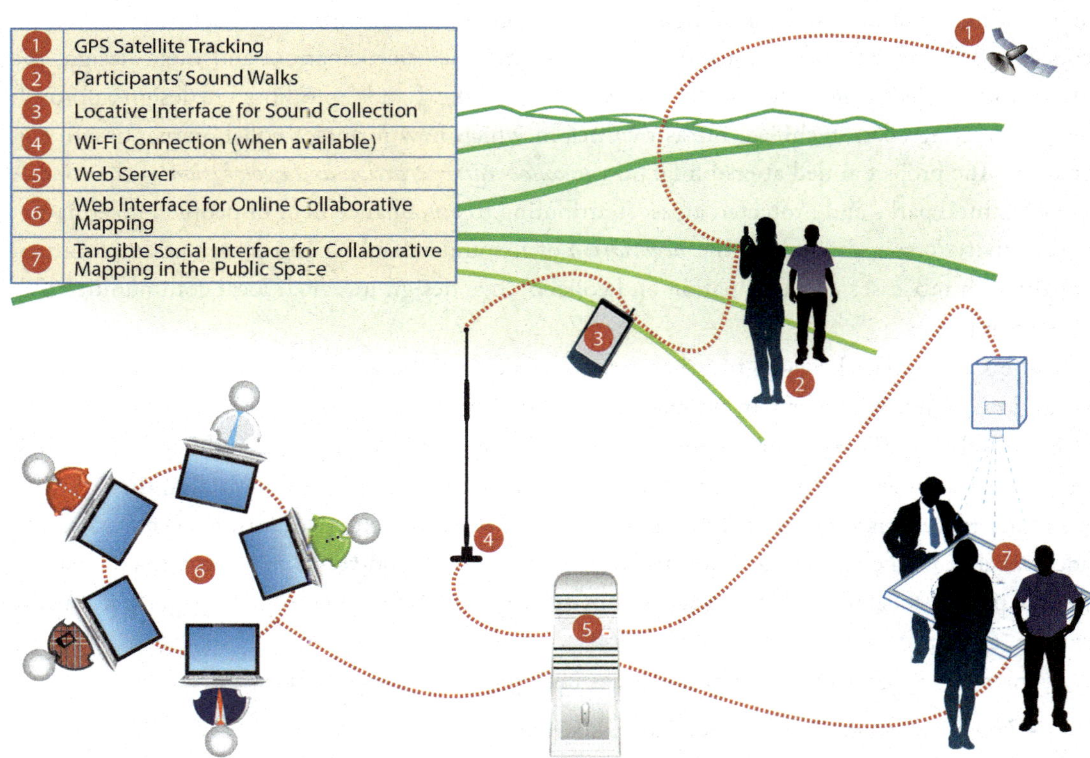


Figure 7.11: The overall architecture of the CoS systems.

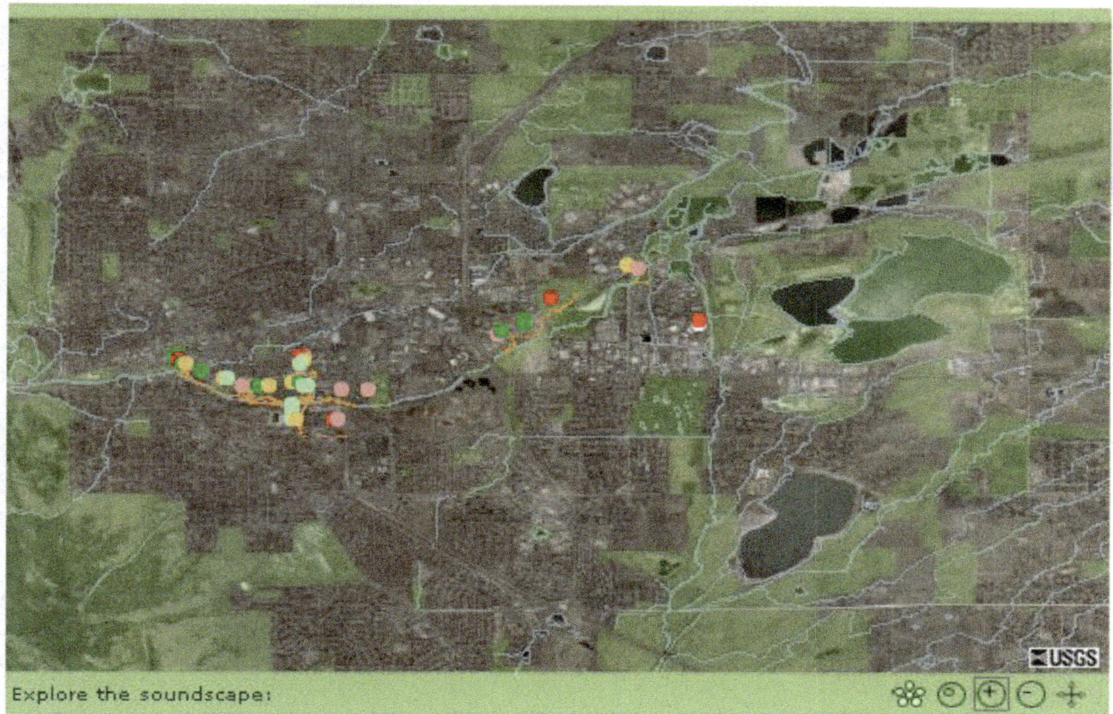


Figure 7.12: The EDC Part of CoS: a view of interactive soundscapes in the action space.

The exploration and manipulation of the soundscape allow participants to play and discuss by means of audio and visual feedback. This results in a comparison among the different interpretations of natural quiet associated with the different paths followed by the individuals in collecting their personal set of sounds and it will eventually allow evaluating the impact of changes in the environment.

The interactive table developed for CoS extended the framework and capabilities of the EDC. A set of *actions* define what may be accomplished by means of the objects mediating the auditory interaction (Figure 7.12); that is, how sounds can be explored and modified, and what effect these operations will have on the entire system. A crucial issue was to reduce the gap between what users desire to do in a particular situation (*situation model*) and what actions the system will effectively enable (*system model*).

The CoS project extended some of the technologies developed at $L^3D$ by combining and integrating interactive audio, interactive graphics, mobile communication, and global positioning system (GPS). The system was developed by successive approximations, following a bottom-up methodology according to which the prototype was simple and led to further development as the project morphed into the final CoS effort, with the tabletop component being implemented using the DiamondTouch table (Figure 7.13 and Section 9.1).

Figure 7.13: The DiamondTouch version of CoS.

As an application of the EDC, CoS enabled people to capture and share sonic experiences of the natural environment in which they live, and use these experiences as conversation pieces of a social dialogue about the places they share. The project encouraged people to connect experientially and to unfold new understandings of the places in which they live—thus giving voice to a broad repertoire of personal experiences and interpretations with more than 1,300 sonic experiences collected. Its goal, supported by the EDC was to investigate how aspects of physicality, interpretation, and ascribed value combine to produce and evolve people's meanings and affects in their encounters with the natural heritage. Participants in CoS could capture their sonic experiences with a GPS equipped field-recording device, and then with the EDC's support create, share and remix soundscapes of the places where sounds were recorded. The result was an acoustic map that changed over time according to people's perceptions and interpretations of their environmental setting (Figure 7.12). By combining mobile computing, collaborative web mapping and the EDC's tangible social interface, the project combined for the first time elements of sensorial experience, memory, and imagination to create an engaging social dialogue and sustain it over time (Giaccardi, 2014).

## 7.3    CONCLUSIONS

The inspiration and support of teaching, learning, and research with the EDC in university courses revealed that students were empowered by the EDC to think creatively and engage in collaborative framing research problems of their own interest, and not just in solving problems that were assigned to them. In this manner the classroom application experiences presented instantiate the multi-dimensional aspects of learning as well as the different conceptions of learning explored by the EDC (discussed in Section 4.3). The developments by our collaborators presented in Section 7.2 provided "existence proofs" that the EDC served as an *inspirational prototype* for technological developments in new application domains.

Finally, as demonstrated in the Mr. Roger's and Urban Dynamics cases, it is important to keep in mind for future tabletop developments that the EDC has been the source of inspirations in both ways: towards the contributions to the technological developments of the EDC, as well as a source of inspirations to application domains through the use of the EDC.

CHAPTER 8

# Lessons Learned and Contributions

The initial requirements for the EDC originated from the problems that we wanted to tackle: systemic, wicked, open-ended, and controversial design problems. We anchored our efforts in the assessment of the strengths and weaknesses of the existing research paradigms (CoPlan and DODEs described in Section 3.1) and created new computational media (Chapter 6) in response to the emerging design requirements from our evolutionary case-study approach.

Our research with the EDC resulted in an *inspirational prototype* for socio-technical environments based on existence proofs of the possibilities and impact of innovative computational media for design, creativity, and learning in the context of addressing important societal problem with case studies.

## 8.1 FORMATIVE EVALUATIONS AND AFFORDANCES

### Iterative Design Based on Formative Evaluations

Over the last two decades, the EDC has gone through numerous technical and social reconceptualizations and redesigns that can be best understood with the SER model (Section 4.1.5) and instantiated in the evolution of the EDC's architecture in Chapter 6.

While some of the central aspects of the EDC's initial conception remain in place, e.g., the use of objects as a tangible interface and the integration of action and reflection spaces, it has incrementally evolved in the course over the last 20 years from what we envisioned and started with at the beginning of our research. Our research and developments efforts did not proceed according to a waterfall model, but were driven forward by the research methodology illustrated in Figure 3.12 starting with problems, engaging in iterative design cycles based on the intertwining of theories, system developments, practice, and assessment, and analyzing the impact of different approaches.

Other major sources for insights and inspirations for iterative improvements of the EDC were derived from:

- the *interplay* between the EDC as a socio-technical environment and individual case studies (representing discrete experiences over time that now can be analyzed in a comprehensive manner) conducted within the EDC (Figure 4.5);

- the *communities* (involved in the different case studies reported in the book) who engaged in elaborated demonstrations and design sessions in our laboratory (Chapter 5); and

- the *EDC-inspired developments* that our students and other researchers carried forward (Chapter 7).

**Affordances Provided by the EDC**

The EDC provides the following *affordances* (Norman, 1990):

- it engages small numbers of participants in framing and solving ill-defined, wicked problems by exploring multiple solutions and engaging in conflict resolution;

- it supports social interactions between participants gathered around the tabletop computing environment to facilitate participants to see each other; to talk to each other (but these conversations are not captured computationally; see Figure 9.2); to observe each others actions and individuals are aware of group activities (facilitating the design principle of "what you see is what I see" (WYSIWIS) (Stefik et al., 1987)—all of these activities representing important aspects of face-to-face interaction (Olson and Olson, 2001);

- it allows developers (acting as meta-designers) based on EDC architecture (Figure 6.6) to create with a reasonable effort seeded environments for specific application domains that are tailored to their goals and objectives; and

- it empowers participants to sketch and use physical objects for tangible interactions in interacting with the EDC thereby supporting human problem-domain interaction in the context of different case studies (Figure 5.1).

## 8.2 EVALUATION OF THE EDC AS A CREATIVITY SUPPORT ENVIRONMENT

A Ph.D. student from the University of Bath, England (who visited the L$^3$D center) undertook an empirical study of the EDC to assess its support for creative behavior of different users. This study was guided by the theoretical framework developed in his Ph.D. thesis (Warr, 2007) and assessed different attributes related to the design of the EDC as a *creativity support environment* (Shneiderman, 2007). The evaluations were conducted through the use of video observations and post-session questionnaire to capture both quantitative and qualitative data. The study identified strengths and weaknesses of the EDC, and based on these findings, improvements to the EDC and recommendations for the design of other creativity support environments were made. Following, a summary analysis of some of the investigations and findings of the study are briefly described (for detailed results see Warr, 2007).

## Supporting Social Creativity

Warr's research evaluated the EDC to support social creativity (Section 4.2) with a specific focus on: (i) creating shared understanding among various stakeholders; (ii) contextualizing information to the task at hand; and (iii) creating objects-to-think-with in collaborative design activities.

His analysis revealed that the participants strongly agreed that the EDC supported the creation, integration, and dissemination of knowledge. Participants commented on the ability to make rapid changes without committing to them and to collaborate around boundary objects. They expressed confidence that using the EDC allowed them ideas to be formed and communicate and disseminate them to other participants quickly. An important role to achieve these objectives was played by the sketch tool that allowed lines and shapes to be drawn rapidly, manipulated, and erased. Participants were able to move away from vague mental conceptions of an idea to more concrete representations in the form of sketches. They could then use these sketches as the basis for further collaboration providing evidence that the EDC represents an effective medium for socially constructing and sharing information.

The study involved twenty-eight participants in seven groups of four collaborating who collaborated in deciding on the future development of land-use and new bus routes, including bus stops (Chapter 2). Interaction with the EDC and amongst the participants was captured for post-analysis through the use of two digital video cameras and screen capture software. A questionnaire was given to the participants after completing a trial, evaluating the EDC on various attributes related to the design of the EDC and the support of creativity.

## Supporting and Facilitating Idea Generation

The evaluation of this aspect was grounded in three theoretical concepts:

1. *production blocking* occurring frequently when ideas are expressed in asynchronous interactions in which participants are prohibited from simultaneously expressing their ideas. If individuals articulate their ideas, the others may be "blocked" and less able to provide their own creative contributions;

2. *evaluation apprehension* occurring when participants fear criticism from others preventing individuals from expressing ideas thereby reducing the quantity of ideas produced in a group; and

3. *social loafing* resulting of participants becoming lazy, relying on other members and thereby not contributing as many ideas as they could. When working in a group, some participants assume the group's output to be assessed collectively, whereas when working alone they have to take responsibility for their own individual performance.

This study assessed the effects of production blocking, evaluation apprehension, and social loafing during experimental sessions. *Production blocking* existed in earlier version of the EDC based on: (1) the Smart Board hardware that required sequential interactions; (2) the availability of only one pen for sketching; and (3) the lack of additional technologies to support individual and group activities. Later versions of the EDC addressed some of the limitations with the PitA-Board (allowing actions to proceed in parallel) and the augmentation of the public interaction space provided by the EDC with individual technologies as pioneered by Caretta (Section 7.2.1). Future version of the EDC should explore the use of multiple pens to facilitate multiple sketching allowing participants simultaneous access to the same functionality, thereby reducing the impact of technological production blocking.

Participants in the study documented that they were able to contribute ideas without fear of criticism indicating that little *evaluation apprehension* existed. This finding may be considered surprising as the EDC comprises a public interaction space, allowing all the other group members to see the ideas generated. A follow-up analysis of the qualitative feedback data suggested that this was because of the positive, supportive environment in which the participants were working. Participants mentioned that the ability to contribute ideas without fear of criticism was a result of the people, not the EDC: "because this was a friendly group, the EDC was not a factor here."

The study showed little agreement by participants that everyone in the group contributed equally suggesting a perception of social loafing. In contrast, all participants considered themselves to be active contributors and they did not expand upon why they thought not everyone contributed equally. Participants commented that they were concerned with their personal agendas and therefore considered themselves actively to be contributing towards the task at hand when the discussion affected them. This may have left other group members with the opinion that they did not contribute as much as they actually did.

### Group Composition around the Interaction Space

One aspect of our research with the EDC is focused on gaining a better understanding and creating more extensive support to change the relationship between individual and social creativity from a "versus" into an "and" one (Section 4.2). Of particular interest was the support of individual, sub-group, and group creativity, extending our work on integrating individual and social creativity (Fischer et al., 2005).

Centered on a tabletop computing environment, the EDC provides a public interaction space and the participants in the study gave a high rating to the support the EDC provided for working as a group. However, the support provided by the EDC for sub-groups and individual work was rated poorly. Additional analysis revealed that the participants believed the EDC provoked individual insight (e.g., through the externalization of boundary objects) but the support for working on these externalizations in private was lacking. Participants also commented that they worked as a group, but sub-conversations did occur. The public interaction space supported the group work, but could not accommodate the sub-group collaboration.

The findings of this study have provided theoretically grounded insights underlying the evolution of the EDC's architecture described in Chapter 6 and motivated EDC-inspired developments such as Caretta (Section 7.2.1). Many more studies could and should be conducted to understand all the interesting issues to move the EDC from an inspirational prototype to a more deeply theoretically grounded and empirically evaluated socio-technical environment for human-centered informatics.

## 8.3    DESIGN REQUIREMENTS (DRS)

This section briefly summarizes design requirements (summarized in Table 8.1) that emerged from the conceptual frameworks described in Chapter 4, and as results from our assessment of the strengths and weaknesses that we derived from: (1) the two research pardigms, CoPlan and DODEs, in Sections 3.1 and 3.2; (2) the software and hardware architecture evolution in Chapter 6; (3) the case studies in Chapter 5; (4) the EDC inspired developments documented in Chapter 7; and (5) the studies reported in the previous two sections of this chapter.

| Table 8.1: Overview of specific design requirements (DRs) | |
|---|---|
| DR-1: | Integrate Physical and Computational Media |
| DR-2: | Support Openness and Extensibility |
| DR-3: | Seeding Content for a Domain Application: Enhancing Data and Information Management Capabilities |
| DR-4: | Changing Human Behavior and Establish New Discourses |
| DR-5: | Exploit the Synergy between Individual and Collaborative Activities |
| DR-6: | Enhance Learning and Shared Understanding between Stakeholders with Different Knowledge and Different Interests |
| DR-7: | The Value and Contributions of Role Playing |

## DR-1: Integrate Physical and Computational Media

Sections 3.1 and 3.2 and Figure 3.1 described how the EDC originated from research activities to identify the strengths and weaknesses of different media (physical and computational) and build a new integrated environment synthesizing the best of both possible worlds. A design requirement guiding the development of the EDC was to design and build low-cost modifiable models for framing and solving complex wicked problems by a community of participants. The EDC reduced the costs (in time, effort, and money) to create new contextualized environments by taking advantage (1) of the integration of existing resources (such as geographic information systems) and (2) by automatically creating alternative representation (e.g., land use distributions represented as histograms in Figure 2.6). Additional opportunities created by DR-1 are:

- *reducing areas of disagreement* by incrementally developing a shared understanding and a common language with the integration of tangible objects; and

- *supporting a conversation* with the evolving externalized artifact.

## DR-2: Support Openness and Extensibility

Given the open ended nature of ill-defined, wicked problems, the research and developments with the EDC have explored architectures and substrates for open systems in which changes can be made with a reasonable effort. As participants contribute new ideas or want to explore new domains, the system must be able to capture these changes. One of the reasons why the simulation game SimCity is not well suited for urban planning is because it is incapable of allowing participants to engage in authentic and personally meaningful design problems. Without being able to capture (or react to) information contributed by participants, closed tools are limited in their ability to capture dynamic open-ended collaborations. By being open, the EDC allows participants to pursue design alternatives by exploring a *set of possible worlds*. This requirement accounts for the fact that design is an argumentative process, where the objective is not to prove a point but to create an environment for design dialogs (examples described are the relevance of building heights (Figure 5.4) or the issue whether a golf course is commercial or recreational land use (Figure 4.6)).

By transcending the functionality and content of existing systems, *control* is distributed among all stakeholders in the design process and it erodes monopoly positions held by expert professionals. Empirical evidence gathered in the context of the different design activities (Ariely, 2010) indicates that these possibilities are less successful when users are brought into the process late (thereby denying them ownership) and when participants are "misused" to fix problems and to address weaknesses of systems that the developers did not fix themselves. To create environments in which people can be supported to contribute in whatever ways are appropriate represents the design requirement that we have pursued with meta-design (Section 4.1.2). The coordination between diverse groups of stakeholders (representing a community of interest and not a community of practice (Section 4.1.3) is difficult. Technical experts should not be gatekeepers in the EDC or artifacts will be created where technical experts have control and participants do not feel they are problem owners. This became apparent to us from our experiences with the Cole Neighborhood presented in Section 3.1.

### DR-3: Exploit Generic Architectures and Seeded Information Environments For Creating New Domain Applications

An important feature of the EDC has been that the modeled environments were highly contextualized to the specific problems the participants wanted to investigate. A new bus route was planned in *their* neighborhood (Chapter 2); the university administration was engaged in development of taking place in their research park (Section 5.1); the emergency management case study was focused on wildfires being one of the most dangerous natural disasters in Colorado (Section 5.2); and the energy case study was grounded in new developments based on smart grids and smart meters in Boulder (Section 5.3).

The generic architecture of the EDC (Figure 6.6) as it evolved over numerous design cycles empowers designers to create contextualized domain applications with a reasonable amount of effort. It supports that: (1) action and reflection spaces can be created and linked; and (2) external information spaces (provided and maintained by others, e.g.: GIS systems (Figure 5.7) and Comet (Figure 5.9) can successfully be integrated.

### DR-4: Changing Human Behavior

Technology alone does not determine social structure nor does it change human behavior: it creates *feasibility spaces* for new social practices (Benkler, 2006) and it can persuade and motivate changes at the individual, group, and community level. The design opportunities created with the EDC should have an impact on people's lives by: (1) making it easier for people to do things; (2) allowing people to explore cause-and-effect relationships; and (3) providing value that cannot be accounted for in monetary terms. Human beings are diversely motivated beings. We act not only for material gain, but for psychological well-being, for social integration and connectedness, for social capital, for recognition, and for improving our standing in a reputation economy. The motivation for going the extra step to engage in participation and collaboration is based in part on evidence of the IKEA effect (Ariely, 2010) that people are more likely to like a solution if they have been involved in its generation; even though it might not make sense otherwise (this observation is also supported by the quote from the President's Council on Sustainable Development in Chapter 1).

Design requirements pursued in the EDC that are grounded in research in behavioral psychology (Ariely, 2010) need to address the following objectives:

- what will make people want to share and what will motivate people to make their knowledge explicit and contribute it to a shared information environment—especially, if they have to do the work but are not necessarily the beneficiaries of it (Grudin, 1989);

- to which extent can users actively desire and control their activities by providing feedback, goal setting, and tailored information;

- how can information be contextualized to the task at hand so that participants can see the benefit of learning something new to their current working situation; and

- to allow participants to focus on their tasks rather than on low-level computational features by supporting human problem domain communication.

## DR-5: Exploit the Synergy between Individual and Collaborative Activities

The EDC transcended our earlier work with DODEs (Section 3.1.2) that were focused on supporting individual designers by employing tabletop computing environments to support collaborative design activities. One can argue that certain application domains are "inherently collaborative" requiring collaboration because diverse groups of people are intimately affected by these problems, and the opinions of all of the participants are necessary to solve these problems.

A requirement to pursue based on our research with the EDC is to not see a "versus" relationship between individual and collaborative activities, but to explore opportunities and support environments for an "and" relationship and findings ways to exploit the synergy between individual and collaborative activities. The main motivation behind the development of Caretta (Section 7.2.1) was to explore this synergy. It allows stakeholders to discuss and negotiate around the shared space by manipulating physical and virtual objects, while providing the opportunity to examine ideas in their own personal spaces.

Activities conducted by participants represent an important advantage of tabletops, because they allow a smooth coordination among actors. In doing so, tabletops make publicly visible the errors made by user. Making a public mistake is a culture-sensitive issue and it is hence not surprising that a cultural requirement emerged in Japan was Caretta tabletop which allows pretesting a solution in one's own private space (a PDA) before applying it to the tabletop.

It is important to make a fundamental distinction with respect to collaborative activities: in EDC-like environments, all stakeholders work together on *one complex systemic problem*, whereas in other environments created by cultures of participation (such as Wikipedia, Scratch, 3D Warehouse (Fischer, 2011)) individuals create components (often working alone on one component) and the collective activity consist in the sharing of the individual contributions in an aggregate site.

### DR-6: Enhance Learning and Shared Understanding between Stakeholders with Different Knowledge and Different Interests

Systemic problems (the type of problems that we have pursued with the EDC) make collaboration not a luxury but a necessity. Communities of interest (represented by the diversity of EDC stakeholders), characterized by "a symmetry of ignorance" (Rittel, 1984) (in which no single participant has comprehensive knowledge of the problem to be investigated) require creating shared understanding with common languages based on boundary objects. These objects need to facilitate dialogues between different stakeholders as explored in the EDC between city officials, transportation experts, citizens, developers, environmental advocates, and commercial interests who all play a role in solving transportation-related problems. By creating an environment in which these different stakeholders can learn from each other turns the "symmetry of ignorance" into an opportunity rather than a limitation.

Other requirements to enhance learning are represented by:

- *computational critics* (representing virtual stakeholders) (Fischer et al., 1998) that can identify breakdown situations based on the violation of established principles (e.g.: how far should two bus stops be apart);

- *linking of the reflection space with the action space* (Fischer et al., 1996; Schön, 1983) thereby contextualizing information to the task at hand, making argumentation serve design, and supporting learning on demand (e.g., as shown in Figures 2.5 and 2.6); and

- *learning from each other* to reflect on and reduce pre-conceived notions and turn conflicts into informed compromises (as illustrated in Figure 5.2) by the interaction between the Regents of CU and the members of the City Council of Boulder.

### DR-7: The Value and Contributions of Role Playing

To create long-term uses for socio-technical environments for realistic problem-solving tasks with authentic stakeholders is an important requirement but a difficult one to realize. An interesting hurdle to overcome is that it is not known what activities need to be supported without long-term users, but one cannot get long-term users without creating a system with adequate support.

To explore this requirement, we conducted several studies of the EDC in *semi-authentic settings*. These situations were instigated by studying gesture in collaborative design situations (Hornecker et al., 2002) and the insights gained led to a set of *role-playing experiments*. Instead of engaging neighbors to solve a design task, we created a scenario where participants would play roles in a neighborhood created by us. Despite the fact that these role-playing scenarios represented artificial situations and lacked the authenticity of real communities of users, these experiments have proven to be valuable to enhance the EDC. They provided us with: (1) insights to determine appropriate information for the reflection and action spaces; and (2) the interactions observed in the role playing experiments helped us to understand that the physical components of the EDC should be carefully designed to encourage and not stifle face-to-face communication (Eden et al., 2002). The lesson learned from these experiments was that role-playing with semi-authentic participants is not the ideal solution, but doing so is more valuable than working with no participants at all.

## 8.4   CONCLUSIONS

Assessment as a comprehensive understanding from evaluation outcomes forms the basis for the lessons learned and their associated design requirements. This chapter integrates the specific evaluation outcomes from our longitudinal experiences integrating theories, applications and developments in the EDC's evolution. It provides a contribution towards various emerging design requirements resulting from the strengths and weaknesses we learned from: (1) the two research pardigms, CoPlan and DODEs in Sections 3.1 and 3.2; (2) the software and hardware architecture evolution in Chapter 6; (3) the real-world application experiences of the EDC in Chapter 5; and (4) the inspired developments from our classroom experiences and those of other researchers documented in Chapter 7. The contributions from these lessons have been translated into design requirements described above. Future developments (as indicated in Chapter 9) resulting from a synthesis of these individual design requirements should include: (1) finding a path that proceeds from artificial experiments to authentic design contexts; (2) creating models of increasing sophistication; and (3) moving from single studies to multi-sessions and longitudinal studies.

CHAPTER   9

# Looking Ahead

Despite the fact that the EDC research and development activities have been going on for over 20 years, numerous interesting research challenges remain. This final chapter delves into topic areas (Figure 9.1) that deserve further exploration when thinking about future developments to tabletop computing environments in the advancement of human-centered informatics:

- will *tabletop environments* become broadly available and more integrated into people's work activities?;

- several *extensions to the EDC* at the software and architectural level; and

- challenges associated with increasing the use of the EDC in *real–world environments*.

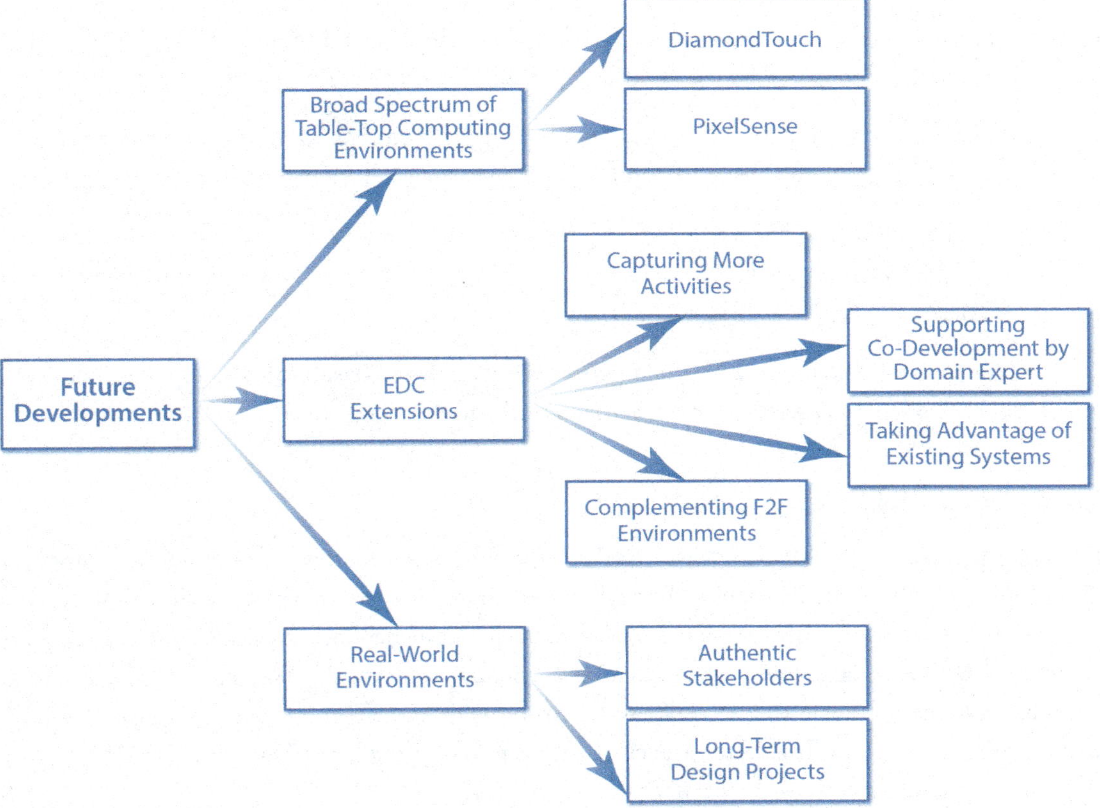


Figure 9.1: Looking ahead: future developments.

## 9.1    NEW DEVELOPMENTS IN TABLE-TOP COMPUTING

When the EDC project began in the 1990's (Figure 6.1), the options for buying commercially interactive horizontal displays were non-existent. Today, there is more research and development into tabletop computing (including a conference series on "Interactive Tabletops and Surfaces" (https://www.interaction-design.org/references/conferences/series/tabletop.html) (Müller-Tomfelde and Fjeld, 2012) and more options are commercially available. We have explored a few of these in various projects in $L^3D$ over the last few years.

A consequence of the limited availability was that few studies (specifically with end-users using these computational environments for extended periods of time) exist exploring at a broad scale the opportunities for tabletop technologies. The following questions related to the technological issues can and should be investigated.

- What are the *benefits* of horizontal interactive surfaces (e.g., low threshold for learning to interact with the technology, multi-touch direct manipulation, tangible interaction, and support for collaborative work)?

- How extensively are tabletop systems being *used*, and what are they used for? What are the communities (CoPs or CoIs) that are using these systems?

- Which features are needed to *integrate individual and collaborative use* and in what domains are tabletops used to attain such integrations?

- What features are needed to better *ground design requirements in complex real world problems* by emphasizing cognitive and social approaches in human-centered informatics?

- What role will *new technological developments* play in the design of tabletop technologies in order to enhance human-centered informatics?

### DiamondTouch Table

The DiamondTouch Table (http://www.circletwelve.com/) as a hardware development supports socio-technical environments such as the EDC to facilitate face-to-face collaboration, brainstorming, and decision making. The principal feature that distinguishes the DiamondTouch table from other tables is that it can identify who is touching where. It achieves this feature through capacitive coupling between a transmitter array located in the touch surface and separate receivers located in the chair of each user. This latter aspect of the technology, while it offers new affordances also represents limitations such as the number of participants.

The DiamondTouch Table was used in a Senior Capstone class at CU Boulder to create an intuitive and collaborative software program that explores and exploits the functionality of the hardware. The primary objectives for this project were: (1) to explore the unique capabilities, limitations, and best uses of the hardware functionality; and (2) to create a uniquely intuitive user interface that amplifies human capabilities. The project (Figure 9.2) created an image-editing software package that recognizes and utilizes gesture-based operations from multiple users and developed best practices for gesture-based interface design and it succeeded in winning the "People's Choice Award" at the CU's Design Expo (http://www.colorado.edu/engineering/academics/personalize/design-projects/senior).

Figure 9.2: An image-editing environment driven by gestures.

## Perceptive Pixel

Perceptive Pixel (PPI; http://www.businessproductivity.com/what-is-perceptive-pixel-ppi-and-what-are-the-benefits/), the maker of very large, sensitive device was acquired by Microsoft in 2012. The plans for the future with PPI were articulated by PPI founder Jeff Han: "Touch will be everywhere. We expect it everywhere and consumers expect it everywhere. There's no reason why large-scale devices like PPI shouldn't be in every meeting room, every conference room, every classroom. We're working hard to make this stuff really accessible."

However, when we talk about the future of technology we need to be careful and ask "Why a PPI device in every room? To do what?" When thinking about the future these are the questions that are central to be asked. Microsoft attempts with its research and development efforts centered around the Microsoft Surface Hub (http://www.microsoft.com/microsoft-surface-hub/en-us): (1) to bring the cost down for large displays (they are targeting mostly wall-mounted settings, but horizontal displays is also considered); (2) to support higher resolution and hundreds of simultaneous touches; and (3) to make the Surface Hub customizable with a wide array of applications.

## 9.2    EDC EXTENSIONS

Looking ahead at the EDC's future evolution, Table 9.1 compares the *current* with the *future* EDC. It summarizes the research in four major capabilities behind the development of the EDC-CURRENT documented in this monograph, and it introduces possible extensions for the EDC-FUTURE that are briefly described below.

Table 9.1: Overview of EDC-CURRENT and EDC-FUTURE

|  | EDC-CURRENT | EDC-FUTURE |
|---|---|---|
| **Capturing more activities** | Computer stores artifacts | Computer mediates design and communication |
| **Supporting co-development** | Most design activities and extensions require expertise in software engineering | System components to support end-user (domain experts, power users) developments including incremental formalization |
| **Creating linkages for the integration of existing systems** | Requires detail knowledge (e.g.: use of GIS, 3D Warehouse, and COMET) | Creating interfaces and interaction techniques to achieve these linkages at the problem domain level |
| **Location of participants** | Face-to-face interactions requiring shared location of all stakeholders | Creating a virtual reality EDC supporting distributed communities with shared interests |

### 9.2.1    CAPTURING MORE ACTIVITIES

A major activity facilitated and supported by the EDC is to create externalizations (Bruner, 1996) by participants. In cases when these externalizations are created "inside" the EDC (based on interpreting object placements and movements), they can be digitally recorded and can be inspected at later points of time (e.g., to retrieve the design rationale for certain decisions). But another important part of the design activities is the communication going on between the participants around the table. Important elements of face-to-face communication (such as speech, gesture, eye contact, and posture) are *not captured* using the EDC. These conversations are ephemeral and will therefore be forgotten and lost (unless one of the participants serve as a recorder).

Furthermore, the temporal element is absent from what is stored in the EDC. Participants can save a final construction, but any rationale in the evolution of that construction is lost. The EDC lacks a single object that can be downloaded and used to understand the overall solution to a problem.

An important extension to the current EDC would be to *integrate design activities* (represented computationally with the table) and *communication* between stakeholders (gathered around the table) to record more activities (Bell and Gemmell, 2009) as illustrated in Figure 9.3. One example of such extensions is supported by the DiamondTouch Table (Section 9.1) that identifies which person is touching where.

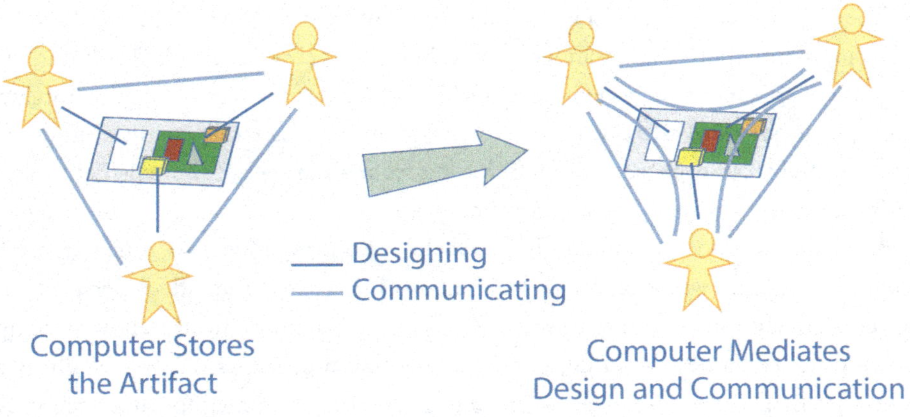



Figure 9.3: Capturing more of the design and communication activities.

To record more data about the interactions going on between the participants is more important for the EDC (supporting communities of designers) than for DODEs (supporting individual designers) because a "group has no head" (Fischer, 1999) that would remember (at least some) the ephemeral information.

## 9.2.2  SUPPORTING CO-DEVELOPMENT BY PARTICIPANTS

As argued through the book, complex design problems are *unique*; for example, each urban-planning problem has to take into consideration the geography, culture, and population of a specific city. Developers in EDC-Current have to customize the system at the source-code level. In most cases, EDC developers (i.e., participants with software design expertise) do not have sufficient knowledge of the problem and the social context and they do not know which issues are of greatest concern to city planners and citizens and which conflicts can and need to be resolved through the EDC system. The domain and context-specific knowledge is sticky and difficult to transfer from local urban planners to EDC developers. Meta-design (Section 4.1.2) addresses these challenges by focusing on "design for designers" and by creating contexts in which all participants, specifically the domain experts, can create content.

Supporting complex design situations requires establishing a context and bringing together various information resources (maps, archival and real-time data, argumentations, and opinions). It entails designing group processes, facilitation strategies, and activities to draw out and explore aspects of problem solving, such as tacit knowledge (Polanyi, 1966). EDC-Future may be envisioned as empowering participants to bring together these aspects in order to support that systems can be configured dynamically to fit specific situated needs without requiring that participants will have a detailed knowledge of programming.

The following *scenario* (extending the scenario described Section 5.1) describes the extensions and developments that urban planners would be able to construct in EDC-Future. Charged with community engagement for a new development, the planners will be able to integrate geographic information system (GIS) resources (maps, plans, census data, existing buildings, traffic statistics, etc.) related to a proposed project. Selecting from a number of pre-existing tools, models, and simulations, planners assemble an environment for a series of community meetings to allow neighborhood groups to understand and provide feedback on the impacts of a new development.

These developments would allow participants to bring their individual perspectives to the process and collectively interact with the design. Sketching support would allow participants to draw the ground floor of a new building, such as a new stadium, and associate a height with it. To allow the other participants to visualize the impacts of the design on neighborhood views and local environments, the sketch would be shown in Google Earth as a simple 3D model (Figure 9.4). This would allow discussion of, for example, whether the proposed design would block the view of the mountains from certain neighborhoods.

As the design process progresses, the crude sketch in Figure 9.4 could be used to locate exemplars in the Google 3D Warehouse (http://sketchup.google.com/3dwarehouse/) to *incrementally refine* the initial design (Shipman, 1993) (Figure 9.5). For a situation in which no adequate model exists in the 3D Warehouse, participants will be able develop their own models in SketchUp and import them into the design under development.

Figure 9.4: A simple 3D model.

Figure 9.5: Incremental refinement: importing objects from the 3D Warehouse.

In addition, EDC-Future needs to support the creation of dynamic participatory web spaces to document discussion of issues surrounding the proposed development in the associated reflection space. These websites will be integrated with the action space and Google Earth to capture the results of design sessions and provide access to broader participation by all stakeholders. They will extend the information in the reflection space and allow those who could not participate in the meeting to view the sketches in Google Earth and provide their comments and ideas as feedback.

The collected feedback will then be linked to the project, and future discussions of the development will display relevant comments that are contextualized to specific design elements.

Another co-development activity that should be supported by EDC-Future is support for designing interaction scenarios representing processes that involve not only adding content to a project under development but also designing and organizing interaction (for example, the "workflow" of a meeting). The interaction support module would step designers through various scenario design choices, providing them with advice on various possibilities as well as linkages to discussion pages for others who are involved in the creation of a scenario.

### 9.2.3    EDC-VIRTUAL: EXTENDING PARTICIPATION

Our work on the EDC to this point has focused primarily on an augmented reality approach inspired by the vision articulated by Mark Weiser a number of years before our research on the EDC started: "The most profound technologies are those that disappear. They weave themselves into the fabric of everyday life until they are indistinguishable from it." (Weiser, 1991). Our research was driven by the objectives: (1) making the "computer disappear" (Streitz et al., 2007; Streitz and Nixon, 2005) in the background and bring tasks to the forefront by supporting human problem-domain interaction (Fischer and Lemke, 1988); and (2) focusing on "face-to-face meetings" (Olson and Olson, 2001).

An exclusive focus on face-to-face meetings resulted in a limited scope of participation. This limitation became obvious when the $L^3D$ center engaged in a close collaboration with the University of Costa Rica. The need and rationale for such a collaboration was derived from the fact that many design topics (e.g., *environmental sustainability* played an important role in our collaboration) transcend a sole dependence on *local knowledge* and rely heavily on understanding and involvement by communities located in different environments (Olson and Olson, 2013), requiring reflection on behavior, understanding implications and breakdowns caused by individual and collective actions (or lack thereof), and resolutions to improve behaviors to move toward more sustainable situations. Such settings provide unique opportunities to foster, support, and study techniques to bridge conceptual distances among communities of interest (Section 4.1.3). Presently, we are exploring the possibilities of the EDC-Virtual in the context of the Urban Observatory of the Great Metropolitan Region (OUGAM; http://ougam.ucr.ac.cr/) at the University of Costa Rica. An aim of the observatory is to enhance informed participation of citizen when contributing with their critical thinking on future sustainable developments of the metropolitan region and their communities. The OUGAM is developing a "Collaboratory Space" as one of its interactive spaces to attain such aim. Part of the idea is the partnership between the OUGAM and the new digital newspaper CRHoy which is at present the most visited news site in Costa Rica (http://www.crhoy.com/en-2015-el-97-de-la-generacion-electrica-provendra-de-fuentes-limpias/). In addition to the Collaboratory Space, the OUGAM has been designed as an "interactive citizen tool" with spaces for different audiences (e.g., (1) the "classroom for elementary school children and teachers;" (2) the "community space for neighbors to think and plan their communities;" and (3) the "laboratory for researchers in public and private sectors to address research concerns). OUGAM manages information and data on socio economic and physical systems, both natural (rivers, air, etc.) as well as created (transportation, energy, etc.).

Bringing spatially distributed people together with the support of computer-mediated communication would allow people to interact on shared concerns and not just at shared locations (Olson and Olson, 2001).

EDC-Virtual represents a research objective to complement the face-to-face EDC by supporting a virtual reality approach in which interaction takes place in a fictional, computer-generated world. A mock-up of our envisionment of EDC-Virtual is shown in Figure 9.6. The further development of EDC-Virtual would expand our test-bed environment to instantiate, evaluate, and further develop our theoretical framework for how to design appropriate socio-technical environments for participative roles and migration among them. The ability to allow *more people* to participate and the utilization and development of substrates that support a range of roles, would provide an environment to study and develop specific interventions to encourage and cultivate increasing involvement.

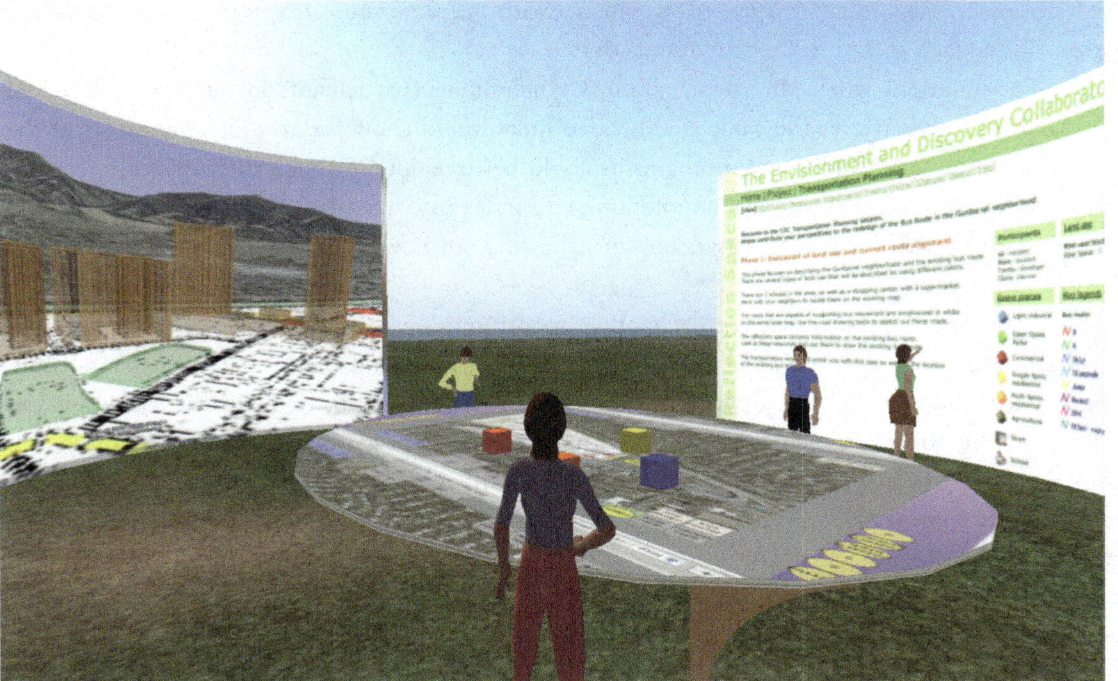

Figure 9.6: A mock-up of EDC-Virtual.

Research that has shown how the "online" and "offline" social worlds are related as well as how they are different (Bergatti et al., 2009). To understand the evolution of new forms of social interaction in on-line virtual reality and their historical and continuing relations to the off-line world, the EDC-Virtual would be integrated with the face-to-face version of EDC-Current. This would allow on-line, face-to-face, and combined participation to take place, building synergy among the strengths of the respective environments and allowing the study of the impact of these approaches on role development and migration. These developments would extend the EDC to include greater flexibility (Bonifacio and Molani, 2003) and explore the way in which technical and social infrastructures can be integrated to sustain *usefulness*, *sociability*, and *meaningfulness* (Preece and Maloney-Krichmar, 2003), and thus create new prospects for social creativity and collaborative design (Fischer, 2005).

## Brief Description of the Technical Approach

EDC-Virtual could utilize OPENCOBALT (www.opencobalt.org) as a migration platform from the face-to-face to the virtual environment. (OpenCobalt is based on Squeak and could provide a reasonable path to virtual environments from our current implementation). The initial version would provide an EDC-Current like tabletop in the virtual environment (Figure 9.6) to allow the participants in the virtual environment to interact with the same simulation with which the participants in the face-to-face setting are interacting.

For situations where the participation is synchronous (participants in the face-to-face and virtual EDC are active at the same time), video links would show the respective group(s) in the other's environment. Additional mechanisms could be developed to track interactions for replay, store intermediate results, support annotations, and index into a session video to allow those who are interacting with the scenario asynchronously to find out how choices or decisions were arrived at in another time and setting.

In addition to this initial approach, other opportunities present themselves. For example, the virtual world could itself become the simulation environment and the virtual participants could explore the simulation by flying over it, walking through it, and interacting with virtual simulation elements. This could complement the table-centered meeting space rather than replacing it, so that discussions requiring an overview of the setting could still take place. This meeting space could also act as a prototype for more extensive visualization support than is currently available in the face-to-face EDC.

Table 9.2 shows an initial analysis of some of the strengths and weaknesses of the two environments to guide the further development.

Table 9.2: Strengths and weaknesses for the EDC-Current and EDC-Virtual

|  | EDC-Current | EDC-Virtual |
|---|---|---|
| **Strengths** | • Straightforward, tangible interaction<br>• Face-to-face interaction across the representation of the situation focuses conversation<br>• Implicit communication: people can see what other people do as part of "shared interaction" and can communicate implicit cues (e.g., body language)<br>• View and interaction generally from a broad overview perspective | • Participation at a distance<br>• Participation can happen at varied times<br>• No specialized equipment (tabletop computing) needed<br>• Larger community involved in writing scripts/behavior to draw on<br>• Can explore/interact/reflect in an embedded fashion (you can walk through the virtual neighborhood, not just look at it from above) |
| **Weaknesses** | • Participants have to come to EDC site<br>• Specialized hardware required, difficult to replicate<br>• Number or participants around the table limited<br>• Need for spatial co-location places greater temporal constraints on when interaction can take place<br>• Model development has been limited to EDC developers<br>• Individual reflection and exploration not strongly supported | • Greater overhead to learn virtual environment interaction<br>• Interaction not tangible or as direct<br>• Challenge to integrate remote participants into table conversation (part of "distances matter")<br>• Need to find ways to integrate asynchronous (participation during interval) with face-to-face, synchronous meetings (temporal distance matters)<br>• Sketching might be more difficult |

## 9.2.4 ENGAGEMENT WITH REAL STAKEHOLDERS AND INTEGRATION INTO REGULAR WORK ENVIRONMENTS

Based on the low availability of tabletop computing environments (specifically in the early years of our developments), our research was limited by being forced to bring stakeholders to our laboratory rather than integrating the EDC into their work environment and thereby we were often unable to work with real stakeholders (and had to engage in role play instead; see Section 8.3). Based on these limitations, most of populations participating in our case studies did not represent the target end users of tabletop technologies but they were restricted to tabletop researchers, developers, and designers and small numbers of individuals and communities who explored their design activities with the EDC in our laboratory.

To be successful in moving the EDC from our laboratory to work environments (such as the Campus Planning office involved in the case study described in Section 5.1) will require a substantially increased level of scaffolding and robustness that goes beyond a laboratory prototype.

Another difficult challenge is to create environments in which diverse groups of stakeholders can contribute in whatever ways are appropriate for them (as indicated in Section 9.2.2). Technical experts should not be gatekeepers in the EDC or settings will be created where technical experts have control and participants do not feel they are problem owners (von Hippel, 2005).

To support sessions with participants who were not too familiar with the EDC or to provide support to complex design sessions, we have created a collaborative process relying on a trained *facilitator* and multiple *explicit phases of collaboration*. These phases included a general overview of the system, an overview of the technology, an initial collaborative construction of the scenario, a profile gathering phase, player introductions, and multiple phases of transportation modeling and subsequent reflection (theses phases serve as the structuring mechanisms of the scenario in Chapter 2). The facilitator was familiar with the technology, provided domain information not familiar to the participants, and kept participation focused.

My making the engagement with real stakeholders and the integration of the EDC into regular work environments a reality, numerous additional research challenges can be studied. We will be able to investigate the assumption (mentioned in Section 1.1) that "Americans want to take control of their lives" (PCSD, 1996) by analyzing in specific settings what motivates people to participate in democratic planning, decision making, and design processes? We believe that good interaction mechanisms (e.g., support for tangible interaction, sketching, visualizations) are necessary, but they are not sufficient. Participation is personal. Someone might participate in a project as part of a job (in the case of a transportation planner), or because the issues impact their daily life (in the case of a citizen), or because people find issues interesting (such as an environmental advocate). People are motivated to participate because they have some stake in the outcome. Judging from our experience gained from the use of the EDC so far, the *immersive experience* provided by the EDC makes participation in the collaborative design process enjoyable.

## 9.2.5   SUPPORTING DESIGN PROJECTS FROM BEGINNING TO END

To move from experimental situations to authentic design contexts in future developments will require moving from single studies to multiple sessions and longitudinal studies. EDC-Future needs to be able to track system developments from early envisionment throughout their lifetime. Complex design projects are never finished: they will always evolve. The EDC would serve as a coherent, evolving artifact memory, including the documentation of design rationale. Making an explicit connection between the evolving artifact and the communication around that artifact

(Figure 9.3) may provide a way to create a memory that captures, stories, and helps to manage all produced information thereby supporting evolutionary changes and assisting new participants to get acquainted with the history of a long term development process.

## 9.3    CONCLUSIONS

At this point of time, it is fair to say that tabletop computing has not "taken off" as many (including us) expected—evidence for this claim is provided by the following observations:

- despite the fact that there is now a conference about tabletop computing (https://www.interaction-design.org/references/conferences/series/tabletop.html), the marketplace for hard- and software environments for tabletops is still quite limited (e.g.: the engagement of Microsoft starting many years ago with the "Surface" has not lived up to expectations);

- the "killer apps" for tabletop computing are still missing; and

- tabletop computing cannot be compared in its success to Smartphones even though both provide support for collaboration and communication.

But whatever will be ahead when reflecting about technology in the context of human-centered informatics, the core objective pursued with the EDC "to explore, create, and foster immersive socio-technical environments in which stakeholders can collaboratively frame and solve problems and discuss and make decisions in a variety of application domains and different disciplines" will remain a challenge and an opportunity to be addressed.

When looking ahead at future versions of the EDC, or any tabletop technological development in the future, there is an inherent need to continue understanding that the nature of participation with any technology will continue to be contingent on: (1) the attributes of the individuals such as competence (Lawton, 1975) and motivation (Maslow, 1970); (2) the characteristics of groups such as size and levels of control (Arias, 1984); (3) the nature of problems such as "wicked" or "tame" (Rittel and Webber, 1984); and (4) the organizational or institution setting in which participation takes place (Arias, 1989).

# CHAPTER 10

# Conclusions

To make further progress in human-centered informatics will require exploring and supporting the co-evolutionary processes between fundamental human activities and their relationships and inter-dependencies with new media. This will require a deeper understanding of new theories, innovative systems, practices, and assessment. New intellectual spaces, new physical spaces, and new organizational forms are needed to allow all stakeholders to engage in personally meaningful problems, and to provide incentives and reward for their participation.

The research efforts centered around the EDC for the last two decades have brought many efforts by research communities and by our team together in a number of different, but related disciplines, including: human-computer interaction; design; creativity; learning; urban planning; and tabletop computing.

The EDC has served as *inspirational prototype* for other researchers and for the participants in our case studies. We hope that the research documented in this book is a stepping stone forward in human-centered informatics. Our concern throughout the development of the EDC as presented in the book has been on enhancing peoples' lives: how they think, learn, work, and make decisions to better plan and design their futures. Our research to envision innovative socio-technical systems was ground in the basic belief that the *future is not out there to be discovered, but it will be designed and created.*

As indicated by the brief discussion about EDC extensions in Chapter 9, much more work could and should be done. While the EDC has been used for complex, real-world problems and has involved participants having a stake in these problems, our design sessions have taken place in our laboratory and not in the work environment of the respective communities. To build systems that will be used in the real world (specifically when they rely on not widely available hard- and software) need to be stable, scalable, usable, and useful without requiring the assistance from the developer at all times. These requirements represent demands that are difficult to meet by small research teams and are often in conflict with the goal to advance the research agenda instead of promoting and supporting the broad based use of existing prototypes.

In developing socio-technical environments such as the EDC we must be cautious to *avoid over-generalizations and over-expectations of the impact of new technologies* (such as tabletop computing environments). Innovative technologies by themselves may be necessary to create new affordances but they are not sufficient to change human behavior and create new opportunities and new effectiveness in design, creativity, and learning.

CHAPTER   11

# Appendices

## 11.1   APPENDIX 1: ABBREVIATIONS AND PLACES USED IN THE BOOK

### Abbreviations of Concepts

- COMET a program at the University Center for Atmospheric Research (UCAR) that supports education and training for the environmental sciences, delivering scientifically relevant and instructionally progressive products and services. (http://www.comet.ucar.edu)

- CoPlan = Community Planning

- CoS = Community of Soundscapes

- DODEs = Domain-Oriented Design Environments

- GIS = Geographic Information Systems

- EUD = End-User Development

- InterSim = INTERactive SIMulation Station

- $L^3D$ = Center for Lifelong Learning and Design

- Meterological education (MetEd) (a part of COMET) = a free collection of learning resources for the geoscience community serving both experienced meteorologists extending existing skills and students https://www.meted.ucar.edu/

- PitA = "Participate-in-the-Action (PitA)"-Board

- SimLab = Urban Simulations and Information Systems Laboratory

- STEM = science, technology, engineering, mathematics (NSF funding theme)

- VAT = Visual AgenTalk

**Places**

- Department of Computer Science at CU Boulder

- Institute of Cognitive Science at CU Boulder

- College of Architecture and Planning at CU Boulder

- Center for LifeLong Learning and Design ($L^3D$)—a research center being part of the Department of Computer Science and the Institute of Cognitive Science at CU Boulder

- SimLab: Urban Simulations and Information Systems Laboratory at the College of Architecture and Planning, CU Boulder

- COLE Neighborhood: The Cole Neighborhood is an area in northwest Denver that has had significant need for economic and community redevelopment. In the mid-1980s under Mayor Peña, funds for infrastructure and bank loan packages for property improvements were made available to the area, and the decisions about how the money would be spent were to be made by community participants. The SimLab was asked to participate in creating processes to elicit meaningful participation by the community. Through the creation of physical models of homes, neighborhoods, and infrastructure, along with the training of citizens as facilitators, community participants were engaged in a process of description, evaluation, and prescription, resulting in decisions on funding priorities.

- Program of Environmental in the College of Architecture and Planning (ENVD)

- National Center for Atmospheric Research (NCAR)

- University Corporation for Atmospheric Research in Boulder, Colorado (UCAR)

- Boulder County Healthy Communities Initiative (BCHCI),

- Wildland Fires Initiative of the National Center for Atmospheric Research and the University Corporation of Atmospheric Research in Boulder, Colorado.

## 11.2   APPENDIX 2: GLOSSARY OF CONCEPTS

**Remark.** The glossary briefly describes the basic concepts used in the book and in our research. The field "related terms" mentions either synonyms or antonyms of the concept and the field "sources" provides two references: (1) one from the scientific community at large; and (2) one from our own work.

**Argumentation:** Design is best understood as an argumentative process where no optimal solutions exist, and the consideration of trade-offs is essential. The multi-faceted architecture of the EDC contains a specific argumentation component (implemented as a hypermedia system). Argumentation is linked with the constructive activities with critics. Argumentation supports reflection as a cognitive process.

Related terms: reflection-in-action, making argumentation serve design, design rationale

Sources: Moran and Carroll (1996); Fischer et al. (1996)

**Artifact:** In design processes, artifacts are created. Artifacts provide externalization of our thoughts and they "talk back" to participating stakeholders. They can be shared among groups of people and they are essential components of distributed cognition. The EDC is a socio-technical environment supporting the construction, assessment and evolution of artifacts.

Related terms: externalization, knowledge in the world

Sources: Bruner (1996); Arias et al. (2001)

**Augmentation of Human Intelligence:** Human intelligence can be augmented and amplified by cognitive artifacts. A famous quote of Einstein states: "My pencil is cleverer then I." Examples of cognitive artifacts are: calculators, external information stores (to compensate for the limitations of short term memory), navigation systems, etc. The EDC explores how to identify and create unique possibilities for computational media as a cognitive artifact.

Related terms: distributed cognition

Sources: Norman (1993); Fischer and Nakakoji (1992)

**Boundary Objects:** Boundary objects are objects that facilitate shared understanding and help to establish common ground among stakeholders from different communities of practice as they get together in communities of interest. The EDC as a whole can be considered as a boundary object as well as a boundary-object creation tool.

Related terms: communities of interest, shared understanding

Sources: Star (1989); Arias and Fischer (2000)

**Backtalk of a Situation:** Making thoughts, ideas and plans explicit by writing them down or by developing an artifact, stakeholders create situations that talk back to them. Often this backtalk is limited, and critics are needed to enhance the backtalk.

Related terms: critics, externalization

Sources: Schön (1983); Fischer and Nakakoji (1992)

**Breakdowns:** Designers act until they experience a breakdown (e.g., they are lacking knowledge to proceed, or they cannot satisfy conflicting requirements). These breakdowns are either noticed by the designers themselves through the backtalk of the situation, or they are signaled by a human collaborator or a computational critic. Breakdowns play an important role in deepening our understanding and can serve as a source for creativity.

Related terms: tacit knowledge, creativity, learning on demand

Sources: Popper (1965); Fischer et al. (1998)

**Community of Interest:** Communities of interest are groups of people (typically coming from different disciplines) that engage in a joint activity. The "symmetry of ignorance" among the different stakeholders within communities of interest serves as a challenge to create new knowledge and shared understanding.

Related terms: community of practice

Sources: Resnick et al. (1991); Fischer (2001a)

**Community of Practice:** Communities of practice are groups of practitioners who work as a community in a certain domain. One objective of the EDC is to support communities of practice through its domain-orientation that supports interaction at the level of the problem domain of the community of practice and not only on a computational level.

Related terms: community of interest

Sources: Wenger (1998); Fischer (2001a)

**Collaboratory:** A collaboratory (a new word originating from the fusion of "collaboration" and "laboratory") represents a socio-technical environment where groups of people can explore (with the help of powerful information and communication technologies) complex systemic problems transcending the capabilities of individual human minds.

Related terms: face-to-face communication

Sources: Wulf (1993); Arias et al. (2001)

**Construction Kits:** A construction kit is a set of components that can be used to create artifacts. Construction kits include a presentation component that allows its users to see what parts are available. The elements of a construction kit are at a higher (more domain-oriented) level than programming language constructs.

Related terms: human problem-domain communication, design by composition

Sources: Eisenberg et al. (2002); Fischer and Lemke (1988)

**Creativity:** Creativity produces work that is both novel (i.e., original, unexpected) and appropriate (i.e. useful, adaptive concerning the task constraints). It is wide in scope and important at both the individual and societal levels for a wide range of domains.

Related terms: social creativity, design, innovation

Sources: Sternberg (1988); Fischer et al. (2005)

**Critical Coalition:** Central participatory planning approaches identify those interest groups *effecting* or *affected by* the impacts of a planning policy or a development action. Their importance in participation is that they represent the community's needs, attitudes, values, and shared common interests. Through their participation in the decision-making process, the critical coalition provides specific knowledge to identify shared problems and objectives of diverse interest groups, as well as the political base for implementation of decisions and policies.

Related terms: participatory planning, empowerment

Sources: Grigsby et al. (1977); Arias (2005)

**Critiquing and Critiquing Systems:** A computational mechanism that gives context-sensitive advice regarding a product under development. Critics need a metric to evaluate the quality of a solution. Specific classes of critics are: generic critics, specific critics, interpretive critics, and pluralistic critics. Critiquing systems can use different critiquing strategies (based on different metrics for evaluating an artifact) for determining when a critique is necessary and when and how users should be informed.

Related terms: reflection-in-action, breakdowns

Sources: Miller (1986); Fischer et al. (1998)

**Cultures of Participation:** Cultures of participation provide opportunities, means, and rewards for all people to participate and to contribute actively in personally meaningful problems.

Related terms: consumer cultures, meta-design

Sources: Jenkins (2009); Fischer (2011)

**Design:** Design is concerned with "how things ought to be." Design (as understood in this book) is understood in this very broad sense and is a central activity and provides a conceptual framework for how we conduct our lives, how we organize our societies, and how we create specific artifacts.

Related terms: artifacts, externalizations, design methodologies

Sources: Simon (1996); Arias et al. (1997a)

**Design Rationale:** A record of the reasoning underlying the design of an artifact. Successful computational artifacts will evolve over long periods of time. To support changes, the rationale behind the artifacts is an important source of information to support their evolution. In the EDC, design rationale is recorded in the argumentation component.

Related terms: argumentation, indirect long-term collaboration

Sources: Moran and Carroll (1996); Fischer et al. (1996);

**Distributed Cognition:** The knowledge which we have and need is not all in our head, but to a large extent resides in the world: in artifacts of all kinds and in the heads of other people. A distributed cognition perspective raises many interesting issues, such as how the knowledge in the head and the knowledge in the world are related to each other, how knowledge in the world can be learnt on demand, and whether we actively access the knowledge in the world or whether it is delivered to us.

Related terms: externalization, cognitive artifacts, tacit knowledge

Sources: Salomon (1993); Arias et al. (2001)

**Domain-Oriented Design Environments (DODEs):** DODEs are computational media that allow people to be engaged in more authentic tasks in their work practices by allowing them to deal with domains, not to fight with tools. DODEs make computers invisible and enable users to communicate with the problem domain rather than with computer tools. They extend construction kits by supporting not just the design of an artifact, but the design of a "good" artifact by increasing the back-talk of an artifact using critics. They support reflection-in-action as a design method.

Related terms: construction kits, critiquing, human problem-domain interaction

Sources: Winograd (1995); Fischer (1994a)

**End-User Development (EUD):** Mechanisms allowing users of all levels of technical competence to make substantial modifications to a system. EUD is necessary for design environment seeds to evolve. EUD systems enable a mode of design called "design in use," in which users modify and evolve their systems as they use them.

Related terms: cultures of participation, meta-design

Sources: Lieberman et al. (2006); Fischer and Giaccardi (2006)

**Evolutionary Design of (Complex) Systems:** Based on empirical findings that successful systems (software systems, buildings, cities) evolve, a paradigm shift is needed which is based on the following requirements: software systems must evolve; they cannot be completely designed prior to use; they must evolve at the hands of the users and they must be designed for evolution. The EDC, being based on the Seeding, Evolutionary Growth, and Reseeding (SER) model, supports evolutionary processes at the architecture, the domain, and the artifact level.

Related terms: meta-design, SER Model

Sources: Curtis et al. (1988); Fischer et al. (2001)

**Human-Centered Informatics:** Represents the intersection of the cultural, the social, the cognitive, and the aesthetic with computing and information technology. It encompasses a huge range of issues, theories, technologies, designs, tools, environments and human experiences in knowledge, work, recreation and leisure activity, teaching and learning, and the potpourri of everyday life.

Related terms: human-computer interaction, socio-technical systems

Sources: series "Synthesis Lectures on Human-Centered Informatics" (by Morgan and Claypool in which this book is published)

**Human Problem-Domain Interaction:** Brings tasks to the forefront and pushes computer-level objects to the back by providing domain-oriented objects for users to interact with. Reduces the representational gap between the real world and computational representations of it.

Related terms: disappearing computer

Sources: Streitz and Nixon (2005); Fischer and Lemke (1988)

**Ill-defined Problems:** Problems are ill-defined when no specification for them is available. The integration between problem framing and problem solving is critical for ill-defined problems. The

EDC supports coping with ill-defined problems through partial constructions and specifications that can be modified at any time.

Related terms: wicked problems, ill-structured problems

Sources: Rittel and Webber (1984); Arias (1996)

**Informed Participation:** If people want to take control of their lives, informed participation is required. It relies on the potential power of and growing desire for decision processes that promote direct and meaningful interaction involving people in decisions that affect them.

Related terms: participation, conflict resolution, informed compromises

Source: Brown et al. (1994); Arias et al. (1999)

**Learning:** Learning has emerged as the most challenging activity in the world of today where there is too much to know for any individual. The EDC provides the foundation for a variety of innovative learning strategies.

Related terms: lifelong learning, self-directed learning, learning on demand, experiential learning, organizational learning

Sources: Brown (2005); Fischer (2014)

**Making Argumentation Serve Design:** Empirical findings provide evidence that designers do not like to study large information repositories in the abstract (such as many pages of design rationale or lengthy user manuals). Designers get interested in argumentation in situations which are direct relevant to their goals and objectives and which help them understand problematic aspects of the design situation. In order to serve the design activity, argumentation must be available when it is relevant to the specific problem the designer trying to understand.

Related terms: reflection-in-action, design rationale, relevance to the task at hand

Sources: Schön (1983); Fischer et al. (1996)

**Meta-Design:** Meta-design ("design for design after design") is grounded in the basic assumption that future uses and problems cannot be completely anticipated at design time, when a system is developed. At use time, users will discover mismatches between their needs and the support that an existing system can provide for them. By supporting users as active contributors who can transcend the functionality and content of existing systems, control is distributed among all stakeholders in the design process.

Related terms: end-user development, participatory design

Sources: Binder et al. (2011); Fischer and Giaccardi (2006)

**Motivation:** Motivation has been largely ignored or at least not sufficiently emphasized in many research areas such as human computer interaction, computer-supported cooperative work, and design rationale research. But it is one of the most important forces determining human behavior. Ignoring the motivational factors of any stakeholders involved in design processes, will lead to failure of the most sophisticated computational mechanisms.

Related terms: asymmetry between humans and computers

Sources: Csikszentmihalyi (1996); Dick et al. (2012)

**Owner(s) of Problems:** The owner(s) of problems need to remain active participants in the solving of ill-defined problems and they are the stakeholders who drive the evolutionary growth in the SER process. Because they are practitioners (end-users) in specific problem domains, human problem domain communication and end-user modifiability need to be supported to allow them to be articulate.

Related terms: cultures of participation, ill-defined problems, end-user development

Sources: Nardi (1993); Fischer (1994b)

**Participatory Design:** Participatory design (characterized as "design for use before use") supports diverse ways of thinking, planning, and acting by requiring the social inclusion and active participation of the users. It is focused on system development at design time by bringing developers and users together to envision the contexts of use.

Related terms: design methodologies, mutual learning, meta-design

Sources: Binder et al. (2011); Fischer and Giaccardi (2006)

**Planning:** Planning is a problem-solving process that centers around decision-making in the resolution of problems. The implementation of outcomes (policies and plans) is its central aim, and addresses the framing and resolution of problems in a context of conflict at different levels of aggregation from community to city, to urban regions.

Related terms: wicked problems, conflict resolution, decision-making

Sources: Mandelbaum (1983); Arias (1996)

**Planning Problems:** They are collective and wicked by nature. They are owned by many stakeholders who are affected by them. Given their complexity, these problems require more knowledge than any single person posses since the knowledge relevant to their resolution is usually distributed among the stakeholders affected by them.

Related terms: ill-defined problems, transcending the individual human mind

Sources: Rittel and Webber (1984); Arias et al. (2001)

**Problem Framing and Problem Solving:** In the real world, problems are not given but need to be framed. Problem framing often requires attempts to partially solve the problem. Therefore problem framing and solving need to be integrated. The EDC supports this integration with allowing stakeholders to create externalizations that can be analyzed, critiqued, and incrementally refined.

Related terms: externalizations, backtalk of the situation

Sources: Rittel (1984); Fischer (1994a)

**Reflection-in-Action:** Humans like to *act* in design and other activities. In acting, humans may encounter a breakdown (e.g., perceived by analyzing the artifact or by receiving a critiquing message). They can then switch to reflection. The EDC supports reflection-in-action with critics (to interrupt action and notify the designer of a possible breakdown) and argumentation (to support reflection).

Related terms: breakdowns, critics, making argumentation serve design

Sources: Schön (1983); Fischer et al. (1996)

**Seeding, Evolutionary Growth, and Reseeding (SER) Model:** The SER model is a process model for the sustained evolution of computational systems modeling real world environments. It provides a conceptual framework for the development of open (rather than closed) systems. The SER model describes social and technical interactions that take place around the use of the EDC over an extended period of time.

Related terms: design-in-use, meta-design

Sources: Henderson and Kyng (1991); Fischer et al. (2001)

**Situation Awareness:** is the capability of a system to be aware of the user's situation. The EDC is situation aware because the activities (e.g., the design of artifacts) take places to a large part inside the system.

Related terms: embedded communication, relevance to the task at hand, user modeling

Sources: Dey et al. (2001); Fischer (2012);

**Stakeholders:** All people affected by the design and use of a computer system. Typically, stakeholders are grouped into users and developers, where users might include the management as well as operators of a computer system, and developers might include designers, evaluators, maintainers, and so forth.

Related terms: participatory design, mutual learning, symmetry of ignorance

Sources: Greenbaum and Kyng (1991); Fischer (2001a)

**Symmetry of Ignorance:** Real world design problems transcend the knowledge of individuals and specific groups. All participants who have a stake in the design activity should be able to contribute their knowledge. Rittel describes it in this way: "The expertise and ignorance is distributed over all participants in a wicked problem. There is a symmetry of ignorance among those who participate because nobody knows better by virtue of his degrees or his status. There are no experts (which is irritating for experts), and if experts there are, they are only experts in guiding the process of dealing with a wicked problem, but not for the subject matter of the problem."

Related terms: wicked problems, shared understanding, communities of interest

Sources: Rittel (1984); Fischer et al. (2002)

**Tabletop Computing:** Horizontal computing surfaces that support novel forms of interaction (generally emphasizing face to face) and collaboration, and extend computation to new environments. The EDC's predecessor, the InterSim, is one of the earliest systems that are now known as tabletop technologies.

Related terms: InterSim, SmartBoards, PitaBoard

Sources: Müller-Tomfelde and Fjeld (2012); Robinson et al. (1997)

**Tacit Knowledge:** Unspoken knowledge that only surfaces in the context of doing something or when the knower is somehow reminded of it. Much of an expert's knowledge is tacit and cannot be articulated in abstract contexts such as interviews. Therefore knowledge acquisition schemes cannot capture all of what an expert knows. They must therefore be open-ended so experts can add their knowledge as it arises in the contexts of doing work.

Related terms: breakdowns, knowledge construction

Sources: Polanyi (1966); Fischer (1994b)

**Wicked Problems:** Many social problems have no definitive formulation; no simple criteria for success or completion; solutions are better/worse, not true/false; every attempt at a solution is a "one-shot operation," with no opportunity to learn by trial-and-error; the solution space is ill-defined, both in terms of permissible operations and outcomes; constitutes a "universe of one;" may be considered the symptom of another problem; and require framing the problem as part of the solution process: these are wicked problems.

Related terms: ill-defined problems; symmetry of ignorance

Sources: Rittel (1973); Fischer and Herrmann (2011)

# References


Alexander, C. (1964) *The Synthesis of Form*, Harvard University Press, Cambridge, MA. 63

Anselin, L. and Arias, E. G. (1983) "A Multi-Criteria Framework as a Decision Support System for Urban Growth Management Applications: Central City Redevelopment," *European Journal of Operational Research*, 13(3), pp. 300–309. DOI: 10.1016/0377-2217(83)90058-9. 28, 29, 30, 43

Arias, E. and Eden, H. (2002) "Creating Shared Understanding through Collaborative Design" in G. C. Lopez, and R. A. Tenorio (Eds.), *Enseñanza Virtual De La Psicologia*, Volume 1, Amis Impresos, Mexico, DF, pp. 14–33. 31

Arias, E., Eden, H., and Fischer, G. (1995) "Cise Research Instrumentation: Shared Interaction in Support of Design, Learning, and Planning," National Science Foundation, University of Colorado Boulder. 3

Arias, E. G. (1984) "Resident Participation in Public Housing: A Conceptual Approach" in E. Cassetti, M. H. Mickle, and W. G. Vought (Eds.), *Modeling and Simulation*, Volume 15, Instrument Society of America, University of Pittsburgh, Pittsburgh, PA, pp. 131–138. 185

Arias, E. G. (1988) "Resident Participation and Residential Quality in U.S. Public Housing," Dissertation, University of Pennsylvania. 28, 30

Arias, E. G. (1989) "The Contingent Nature of Participation and Housing Research," *Guru Nanak Journal of Sociology—Special Housing Policy Issue*, 10(1-2), pp. 81–99. 185

Arias, E. G. (1994) "Decision Support in Locational Analysis for Urban Growth Management," Technological Challenges and Visions,? Keynote Paper, *GIS 1994 European Conference* (Wiesbaden, Germany), February, 1994. 31, 42

Arias, E. G. (1995a) "A Common Language for Helping Neighbors Help Themselves: Participatory Design Support Tools for Implementation in Contexts of Conflict," *The Wm. G. Grigsby Symposium: Housing Markets, Neighborhood Dynamics and Societal Goals* (The Wharton Real Estate Center, Philadelphia), University of Pennsylvania. 27, 33, 38, 40, 44

Arias, E. G. (1995b) "Designing in a Design Community: Insights and Challenges," *DIS'95 Symposium on Designing Interactive Systems: Processes, Practices, Methods, and Techniques* (Ann Arbor, MI), ACM Press, New York, pp. 259–263. 27, 28, 31, 116

Arias, E. G. (1996) "Bottom-up Neighborhood Revitalization: Participatory Decision Support Approaches and Tools," *Urban Studies Journal—Special Issue on Housing Markets, Neighborhood Dynamics and Societal Goals*, 33(10), pp. 1831–1848. xxii, 3, 29, 36, 37, 43, 46, 195, 196

Arias, E. G. (2000) "The Envisionment and Discovery Collaboratory: Extending the Limits of Participation," *The Analytical Methods and Computer Applications Track, American Association of Collegiate Schools of Planning National Conference* (Atlanta), November. 46

Arias, E. G. (2005) "Critical Coalition (CC)" in R. Caves (Ed.), *Encyclopedia of the City*, Routledge, London, pp. 103–104. 29. 45, 193

Arias, E. G., Eden, H., and Fischer, G. (1997a) "Enhancing Communication, Facilitating Shared Understanding, and Creating Better Artifacts by Integrating Physical and Computational Media for Design" in *Proceedings of Designing Interactive Systems (DIS '97)*, ACM, Amsterdam, The Netherlands, pp. 1–12. 28, 29, 30, 41, 46, 141, 193

Arias, E. G., Eden, H., Fischer, G., Gorman, A., and Scharff, E. (1999) "Beyond Access: Informed Participation and Empowerment" in C. Hoadley (Ed.), *Proceedings of the Computer Supported Collaborative Learning (CSCL '99)* Conference, Stanford, pp. 20–32. DOI: 10.3115/1150240.1150242. 28, 37, 85, 195

Arias, E. G., Eden, H., Fischer, G., Gorman, A., and Scharff, E. (2001) "Transcending the Individual Human Mind—Creating Shared Understanding through Collaborative Design" in J. M. Carroll (Ed.), *Human-Computer Interaction in the New Millennium*, ACM Press, New York, pp. 347–372. xxi, xxii, 7, 55, 57, 61, 71, 157, 191, 192, 193, 196

Arias, E. G. and Fischer, G. (2000) "Boundary Objects: Their Role in Articulating the Task at Hand and Making Information Relevant to It" in *International Icsc Symposium on Interactive and Collaborative Computing (Icc'2000)*, University of Wollongong, Australia, Icsc Academic Press, Wetaskiwin, Canada, pp. 567–574. 13, 57, 71, 74, 191

Arias, E. G., Perrone, C., and Spencer, S. (1997b) "Mr. Rogers Sustainable Neighborhood: A Visual Language Case Study for Community Education," VL '97 (CU Denver). DOI: 10.1109/VL.1997.626609. 141

Ariely, D. (2010) *The Upside of Irrationality—the Unexpected Benefits of Defying Logic at Work and at Home*, HarperCollins, New York, N.Y. 108, 168, 169

Barker, R. (1968) "Ecological Psychology: Concepts and Methods for Studying the Environment of Human Behavior," Stanford University Press, Stanford, CA. 28

Basalla, G. (1988) *The Evolution of Technology*, Cambridge University Press, New York. 75

Bell, G. and Gemmell, J. (2009) *Total Recall*, Dutton, New York. 177

Benkler, Y. (2006) *The Wealth of Networks: How Social Production Transforms Markets and Freedom*, Yale University Press, New Haven, CT. 169

Bennis, W. and Biederman, P. W. (1997) *Organizing Genius: The Secrets of Creative Collaboration*, Perseus Books, Cambridge, MA. 55, 70, 79, 152

Binder, T., DeMichelis, G., Ehn, P., Jacucci, G., Linde, P., and Wagner, I. (2011) *Design Things*, MIT Press, Cambridge, MA. 65, 66, 195, 196

Boden, M. (1991) *The Creative Mind: Myths and Mechanisms*, Basic Book, New York. 78

Bonifacio, M. and Molani, A. (2003) "The Richness of Diversity in Knowledge Creation: An Interdisciplinary Overview," *Proceedings of I-KNOW'03* (Graz, Austria), pp. 379–388. 182

Borgatti, S. P., Mehra, A., Brass, D. J., and Labianca, G. (2009) "Network Analysis in the Social Sciences," *Science*, 323(5916), pp. 892-895. DOI: 10.1126/science.1165821. 182

Bowker, G. C. and Star, S. L. (2000) *Sorting Things out—Classification and Its Consequences*, MIT Press, Cambridge, MA. 71

Brand, S. (1995) *How Buildings Learn: What Happens after They're Built*, Penguin Books, New York. 56

Brooks, F. P., Jr. (1987) "No Silver Bullet: Essence and Accidents of Software Engineering," IEEE Computer, 20(4), pp. 10-19. DOI: 10.1109/MC.1987.1663532. 75

Brown, J. S. (2005) *New Learning Environments for the 21st Century*, http://www.johnseelybrown.com/newlearning.pdf. 87, 195

Brown, J. S., Duguid, P., and Haviland, S. (1994) "Toward Informed Participation: Six Scenarios in Search of Democracy in the Information Age," *The Aspen Institute Quarterly*, 6(4), pp. 49–73. 37, 195

Bruner, J. (1996) *The Culture of Education*, Harvard University Press, Cambridge, MA. 68, 87, 88, 176, 191

Budge, B. (1983) *Pinball Construction* (Computer Program), Electronic ARts, San Mateo, CA. 48

Campbell, D. T. (1969) "Ethnocentrism of Disciplines and the Fish-Scale Model of Omniscience" in M. Sherif, and C. W. Sherif (Eds.), *Interdisciplinary Relationships in the Social Sciences*, Aldine Publishing Company, Chicago, pp. 328–348. 70

Cialdini, R. (2009) *Influence: Science and Practice* (5th Edition), Pearson, Boston. 108

Clark, H. H. and Brennan, S. E. (1991) "Grounding in Communication" in L. B. Resnick, J. M. Levine, and S. D. Teasley (Eds.), *Perspectives on Socially Shared Cognition*, American Psychological Association, pp. 127–149. DOI: 10.1037/10096-006. 55, 70, 71, 106

Collins, A. and Halverson, R. (2009) *Rethinking Education in the Age of Technology: The Digital Revolution and the School*, Teachers College Press New York. 84

COMET-Program (2006) *Introduction to Fire Behavior - Influences of Topography, Fuels, and Weather on Fire Ignition and Spread, University Corporation for Atmospheric Research*, http://meted.ucar.edu/fire/fwx/. 98

Csikszentmihalyi, M. (1996) *Creativity—Flow and the Psychology of Discovery and Invention*, Harper Collins Publishers, New York. 78, 86, 196

CSTB (1990) "Scaling Up: A Research Agenda for Software Engineering (Computer Science and Technology Board)," *Communications of the ACM*, 33(3), pp. 281–293. DOI: 10.1145/77481.77482. 64, 75

Curtis, B., Krasner, H., and Iscoe, N. (1988) "A Field Study of the Software Design Process for Large Systems," *Communications of the ACM*, 31(11), pp. 1268–1287. DOI: 10.1145/50087.50089. 55, 63, 194

dePaula, R. and Fischer, G. (2005) "Knowledge Management: Why Learning from the Past Is Not Enough!" in J. Davis, E. Subrahmanian, and A. Westerberg (Eds.), *Knowledge Management: Organizational and Technological Dimensions*, Physica Verlag, Heidelberg, pp. 21–54. DOI: 10.1007/3-7908-1618-3_2. 99

Dewey, J. (2009) *Democracy and Education: An Introduction to the Philosophy of Education*, WLC Books (original work published 1916), New York. 98

Dey, A. K., Abowd, G. D., and Salber, D. (2001) "A Conceptual Framework and a Toolkit for Supporting the Rapid Prototyping of Context-Aware Applications," *Human-Computer Interaction Journal, Special Issue on "Context-Aware Computing"*, 16(2-4), pp. 97–166. 197

DGT (2015) *Digital Game Technology*, http://www.digitalgametechnology.com. 120

Dick, H. (2013) "Socio-Technical Frameworks and Systems That Motivate People to Reduce Their Energy Consumption," Ph.D., University of Colorado, Boulder. 107

Dick, H., Eden, H., Fischer, G., and Zietz, J. (2012) "Empowering Users to Become Designers: Using Meta-Design Environments to Enable and Motivate Sustainable Energy Decisions" in K. Halskov, H. Winschiers-Theophilus, Y. Lee, Y. Simonsen, and K. Bødker (Eds.), *Proceedings of the Participatory Design Conference (PDC 2012)* Volume 2, Roskilde, Denmark, pp. 49–52. DOI: 10.1145/2348144.2348160. 107, 196

Dillenbourg, P. and Evans, M. (2011) "Interactive Tabletops in Education," *Computer-Supported Collaborative Learning*, 6, pp. 491–514. DOI: 10.1007/s11412-011-9127-7. xxi, 115, 137

Dourish, P. (2001) *Where the Action Is—the Foundations of Embodied Interaction*, The MIT Press, Cambridge, MA. 56

Eden, H. (2002) "Getting in on the (Inter)Action: Exploring Affordances for Collaborative Learning in a Context of Informed Participation" in G. Stahl (Ed.), *Proceedings of the Computer Supported Collaborative Learning (CSCL 2002) Conference*, Boulder, CO, pp. 399–407. 129

Eden, H., Hornecker, E., and Scharff, E. (2002) "Multilevel Design and Role Play: Experiences in Assessing Support for Neighborhood Participation in Design" in *Proceedings of DIS'02 (Designing Interactive Systems)*, ACM Press, London, pp. 387–392. DOI: 10.1145/778712.778768. 172

Ehn, P. (1989) *Work-Oriented Design of Computer Artifacts*, 2nd ed., Arbetslivscentrum, Stockholm. 55, 64

Ehrhardt-Martinez, K., Donnelly, K. A., and Laitner, J. A. S. (2010) *Advanced Metering Initiatives and Residential Feedback Programs: A Meta-Review for Household Electricity-Saving Opportunities*, American Council for an Energy-Efficient Economy. 107

Eisenberg, M., Eisenberg, A., Gross, M., Kaowthumrong, K., Lee, N., and Lovett, W. (2002) "Computationally-Enhanced Construction Kits for Children: Prototype and Principles" in *Proceedings of Icls2002, the Fifth International Conference of the Learning Sciences*, Seattle, Washington, October 23–26. 192

Engelbart, D. C. (1995) "Toward Augmenting the Human Intellect and Boosting Our Collective IQ," *Communications of the ACM*, 38(8), pp. 30–33. DOI: 10.1145/208344.208352. 56

Engeström, Y. (2001) "Expansive Learning at Work: Toward an Activity Theoretical Reconceptualization," *Journal of Education and Work*, 14(1), pp. 133–156. DOI: 10.1080/13639080020028747. 78, 84, 88

Erickson, T. (2006) "From PIM to GIM: Personal Information Management in Group Contexts," *Communications of the ACM*, 49(1), pp. 74–75. DOI: 10.1145/1107458.1107495. 152

Fischer, G. (1991) "Supporting Learning on Demand with Design Environments" in L. Birnbaum (Ed.), *International Conference on the Learning Sciences* (Evanston, Il), Association for the Advancement of Computing in Education, pp. 165–172. 86, 131

Fischer, G. (1994a) "Domain-Oriented Design Environments," *Automated Software Engineering*, 1(2), pp. 177–203. DOI: 10.1007/BF00872289. 3, 47, 49, 194, 196

Fischer, G. (1994b) "Putting the Owners of Problems in Charge with Domain-Oriented Design Environments" in D. Gilmore, R. Winder, and F. Detienne (Eds.), *User-Centered Requirements for Software Engineering Environments*, Springer Verlag, Heidelberg, pp. 297–306. DOI: 10.1007/978-3-662-03035-6_23. 74, 196, 198

Fischer, G. (1999) "A Group Has No Head—Conceptual Frameworks and Systems for Supporting Social Interaction (in Japanese; Translated by Masanori Sugimoto)," *Information Processing Society of Japan (IPSJ) Magazine*, 40(6), pp. 575–582. 177

Fischer, G. (2000a) "Lifelong Learning - More Than Training," *Journal of Interactive Learning Research, Special Issue on Intelligent Systems/Tools In Training and Life-Long Learning* (eds.: Riichiro Mizoguchi and Piet A.M. Kommers), 11(3/4), pp. 265–294. 99

Fischer, G. (2000b) "Social Creativity, Symmetry of Ignorance and Meta-Design," *Knowledge-Based Systems Journal (Special Issue on Creativity and Cognition)*, Elsevier Science B.V., Oxford, UK, 13(7-8), pp. 527–537. 71, 79, 106

Fischer, G. (2001a) "Communities of Interest: Learning through the Interaction of Multiple Knowledge Systems," *24th Annual Information Systems Research Seminar In Scandinavia (IRIS'24)* (Ulvik, Norway), Department of Information Science, Bergen, Norway, pp. 1–14. 68, 192, 197

Fischer, G. (2001b) "User Modeling in Human-Computer Interaction," *User Modeling and User-Adapted Interaction (UMUAI)*, 11(1), pp. 65–86. DOI: 10.1023/A:1011145532042. 106

Fischer, G. (2002) "Beyond 'Couch Potatoes': From Consumers to Designers and Active Contributors, in Firstmonday" (peer-reviewed journal on the Internet), http://firstmonday.org/htbin/cgiwrap/bin/ojs/index.php/fm/article/view/1010/931. 86, 99

Fischer, G. (2005) "Distances and Diversity: Sources for Social Creativity" in *Proceedings of Creativity and Cognition*, ACM, London, April, pp. 128–136. DOI: 10.1145/1056224.1056243. 79, 82, 83, 84, 182

Fischer, G. (2011) "Understanding, Fostering, and Supporting Cultures of Participation," *ACM Interactions XVIII.3* (May + June 2011), pp. 42–53. 56, 107, 108, 193

Fischer, G. (2012) "Context-Aware Systems: The 'Right' Information, at the 'Right' Time, in the 'Right' Place, in the 'Right' Way, to the 'Right' Person" in G. Tortora, S. Levialdi, and M. Tucci (Eds.), *Proceedings of the Conference on Advanced Visual Interfaces (AVI 2012)*, ACM, Capri, Italy (May), pp. 287–294. DOI: 10.1145/2254556.2254611. 197

Fischer, G. (2013) "From Renaissance Scholars to Renaissance Communities: Learning and Education in the 21st Century" in W. Smari, and G. Fox (Eds.), *International Conference on Collaboration Technologies and Systems*, IEEE, San Diego, pp. 13–21. DOI: 10.1109/cts.2013.6567198. 87

Fischer, G. (2014) "Supporting Self-Directed Learning with Cultures of Participation in Collaborative Learning Environments" in E. Christiansen, L. Kuure, A. Mørch, and B. Lindström

(Eds.), *Problem-Based Learning for the 21st Century - New Practices and Learning Environments*, Aalborg University Press, pp. 15–50. 195

Fischer, G., Ehn, P., Engeström, Y., and Virkkunen, J. (2002) "Symmetry of Ignorance and Informed Participation" in T. Binder, J. Gregory, and I. Wagner (Eds.), *Proceedings of the Participatory Design Conference (Pdc'02)*, CPSR, Malmö University, Sweden, pp. 426–428. xxii, 197

Fischer, G. and Giaccardi, E. (2006) "Meta-Design: A Framework for the Future of End User Development" in H. Lieberman, F. Paternò, and V. Wulf (Eds.), *End User Development*, Kluwer Academic Publishers, Dordrecht, The Netherlands, pp. 427–457. http://l3d. cs.colorado.edu/~gerhard/papers/EUD-meta-design-online.pdf. DOI: 10.1007/1-4020-5386-X_19. xxii, 56, 66, 194, 195, 196

Fischer, G., Giaccardi, E., Eden, H., Sugimoto, M., and Ye, Y. (2005) "Beyond Binary Choices: Integrating Individual and Social Creativity," *International Journal of Human-Computer Studies (IJHCS) Special Issue on Computer Support for Creativity* (E.A. Edmonds and L. Candy, Eds.), 63(4-5), pp. 482–512. DOI: 10.1016/j.ijhcs.2005.04.014. xxii, 79, 152, 155, 166, 192

Fischer, G. and Girgensohn, A. (1990) "End-User Modifiability in Design Environments" in *Human Factors in Computing Systems, (Chi'90)* (Seattle, Wa), ACM, New York, pp. 183–191. DOI: 10.1145/97243.97272. 51

Fischer, G., Grudin, J., Lemke, A. C., McCall, R., Ostwald, J., Reeves, B. N., and Shipman, F. (1992) "Supporting Indirect, Collaborative Design with Integrated Knowledge-Based Design Environments," *Human Computer Interaction, Special Issue on Computer Supported Cooperative Work*, 7(3), pp. 281–314. DOI: 10.1207/s15327051hci0703_2. 68

Fischer, G., Grudin, J., McCall, R., Ostwald, J., Redmiles, D., Reeves, B., and Shipman, F. (2001) "Seeding, Evolutionary Growth and Reseeding: The Incremental Development of Collaborative Design Environments" in G. M. Olson, T. W. Malone, and J. B. Smith (Eds.), *Coordination Theory and Collaboration Technology, Lawrence Erlbaum Associates*, Mahwah, NJ, pp. 447–472. 52, 55, 56, 194, 197

Fischer, G. and Herrmann, T. (2011) "Socio-Technical Systems: A Meta-Design Perspective," *International Journal of Sociotechnology and Knowledge Development*, 3(1), pp. 1–33. DOI: 10.4018/jskd.2011010101. 1, 56, 61, 198

Fischer, G. and Lemke, A. C. (1988) "Construction Kits and Design Environments: Steps toward Human Problem-Domain Communication," *Human-Computer Interaction*, 3(3), pp. 179–222. DOI: 10.1207/s15327051hci0303_1. 3, 51, 192, 194

Fischer, G., Lemke, A. C., McCall, R., and Morch, A. (1996) "Making Argumentation Serve Design" in T. Moran, and J. Carrol (Eds.), *Design Rationale: Concepts, Techniques, and Use*, Lawrence Erlbaum and Associates, Mahwah, NJ, pp. 267–293. 51, 106, 131, 171, 191, 193, 195, 197

Fischer, G. and Nakakoji, K. (1992) "Beyond the Macho Approach of Artificial Intelligence: Empower Human Designers - Do Not Replace Them," *Knowledge-Based Systems Journal, Special Issue on AI in Design*, 5(1), pp. 15–30. DOI: 10.1016/0950-7051(92)90021-7. 51, 191

Fischer, G., Nakakoji, K., Ostwald, J., Stahl, G., and Sumner, T. (1998) "Embedding Critics in Design Environments" in M. T. Maybury, and W. Wahlster (Eds.), *Readings in Intelligent User Interfaces*, Morgan Kaufmann, San Francisco, pp. 537–559. 49, 51, 82, 171, 192, 193

Fischer, G. and Ostwald, J. (2005) "Knowledge Communication in Design Communities" in R. Bromme, F. W. Hesse, and H. Spada (Eds.), *Barriers and Biases in Computer-Mediated Knowledge Communication*, Springer, New York, pp. 213–242. DOI: 10.1007/0-387-24319-4_10. xxii

Fischer, G. and Sugimoto, M. (2006) "Supporting Self-Directed Learners and Learning Communities with Sociotechnical Environments," *International Journal Research and Practice in Technology Enhanced Learning (RPTEL)*, 1(1), pp. 31–64. DOI: 10.1142/S1793206806000020. xxi, 86, 154

Foy, J. (1991) "Cole Neighborhood Instruments: A Final Report on the Research" in A. Davidson (Ed.), *Experiential Learning of the Urban Planning Process. Simlab Working Papers Series*, College of Architecture and Planning, University of Colorado, Boulder. 37, 44

Gans, H. J. (1991) *People, Plans, and Policies*, Columbia University Press, New York. 12, 64

Gardner, H. (1993) *Creating Minds*, Basic Books, Inc. New York. 78

Gardner, H. (1995) *Leading Minds: Anatomy of Leadership*, Basic Books, Inc. New York. 78, 79

Giaccardi, E. (2007) "Cross Media Interaction in the Virtual Museum: Reconnecting to Natural Heritage in Boulder, Colorado" in E. Giaccardi (Ed.), *New Heritage: New Media and Cultural Heritage*, Routledge, London, pp. 112–131. 137, 152, 156

Giaccardi, E. (2014) "Practising Heritage: Weaving Actions and Meaning in the Silence of the Lands" in G. Schiller, and S. Rubidge (Eds.), *Choreographic Dwellings: Practising Place*, Palgrave Macmillan, Hampshire, UK. DOI: 10.1057/9781137385673.0010. 160

Greenbaum, J. and Kyng, M. (Eds.) (1991) *Design at Work: Cooperative Design of Computer Systems*, Lawrence Erlbaum Associates, Inc., Hillsdale, NJ. 197

Grigsby, W. G., White, S. B., Levine, D. U., Kelly, R. M., Perelman, M. R., and Claflen, G. L. (1977) *Re-Thinking Housing and Community Development Policy*, University of Pennsylvania, Department of City and Regional Planning, Philadelphia. 29, 193

Grudin, J. (1989) "Why Groupware Applications Fail: Problems in Design and Evaluation," *Office: Technology and People*, 4(3), pp. 245–264. 170

Gutwin, C. and Greenberg, S. (1998) "Design for Individuals, Design for Groups: Tradeoffs between Power and Workspace Awareness" in *Proceedings of Cscw'98*, Seattle, Wa, pp. 207–216. DOI: 10.1145/289444.289495. 119

Habraken, N. J., Gross, M. D., Anderson, J., Hamdi, N., Dale, J., Palleroni, S., Saslaw, E., and Wang, M.-H. (1987) *Concept Design Games Book Two: Playing, Department of Architecture*, MIT, Cambridge, MA. 30

Harriss, R. and Arias, E. G. (2004) *Creating Hazard Resistant and Resilient Communities: Modeling and Decision Support Tools for Assessment and Mitigation of Wildfire Risk in Alternative Settlement Patterns*. 140, 151

Henderson, A. and Kyng, M. (1991) "There's No Place Like Home: Continuing Design in Use" in J. Greenbaum, and M. Kyng (Eds.), *Design at Work: Cooperative Design of Computer Systems*, Lawrence Erlbaum Associates, Inc., Hillsdale, NJ, pp. 219–240. 64, 65, 77, 197

Hirsch, E. D. (1988) *Cultural Literacy: What Every American Needs to Know*, Vintage, New York. 87

Hornecker, E. (2011) "The Role of Physicality in Tangible and Embodied Interaction," *Interactions* (March+April ), pp. 19–23. DOI: 10.1145/1925820.1925826. 3, 11, 29, 116, 129

Hornecker, E., Eden, H., and Scharff, E. (2002) "'In My Situation I Would Dislike Thaaat!'—Role Play as Assessment Method for Tools Supporting Participatory Planning." in *Proceedings of PDC 2002, CPSR*, Malmö Sweden, pp. 243–247. 171

Janis, I. (1972) *Victims of Groupthink*, Houghton Mifflin, Boston. 70, 79, 83

Jenkins, H. (2009) *Confronting the Challenges of Participatory Cultures: Media Education for the 21st Century*, MIT Press, Cambridge, MA. 193

John-Steiner, V. (2000) *Creative Collaboration*, Oxford University Press, Oxford. 78

Kafai, Y. B. (1995) *Minds in Play: Computer Game Design as a Context for Children's Learning*, Lawrence Erlbaum Associates, Inc., Hillsdale, NJ. 141

Landauer, T. K. (1995) *The Trouble with Computers*, MIT Press, Cambridge, MA. 44

Lang, J. T. (1987) *Creating Architectural Theory: Role of the Behavioral Sciences in Environmental Design*, Van Nostrand Reinhold Co., New York. 29

Lave, J. and Wenger, E. (1991) *Situated Learning: Legitimate Peripheral Participation*, Cambridge University Press, New York. DOI: 10.1017/CBO9780511815355. 68, 87

Lawton, M. P. (1975) "Assessing the Competence of People" in D. P. Kent (Ed.), *Research Planning and Action for Older People*, Behavioral Publications, New York. 185

Lieberman, H., Paterno, F., and Wulf, V. (Eds.) (2006) *End User Development*, Kluwer Publishers, Dordrecht, The Netherlands. 194

Mandelbaum (1983) "The Design of the Designing Community" in M. C. J. Elton, W. A. Lucas, and D. W. Conrath (Eds.), *Evaluating New Telecommunications Services*, Plenum Press, New York, pp. 563–679. 196

Mandelbaum, S. J. (1984) "Temporal Conventions in Planning Discourse," *Environment and Planning B: Planning and Design*, 11(1), pp. 5–13. DOI: 10.1068/b110005. 28, 29

Maslow, A. (1970) *Motivation and Personality*, 2nd ed., Harper and Row, New York. 185

Mayer, R. E. (2004) "Should There Be a Three-Strikes Rule against Pure Discovery Learning?—the Case for Guided Methods of Instruction," *American Psychologist*, 59(1), pp. 14–19. DOI: 10.1037/0003-066X.59.1.14. 106

McHarg, I., Todd, T., Partners in Charge (1978) "Master Plan for Abuja: The New Capital City of Nigeria," The Federal Capital Development Authority of Nigeria, International Planning Associates, Philadelphia, PA. 76

Miller, P. (1986) *Expert Critiquing Systems: Practice-Based Medical Consultation by Computer*, Springer-Verlag, New York–Berlin. DOI: 10.1007/978-1-4613-8637-7. 193

Moran, T. P. and Carroll, J. M. (Eds.) (1996) *Design Rationale: Concepts, Techniques, and Use*, Lawrence Erlbaum Associates, Inc., Hillsdale, NJ. 55, 75, 191, 193

Müller-Tomfelde, C. and Fjeld, M. (2012) "Tabletops: Interactive Horizontal Displays for Ubiquitous Computing," *Computer* (2), pp. 78–81. DOI: 10.1109/MC.2012.64. 115, 174, 197

Mumford, E. (1987) "Sociotechnical Systems Design: Evolving Theory and Practice" in G. Bjerknes, P. Ehn, and M. Kyng (Eds.), *Computers and Democracy*, Avebury, Aldershot, UK, pp. 59–76. 1, 56

Nakakoji, K. (1993) "Increasing Shared Understanding of a Design Task between Designers and Design Environments: The Role of a Specification Component," Ph.D. Dissertation, University of Colorado at Boulder. 52, 106

Nardi, B. A. (1993) *A Small Matter of Programming*, The MIT Press, Cambridge, MA. 73, 77, 152, 196

National-Research-Council (2003) *Beyond Productivity: Information Technology, Innovation, and Creativity*, National Academy Press, Washington, DC. 81, 86

National-Research-Council (2009) *Learning Science in Informal Environments—People, Places, and Pursuits*, National Academy Press, Washington, DC. 78

Norman, D. A. (1990) *The Design of Everyday Things*, Currency Doubleday, New York. 164

Norman, D. A. (1993) *Things That Make Us Smart*, Addison-Wesley Publishing Company, Reading, MA. 191

Norman, D. A. and Draper, S. W. (Eds.) (1986) *User-Centered System Design, New Perspectives on Human-Computer Interaction*, Lawrence Erlbaum Associates, Inc., Hillsdale, NJ. 65

Olson, G. M. and Olson, J. S. (2001) "Distance Matters" in J. M. Carroll (Ed.), *Human-Computer Interaction in the New Millennium*, ACM Press, New York, pp. 397–417. DOI: 10.1207/S15327051HCI1523_4. 164, 180, 181

Olson, J. S. and Olson, G. M. (2013) *Working Together Apart: Collaboration over the Internet*, Morgan & Claypool Publishers, San Rafael, CA. DOI: 10.2200/S00542ED1V01Y-201310HCI020. 180

Ostwald, J. (1996) "Knowledge Construction in Software Development: The Evolving Artifact Approach," Ph.D. dissertation, University of Colorado at Boulder. 71, 77

PCSD (1996) "Sustainable America: A New Consensus for Prosperity, Opportunity, and a Healthy Environment for the Future," The President's Council on Sustainable Development, USGPO, Washington, DC. 1, 184

Perrone, C., Clark, D., and Repenning, A. (1996) "Webquest: Combining the WWW with Interactive Simulation Games," *Computer Networks and ISDN Systems*, 28(7–11), pp. 1307-1319. DOI: 10.1016/0169-7552(96)00053-0. 141, 146

Polanyi, M. (1966) *The Tacit Dimension*, Doubleday, Garden City, NY. 27, 68, 178, 198

Popper, K. R. (1959) *The Logic of Scientific Discovery*, Basic Books, New York. 53, 91

Popper, K. R. (1965) *Conjectures and Refutations*, Harper and Row, New York, Hagerstown, San Francisco, London. 64, 192

Postman, N. (1985) *Amusing Ourselves to Death—Public Discourse in the Age of Show Business*, Penguin Books, New York. 62, 78

Preece, J. and Maloney-Krichmar, D. (2003) "Online Communities" in J. Jacko, and A. Sears (Eds.), *Handbook of Human-Computer Interaction*, Lawrence Erlbaum Associates Inc., Mahwah: NJ, pp. 596–620. 182

Preece, J. and Shneiderman, B. (2009) "The Reader-to-Leader Framework: Motivating Technology-Mediated Social Participation," *AIS Transactions on Human-Computer Interaction*, 1(1), pp. 13–32. 84

Raymond, E. S. and Young, B. (2001) *The Cathedral and the Bazaar: Musings on Linux and Open Source by an Accidental Revolutionary*, O'Reilly and Associates, Sebastopol, CA. 68

Reeves, B., Robinson, T., Banerjee, B., and Sweeney, J. (2009) *Large-Scale Energy Reductions through Sensors, Feedback, and Information Technology*, http://arpa-e.energy.gov/LinkClick.aspx?-fileticket=xpbAhwLKiwE%3d&tabid=200. 107

Reeves, B. N. (1993) "The Role of Embedded Communication and Artifact History in Collaborative Design," Ph.D. dissertation, University of Colorado at Boulder. 68

Repenning, A. (2014) *Agentsheets Web Site*, http://www.agentsheets.com/. 117, 123

Repenning, A. and Sumner, T. (1995) "Agentsheets: A Medium for Creating Domain-Oriented Visual Programming Languages," *IEEE Computer, Special Issue on Visual Programming*, 28(3), pp. 17–25. DOI: 10.1109/2.366152. 123, 142

Resnick, L. B. (1987) "Learning in School and Out," *Educational Researcher*, 16(9), pp. 13–20. 86

Resnick, L. B., M.Levine, J., and Teasley, S. D. (1991) *Perspectives on Socially Shared Cognition*, American Psychological Association, Washington, DC. DOI: 10.1037/10096-000. 70, 83, 192

Rittel, H. (1973) "Dilemmas in a General Theory of Planning," *Policy Sciences*, 4(2), pp. 155–169. DOI: 10.1007/BF01405730. 198

Rittel, H. (1984) "Second-Generation Design Methods" in N. Cross (Ed.), *Developments in Design Methodology*, John Wiley and Sons, New York, pp. 317–327. 47, 63, 64, 70, 71, 84, 122, 171, 196, 197

Rittel, H. and Webber, M. M. (1984) "Planning Problems Are Wicked Problems" in N. Cross (Ed.), *Developments in Design Methodology*, John Wiley and Sons, New York, pp. 135–144. 28, 55, 63, 185, 195, 196

Robinson, C., Arias, E. G., and Eden, H. (1997) "Bridging the Virtual and the Physical: The Intersim as a Collaborative Support Interface" in B. d. Boulay, and R. Mizoguchi (Eds.), *Artificial Intelligence in Education '97*, Kobe, Japan, pp. 556–558. 138, 197

Rogoff, B. and Lave, J. (1984) *Everyday Cognition: Its Development in Social Context*, Harvard University Press, Cambridge, MA. 81

Saaty, T. L. (1977) "A Scaling Method for Priorities in Hierarchical Structures," *Journal of Mathematical Psychology*, 15, pp. 234–281. DOI: 10.1016/0022-2496(77)90033-5. 28

Salomon, G. (Ed.) (1993) *Distributed Cognitions: Psychological and Educational Considerations*, Cambridge University Press, Cambridge, UK. 81, 193

Schön, D. A. (1983) *The Reflective Practitioner: How Professionals Think in Action*, Basic Books, New York. 7, 47, 55, 57, 63, 68, 78, 81, 98, 128, 171, 191, 195, 197

Shipman, F. (1993) "Supporting Knowledge-Base Evolution with Incremental Formalization," Ph.D. Dissertation, University of Colorado at Boulder. 97, 178

Shneiderman, B. (2002) *Leonardo's Laptop—Human Needs and the New Computing Technologies*, MIT Press, Cambridge, MA. 78

Shneiderman, B. (2007) "Creativity Support Tools: Accelerating Discovery and Innovation," *Communications of the ACM*, 50(12), pp. 20–32. DOI: 10.1145/1323688.1323689. 164

Simon, H. A. (1996) *The Sciences of the Artificial*, third ed., The MIT Press, Cambridge, MA. 55, 62, 63, 75, 88, 193

Snow, C. P. (1993) *The Two Cultures*, Cambridge University Press, Cambridge, UK. DOI: 10.1017/CBO9780511819940. 82

Stahl, G. (2006) *Group Cognition: Computer Support for Building Collaborative Knowledge*, MIT Press, Cambridge, MA. 52

Star, S. L. (1989) "The Structure of Ill-Structured Solutions: Boundary Objects and Heterogeneous Distributed Problem Solving" in L. Gasser, and M. N. Huhns (Eds.), *Distributed Artificial Intelligence*, Volume II, Morgan Kaufmann Publishers Inc., San Mateo, CA, pp. 37–54. DOI: 10.1016/b978-1-55860-092-8.50006-x. 71, 79, 84, 191

Stefik, M., Bobrow, D. G., Foster, G., Lanning, S., and Tatar, D. (1987) "WYSIWIS Revised: Early Experiences with Multiuser Interfaces," *ACM Trans. Inf. Syst.*, 5(2), pp. 147–167. DOI: 10.1145/27636.28056. 164

Sternberg, R. J. (Ed.) (1988) *The Nature of Creativity*, Cambridge University Press, Cambridge, UK. 78, 192

Sternberg, R. J. (Ed.) (1999) *Handbook of Creativity*, Cambridge University Press, Cambridge, UK. 29, 79

Streitz, N., Kameas, A., and Mavrommati, I. (Eds.) (2007) *The Disappearing Computer: Interaction Design, System Infrastructures and Applications for Smart Environments, Volume LNCS 4500*, Springer Heidelberg. DOI: 10.1007/978-3-540-72727-9. 180

Streitz, N. and Nixon, P. (2005) "Special Issue: The Disappearing Computer," *Communications of the ACM*, 48(3), pp. 32–71. DOI: 10.1145/1047671.1047700. 180, 194

Suchman, L. A. (1987) *Plans and Situated Actions*, Cambridge University Press, Cambridge, UK. 57, 65, 66

Sugimoto, M., Hosoi, K., and Hashizume, H. (2004) "Caretta: A System for Supporting Face-to-Face Collaboration by Integrating Personal and Shared Spaces" in *Proceedings of CHI2004*, Vienna, Austria, pp. 41–48. DOI: 10.1145/985692.985698. 137, 152

Sugimoto, M., Kusunoki, F., and Hashizume, H. (2002) "Design of an Interactive System for Group Learning Support" in *Proceedings of DIS2002*, London, UK, pp. 50–55. DOI: 10.1145/778712.778723. 153

Taylor, F. (1967) *Principles of Scientific Management*, Norton and Co., New York (first published 1911). 64, 65

Thaler, R. H. and Sunstein, C. R. (2009) *Nudge—Improving Decisions About Health, Wealth, an Happiness*, Penguin Books, London. 64

Trist, E. L. (1981) "The Sociotechnical Perspective: The Evolution of Sociotechnical Systems as a Conceptual Framework and as an Action Research Program" in A. H. VanDeVen, and W. F. Joyce (Eds.), *Perspectives on Organization Design and Behavior*, Wiley, New York, NY. 1, 56

von Hippel, E. (2005) *Democratizing Innovation*, MIT Press, Cambridge, MA. 86, 184

Wallace, D. W., Huffman, R. W., and Arias, E. G. (1979a) "Miami Park West: A Redevelopment Program for Downtown Miami; a WMRT Report for the Downtown Development Authority and City of Miami Community Development Office," Sponsored by the U.S. Department of Housing and Urban Development. 28

Wallace, D. W., Huffman, R. W., Arias, E. G., and Beckman, J. (1979b) "Downtown Detroit Redevelopment Plan 1979: Growth Management, the Susceptibility to Change and Urban Design for Central Detroit, Mi," A WMRT publication for the City of Detroit, MI. 28

Warr, A. (2007) "Understanding and Supporting Creativity in Design," Ph.D. dissertation, University of Bath, England. 164

Weiser, M. (1991) "The Computer for the 21st Century," *Scientific American*, 265(3), pp. 66–75. DOI: 10.1038/scientificamerican0991-94. 180

Wenger, E. (1998) *Communities of Practice—Learning, Meaning, and Identity*, Cambridge University Press, Cambridge, UK. DOI: 10.1017/CBO9780511803932. 68, 71, 83, 87, 192

Wilson, F. R. (1998) *The Hand: How Its Use Shapes the Brain, Language,* and Human Culture, Pantheon, New York. 29

Winograd, T. (1995) "From Programming Environments to Environments for Designing," *Communications of the ACM*, 38(6), pp. 65–74. DOI: 10.1145/203241.203259. 194

Winograd, T. and Flores, F. (1986) *Understanding Computers and Cognition: A New Foundation for Design*, Ablex Publishing Corporation, Norwood, NJ. 45, 66

Wittgenstein, L. (1953) "Translation of Philosophical Investigations," MacMillan Co., New York. 30

Wulf, W. A. (1993) "The Collaboratory Opportunity," *Science*, 261(August), pp. 854–855. DOI: 10.1126/science.8346438. 192

Yamaguchi, E., Inagaki, S., Sugimoto, M., Kusunoki, F., Deguchi, A., Takeuchi, Y., Seki, T., Tachibana, S., and Yamamoto, T. (2009) "Fostering Students' Participation in Face-to-Face Interactions and Deepening Their Understanding by Integrating Personal and Shared Spaces" in Z. Pan, A. D. Cheok, W. Müller, and A. E. Rhalibi (Eds.), *Transactions on Edutainment Ii*, Springer-Verlag, Berlin Heidelberg, pp. 228–245. DOI: 10.1007/978-3-642-03270-7_16. 155, 156

Ye, Y. and Fischer, G. (2007) *Converging on a "Science of Design" through the Synthesis of Design Methodologies, (CHI'2007 Workshop)*, http://swiki.cs.colorado.edu:3232/CHI07Design/3. 65

Ye, Y., Nakakoji, K., Yamamoto, Y., and Kishida, K. (2004) "The Co-Evolution of System and Community in Open Source Software Development" in S. Koch (Ed.), *Free/Open Source Software Development*, Idea Group Publishing, Hershey, PA, pp. 59–82. 69

# Author Biographies

**Ernesto G. Arias Clare** is Professor Emeritus of Planning and Design and Faculty Fellow of the Institute of Cognitive Sciences at the University of Colorado where he taught Architecture, City Planning, and Computer Science, founded the Urban Simulations Laboratory, and co-founded the Center for LifeLong Learning and Design ($L^3D$). His Ph.D. in City and Regional Planning and Masters in Architecture and Planning are from the University of Pennsylvania. The pursuit of his research experience has been toward a contribution of the *collaborative framing and resolution of design and planning problems through participation*. To this end he has integrated environmental psychology and professional work on urban planning and design with the development of innovative technologies to better understand how we "behave," "think," and "learn" in trying to enhance the human competence and understanding to better design, plan, and use the built environment in the future.

Activities related to the EDC development include past Fulbright Research and Teaching Scholar (*participation*), past chair of the National Track in Urban Design of the American Collegiate Schools of Planning (*design*), and past member of the International Scientific Advisory Board of the National Institute of High Technology of Costa Rica (*information technology*). Some of his major planning and urban design experiences include ABUJA (the New Capital City of Nigeria), and various city redevelopments in the U.S.A (*planning problems*). He is presently a professor at the University of Costa Rica where he founded and coordinates the Urban Observatory of the Great Metropolitan Region in Costa Rica (OUGAM).

**Hal Eden** has been a research associate in the Department of Computer Science and the Center for LifeLong Learning and Design ($L^3D$) at the University of Colorado Boulder. He has been associated with numerous research efforts over the past 30 years, including the design and development of technologies to support learning in the context of working, non-intrusive approaches to distance collaboration, and participatory design environments for face-to-face collaboration. As Associate Director of $L^3D$, he has cultivated and supported a rich organizational, computational, and physical environment to support the $L^3D$ research community. Most recently, he has been studying the use of tangible interfaces in face-to-face collaborative settings to enhance social creativity, with specific emphasis on the assessment of interface usability and effectiveness.

**Gerhard Fischer** (http://l3d.cs.colorado.edu/~gerhard/) is a Professor Adjunct and Professor Emeritus of Computer Science, a Fellow of the Institute of Cognitive Science, and the Director of the Center for Lifelong Learning and Design ($L^3D$) at the University of Colorado at Boulder. He is a member of the Computer Human Interaction Academy (CHI; 2007), a Fellow of the Association for Computing Machinery (ACM; 2009), and a recipient of the RIGO Award of ACM-SIGDOC (2012). In 2015, he was awarded an honorary doctorate from the University of Gothenburg, Sweden.

His research has focused on new conceptual frameworks and new media for learning, working, and collaborating, human-centered computing, and design. His recent work is centered on social creativity, meta-design, cultures of participation, design trade-offs, and rich landscapes for learning (including MOOCs).

CPSIA information can be obtained
at www.ICGtesting.com
Printed in the USA
FSOW04n2112210117
29896FS